THE LITTLE
BOY BOOK

THE LITTLE BOY BOOK

A Guide to the First Eight Years

**Sheila Moore and
Roon Frost**

BALLANTINE BOOKS • NEW YORK

A Ballantine Book
Published by The Ballantine Publishing Group

Copyright © 1986 by Sheila Moore and Roon Frost

All rights reserved under International and Pan-American Copyright Conventions. Published in the United States by The Ballantine Publishing Group, a division of Random House, Inc., New York, and simultaneously in Canada by Random House of Canada Limited, Toronto.

http://www.randomhouse.com

Library of Congress Catalog Card Number: 97-97007

ISBN: 0-345-42350-X

Cover design by Cathy Colbert

This edition published by arrangement with Clarkson N. Potter, Inc.

Manufactured in the United States of America

First Ballantine Books Mass Market Edition: September 1987
First Ballantine Books Trade Paperback Edition: February 1998

10 9 8 7 6 5 4 3 2 1

For our husbands,
Harry and Ed

Our Sons,
Ned, Bruce, and Eric

And in memory of two special boys,
Billy and Tom

Contents

Acknowledgments

The Little Boy Book could never have been written without the interest and support of many individuals. Experts in a variety of fields shared their considerable knowledge, and the work of several contributed substantially toward our main points. Louise Bates Ames, associate director of the Gesell Institute in New Haven, Connecticut, gave us the benefit of her long experience and exceptional insight into the behavior of young children. Martha Bridge Denckla, chief of Developmental Neurology's Section on Autism and Related Disorders at the National Institutes of Health in Bethesda, Maryland, has taken time from her own busy schedule to explain complicated scientific theories about male vulnerability (among them the work of the late Normal Geschwind), and offered her wide range of contacts.

Sheppard Kellam, chairman of the Department of Mental Hygiene at Johns Hopkins University, gave us two lengthy interviews as well as many of his own studies, which highlight the importance of first-grade success to boys. We are also indebted to University of Virginia Commonwealth Professor of psychology Sandra Scarr, whose contributions to the field of behavioral development are definitive, both for her overview of part of our manuscript and her delightful sense of humor.

A number of other authorities were also generous with their time and expertise; without the chance to interview them, we might have missed some of the subtleties of their research. Both Jerome Kagan at Harvard University and Eleanor Maccoby at Stanford University are impeccable sources on the socialization of young children; we are grateful for having had the opportunity to speak with them and appreciate the readability of their work. Benjamin Spock was as genial and helpful over the phone as his books seemed to us as mothers. The work of Burton White served as background for the infancy and preschool chapters.

The long-term studies by Stella Chess and Alexander Thomas on the stability of certain temperamental traits lent important support to the notion that children are born with at least some personality variables all their own.

In sorting out what makes boys different from girls, we are grateful to the work of other researchers. Camilla Benbow of the Johns Hopkins' Study of Mathematically Precocious Youth, Bea Cameron, assistant superintendent for Special Education for Fairfax County, Marilyn Bos from Loudoun County's Search Program, and Diana McGuinness at the University of South Florida have been helpful in explaining the special needs of boys in school. The studies of the late Jeanne Block of the University of California at Berkeley, Christopher Ounsted and David Taylor at Oxford, and California researchers Eleanor Maccoby and Carol Jacklin were key to our understanding of sex differences in behavior; those of Tufts University's David Elkind and New York psychologist Mary Ann Spencer Pulaski to the stages of development in young children; and the work of London Institute of Psychiatry's Michael Rutter and the University of Utah's Michael Lamb to our general understanding of boys. We are grateful to Michael McGuire of the Westwood Neuropsychiatric Institute and J. Neil Maclusky at Yale University for their explanations of hormonal effects on developing children and adult males. Evelyn Goodenough Pitcher, professor emeritus at Tufts University, shared her insights into the differences between preschool boys and girls, and Patricia Quinn, developmental pediatrician in Washington, D.C., was always willing to answer our questions.

Our understanding of education was deepened and expanded by interviews with Jeanne Chall and Robert Rosenthal at Harvard University, Pat Davidson at Boston Children's Hospital, and Dorothy Rich of Washington's Home and School Institute. We give special thanks to Jeannette Jansky at Columbia University for her insights into ways parents can help their preschoolers, and for reviewing our section on reading. Sammie Campbell, assistant superintendent of Georgia's Savannah-Chatham County schools, generously contributed her time and research results to further our work. Nathlie Badian, Elizabeth Decker, and Cindy Mellott provided important viewpoints on a boy's early years in school. To Dr. John Hurley, former director of Research and Testing for Fairfax County, we owe our thanks for information about single-sex classes. Jerry Bruns of the Falls Church City Schools provided information about his study on underachieving students, and the work of Carol Dweck at Harvard was useful in understanding school boys' motivations. We consulted the work of Benjamin Bloom of the University of Chicago for a greater understanding of learning itself as well as the nature of schools.

The findings of researchers such as Diana Baumrind at the University of California and Myrna Shure at Philadelphia's Hahnemann University Hospital seem basic to any efforts by parents or teachers to discipline little boys. Leonard D. Eron and Thomas Radecki at the University of Illinois, Peggy Charren of Boston's Action for Children's Television, E. Mavis Hetherington, James M. Page professor of psychology at the University of Virginia, Judith Wallerstein and Joan Kelly of California's

Children of Divorce Project, and Thomas and Lynette Long of Washington, D.C., have performed an invaluable service by detailing the risks to children, particularly boys, from media violence, divorce, and inadequate supervision. We are especially grateful to Dr. Eron for providing us with data from his long-term studies. The State University of New York's Thomas Lickona has been generous in suggesting ways to teach boys right from wrong, and we relied, as well, on the work of Carol Gilligan and Lawrence Kohlberg at Harvard University, Martin L. Hoffman at the University of Michigan, and Marian Radke-Yarrow and Leon Kuczynski at NIH.

In writing *The Little Boy Book,* we also turned briefly to others for very specific information. Although their expertise was not central to our themes, what we learned from them added to our work. Anna Kanianthra, public health nutritionist for Northern Virginia, is a friend unfailing in her willingness to explain children's nutritional needs. Judith Rapoport at NIH contributed important findings that help those working with learning-disabled youngsters, particularly in regard to the use of stimulant medication. We are grateful for the opportunity to talk with Deborah Waber at Boston Children's Hospital about her theory linking delayed maturity with spatial skills. Kyle Pruett at Yale University has shown that fathers, not just mothers, can be enormously effective parents. VPI's Richard K. Stratton helped us recognize that boys should not be pressured too early into competitive sports, and Irwin Hyman at Temple University told us something of the physical punishment many schoolboys endure. Dr. James Hillis of George Washington University spoke with us about the speech problems of boys. Clinical psychologist Rosemary Burns gave us information about adopted children, and Joan Quill provided material on sex differences and mathematics. There are many more experts—physicians, psychologists, teachers, principals, and parents—who shared their interest and knowledge about boys with us.

We owe a special debt to librarians. Without interlibrary loan facilities and many staffers' tireless efforts to track down seemingly obscure monographs, our work would have taken us much longer and our research been limited in scope. The late Jean Carruthers and Virginia Haley at the Purcellville Library; Diana Welty, Janet Hedrick, Indira Dholakia, and Ellen Henry at Leesburg's Thomas Balch Library; Jane Bosley at the Loudoun County Professional Library; and especially Betty Chilton and Ruth Stanley at the Fairfax County Professional Library were helpful and interested in our work.

We are grateful to Raphael Sagalyn, our agent, and Ann Sleeper, his assistant. Thanks as well to Noelle Vitte, who first took an interest in our project and realized the need for a book like this.

We also want to thank Nancy Novogrod, our editor at Clarkson Potter. Her sensitivity, both as a mother and an editor, coupled with her willingness to offer suggestions based on personal concerns about rearing a little boy have added to this book. She and editorial director Carol Southern have been supportive throughout our association.

We feel a special sense of gratitude to Hank Ketcham, the creator of Dennis the Menace, who early in this project responded enthusiastically to our request to use his cartoons as illustrations. That so many American parents identify with the Mitchells testify to Mr. Ketcham's talented and perceptive portrayal of little boys.

A host of volunteer readers, including members of our own families who know this book almost as well as we do, have also been invaluable from our early drafts through completion of the final manuscript. Special thanks to Kathy C. Barber, Bee Cloutier, Liz Decker, Diane Dennis, Karen Donohoe, Anne McComb Frost, Anna Jullien, Fran and Ron Kunz, Ivey Blake Kelly, Lynn Miller, Raymond Nance, Judith Randall, Rachel and Robert Remuzzi, Marty Russell and Martha Williams for their comments and questions, as well as the examples they shared with us of little boys they knew.

Friends and family members have lent particular support or provided hard-to-find information. Our gratitude goes to Patricia Tewksbury, Lynn Smith, Reneé Holsinger, Michelle Van Wyck, Agnes Cammack, Steve Price, Douglas Blount, Jean Sandstrom, Victoria Heard, and Bitsy Blackmar.

Our children deserve accolades for help of every sort, and for their special sense of humor that brightened many trying days. Most of all we thank our husbands, who showed through long and unfailing support their own deep commitment to equality.

Introduction

If you are the parent of a little boy, you may have discovered that the children described in many books for parents are not like your son at all. More often than not, you find information about children in general—not about boys in particular.

The Little Boy Book is written for parents of sons. Knowing why one boy is so different from others—why there is so much variability among boys in general—and why boys may be more vulnerable than their sisters can help us be more responsive as parents. Discovering that there are methods of discipline that work especially well with boys—and others that do not—can assist us in making family relationships smoother.

Throughout the book we present a range of positive parenting techniques and tell you where to find more information if you need it; prescriptive sections that deal with particular issues and problems are highlighted. You are interested in methods that work with *your* little boy, and from the research we have selected findings that we feel will assist you in meeting your son's individual needs.

Both parents and teachers will find the material on learning useful. The sad consequences of pressuring our sons in academic areas at early ages are widespread— school failure, even of bright middle-class children; an increased incidence of special-education enrollments; and an alarming rise in adolescent suicide. We hope that what you read in *The Little Boy Book* will cause you to take a second look the next time you read an article about the superbaby who learns to read at two.

We are both mothers of sons with backgrounds in education and journalism. Four years ago we began looking at research on child development, educational methods, and sex differences. We spoke with experts at leading universities and research centers throughout the United States in order to put together the kind of book we wished we'd had—one that would complement the child-care books that had been helpful to us, but would also tell parents as much as possible about boys.

Although our book deals with serious issues, we have included drawings by prominent cartoonists that portray the humorous aspects of life with little boys. They reflect the endearing qualities and hilarious antics of boys every parent will recognize.

New findings as well as information seldom included in books for parents will, we believe, give you a clearer understanding of your son. We hope, as well, that you find answers, help, and the satisfaction we experienced in raising our little boys.

Sheila Moore
Roon Frost
July 1985

What Little Boys Are Made Of

In *Huckleberry Finn,* Mark Twain's novel of American boyhood, Huck and his friend Jim hide away on an island in the Mississippi River. Boredom sets in after several weeks and, in Huck's words, "I said it was getting slow and dull, and I wanted to get a stirring up some way... I would slip over the river and find out what was going on." Disguising himself as a girl, he rows to shore and approaches a strange house, where a woman invites him inside.

During the visit, Huck attempts to thread a needle. Unlike a girl, who would bring the thread to the needle, Huck tries to do it by bringing the needle to the thread. Suspicious, the woman complains about the number of rats scurrying about the cabin, some so bold as to peek out at her young visitor. She suggests that Huck throw a heavy lead weight at them. Huck throws the weight with his arm out to one side—like a boy would—and the woman catches him out.

"Why, I spotted you for a boy when you was threading the needle!" she exclaims with satisfaction.

* * *

Whether the tasks be threading a needle, throwing a ball, climbing a tree, or learning to write the alphabet, we often notice that boys and girls do them differently. If you have a daughter as well as a son, you can probably list a number of ways they differ in behavior without thinking about it for very long at all.

In Twain's day, people would have been amused, but hardly surprised, by the clever woman's observations about Huck. Until this century, few questioned the premise that differences in behavior between the sexes were innate—natural, desirable, and even God's plan. Most of the world is still quite comfortable with this point of view of life.

Twentieth-century experts, however, have emphasized the importance of the parents' role in bringing up their children, stressing "nurture" as opposed to "nature." Many American parents have looked to the spoken and silent messages they have transmitted and the environment they have created for the key to their children's behavior. Some of us have even felt guilty about our own actions or attitudes that may have encouraged aggression in our boys or passivity in our girls. If we just gave our daughters trucks and showed them how to be assertive, we reasoned, the girls would be independent like boys. If our sons were only taught concern for others and given dolls to cuddle, they would be less aggressive and more nurturant like their sisters.

"But it's not so simple," declares one mother, who tried to raise her children in a nonsexist way. "The biggest things in my daughters' lives right now are Barbie dolls and nail polish," she sighs. "And Jonathan—he walks like the Incredible Hulk, shovels down his food, and wants to wrestle with every boy he sees—and he's only three-and-a-half!" Speaking of the differences between her two children, a second mother added, "When she plays with something, she wants to feed it; he wants to make it fight."

For women, who do most of the hands-on rearing of

young children, boys have always presented a special challenge. Their behavior sometimes seems mysterious or incomprehensible. "Why is he acting that way?" "Is it normal?" and "What should I do about this?" are questions mothers ask endlessly about their sons. "Don't worry about it," a boy's father will counter. "I did the same thing," or, "Lots of boys do that." Because of their common sexuality, fathers understand intuitively the feelings and motivations of their sons; after all, they were once boys themselves. While it may seem an all too obvious and even trivial observation, whether you are a mother or a father affects your responses as a parent in very profound ways.

The Importance of Heredity

Students of human behavior from a variety of disciplines are now taking a second look at the importance of inborn traits. Investigators of sex differences have established that being male or female is a crucial determinant of behavior. Genetic studies show that our intelligence, adaptability, and approach to people are influenced by traits we inherit. An individual's sex and heredity contribute to his perception of the world as well as his potential to achieve.

Recent findings are causing us to reexamine some of our traditional views of the sexes, including the widely held belief that males are stronger and more powerful than females. Many of us expect more of our sons than we do of our daughters, who are sometimes characterized as weak and fragile. Attitudes such as these not only have the force of custom, they are also routinely inculcated in our children from very early ages. Six-year-olds will tell you that boys are stronger and braver than girls, and that it is men who get to be the bosses.

However, researchers find that, despite their greater strength and power, from conception onward males are more fragile than females in substantial ways. Even before birth, maternal stress and genetic errors create more problems for males than for females. More boys than girls have trouble in school and suffer from speech and learning disabilities. When parents divorce, boys often show the emotional impact of family stress by disruptive behavior, whereas girls less often act out their feelings. In the adolescent years, boys turn to alcohol and drugs more frequently than girls do. Throughout their lifespan, males succumb to stress and disease at higher rates than females.

The traditional male characteristics of power, strength, competitiveness, and independence are counterbalanced by specific vulnerabilities that are present before a child is born. These contrasting qualities of strength and fragility, the techniques we use in rearing a son, and the way a boy views himself all contribute to his development. Underpinning these important variables, however, is each little boy's unique genetic heritage.

Psychologist Sandra Scarr of the University of Virginia points out that a child's individual set of genes helps bring him into contact with different experiences. As parents, our response to each child will vary. The outgoing, smiling, happy baby, for instance, causes adults to smile back, pick him up, and play. The more retiring, shy, or fussy baby makes us react far differently.

If you have more than one child, you are no doubt familiar with the difference in response that each of your children evokes in you. One may be the family extrovert, have a high energy level, be athletic, and possess an assortment of friends. His brother, on the other hand, may be less gregarious, enjoy playing the oboe, and have only one or two close companions. If you are, yourself, an extrovert, and enjoy being with people, you may feel more comfortable around the first of these boys. Having personality traits like your son may not, however, make it easier to raise him. "He is in motion from the time he gets up until he goes to bed," one spirited mother says of her seven-year-old son. "I can remember being like that, and I don't plan to let him out of my sight till he's twenty-five!"

Each of us is born with what Scarr calls a "reaction range of possibilities" in a variety of areas. A child may inherit genes that are likely to help him in becoming a fine long-distance runner. If his family places a great deal of emphasis on the arts and disdains sports, however, his athletic potential may go unrealized. The boy's rather modest musical ability may be encouraged, instead. If, on the other hand, the boy's family nurtures his athletic gifts by encouraging his participation in sports, it is likely that his full range of talent will be developed. Opportunities allow an individual to fulfill his reaction range. By themselves, genes do not cause behavior. They make it possible for a person to develop certain strengths given the right kind of environment.

Genetic information is transmitted through genes, the basic units of heredity, which affect development throughout life. When we learn to walk, the onset of puberty, baldness in men, and menopause in women are all influenced to some degree by the chromosomal package we carry from conception.

Each parent contributes a sex chromosome to his or her offspring. Females transmit one kind of sex chromosome—always an X. Males can transmit either an X or Y. If the mother's egg containing the X chromosome is fertilized by an X from the father, the child will be a girl—XX. A Y-bearing chromosome will produce a boy —XY.

The presence or absence of the Y chromosome influences a number of traits and conditions found more commonly in one sex than the other. Cleft palate, baldness, and gout occur more often in males than in females. Certain undesirable traits transmitted through the mother's X chromosome may or may not be inherited by girls, who have the advantage of a second X chromosome from their fathers. Some disadvantageous characteristics transmitted through a mother's X chromosome to her son, however, will be expressed. A rare, though well-known example of a sex-linked disease is hemophilia; color blindness is also a sex-linked trait.

For the full expression of male or female qualities, genes act in concert with hormones—chemical substances that serve as messengers to the child's developing body. There are a number of traits that are expressed only when the proper hormones are present. Hormones help bring about the growth of beards in adolescent males and breast development in females. The sex hormones influence genital development in the fetus and then assist in further differentiation. Male sex hormones, known as androgens, stimulate the development of many masculine characteristics.

The Y chromosome a boy receives from his father brings about the formation of testes in the male embryo. Instead of having structures that resemble male or female sex organs, embryos in the early stage of development have what is called "ovotestes." This tissue can develop in a male or a female way. Between six and seven weeks after conception, the ovotestes in males enlarge and eventually form the testes. Within a short time, these embryonic testes begin to produce sex hormones.

Becoming Male Involves An Extra Step

The tendency in humans, and mammals in general, is to develop in a female way. Female development appears to be the "basic model." If the testes do not produce enough testosterone, a child will develop as a female even if, genetically, it is a male. Not only must the hormone testosterone be available, but the organs on which it acts must also recognize and respond to this androgen. If there is a defect in these target organs, the fetus will develop as a female in spite of the fact that it secretes testosterone. This tendency toward female development is very strong. The action of both the Y chromosome and androgens are required to redirect development toward maleness.

A result of this redirection—this extra step of changing from a female to a male pattern of development—is that "male development is much more subject to error than female development," according to one leading endocrinologist. Even though more males are conceived, more are spontaneously aborted during pregnancy, and more of them have congenital defects and early respiratory problems.

A second and equally important function of the Y chromosome appears to be that of slowing the pace of development in males. Oxford medical researchers David Taylor and Christopher Ounsted theorize that this longer period of development in males allows more of the potentially available genetic material to be expressed. They explain the action of the Y chromosome's effect in terms of a spiral staircase. Boys plod slowly up the staircase, placing both feet on each step and carefully following the directions given there. Time and again their upward path takes them over similar territory, but each repetition is on a slightly higher level than the one before. The staircase for girls is much the same, but they are told to proceed at a faster pace. They may even skip a step or two, ignoring some of the instructions. At any given point, a boy and a girl will be found in different places on the staircase, and each will have a different amount of information.

Males show greater variability than girls in almost every aspect of their growth. One example is height. Although boys grow more slowly than girls, in adulthood most of them are taller. However, compared to the relative height of females in general, there is greater variation, from short to tall, among males. A teacher in a first-grade classroom will encounter a wide variety of IQ levels among her students, and an equally broad assortment of fine motor skills, loose teeth, and dispositions. Among the boys, though, there will generally be greater variation than among the girls. In characteristics that are related in some way to developmental pace, males will demonstrate more problems than females; reading disorders and antisocial behavior are two examples.

The "Sexing" of the Brain

There are less observable but far more profound differences between the sexes than behavior and physical characteristics. In recent years, technology has revealed the incredible complexity of the human brain. We are only beginning to understand the interrelationships of structure and function. In the brains of animals, numerous chemical and anatomical differences between the sexes have been found. The late Norman Geschwind, a prominent Harvard neurologist, once suggested that similar sex differences exist in many parts of the human brain; a number have already been discovered.

Brain weight and volume are both significantly greater in males by about 10 to 15 percent. Consistent prenatal differences were found between males and females in the shape and size of the corpus callosum, the bundle of nerves connecting the brain's hemispheres. During fetal life when the brain and nervous system are being organized, the female cortex develops in advance of the male cortex. The left half of the cortex, the part of the brain that controls thinking, develops somewhat later than the right. In males, though, there is an even greater lag. "As a result," one neurologist says, "when the right side is ready to hook up with the left side [by sending over connecting nerve fibers], in the male the appropriate cells don't yet exist on the left. So [the fibers] go back and instead form connections within the right hemisphere. You end up with extremely enriched connections within the right."

There are also important differences in the way male and female brains function. The enriched right hemisphere of males is believed to contribute to their spatial ability, which is more pronounced than that of females, and leads to skill in such fields as architecture and engineering. The early left-hemisphere advantage of females contributes to their success in language-related skills. There are differences, too, in how the halves of the brain communicate. Science writer Wray Herbert summed them up by suggesting the two halves of the male brain tend to function more independently of one another than in females, where the two halves "talk" back and forth. This increased communication may give girls an additional advantage in reading, a skill that draws on both sides of the brain.

Pioneering work is also being done on the chemistry of the brain, and major differences are being found here too. Neurotransmitters are chemicals that carry messages throughout the brain. They are believed to influence certain emotions and sometimes act in conjunction with sex hormones. One neurotransmitter, serotonin, which inhibits aggressive and impulsive behavior, has been found in higher levels in females than in males. Some researchers have discovered that serotonin levels are low in suicidal and alcoholic individuals. More men than women become problem drinkers; although more women than men attempt suicide, more men carry it to completion.

For a little boy, the sexing of his brain and the formation of his testes in early fetal life are major steps in a series of physiological events that ultimately result in male behavior and a male gender identity. Long before he is born, a little boy is programmed for maleness, and his sex will affect how he grows.

The Sequence of Development

Every child proceeds through progressive stages of development on a timetable influenced by his sex and his own particular combination of hereditary and environmental factors. In boys, acquiring self-control, learning to handle frustration, and settling in to the demands of school usually take longer than they do in girls. The vulnerability of boys to physical and environmental risks, and their delays in some aspects of development, may well mean that your son is more difficult to take care of than your daughter.

Each phase of growth is sequential, and builds upon

what has gone before. Development proceeds from the simple to the complex. The child must walk before he can run; he will run for many years before he is ready to join a track team. From the awareness of his own body, the infant grows to recognize family members and his home surroundings. His thought processes gradually enlarge to encompass the outer world. If your little boy is approaching school age, you may have noticed that he is now more interested than before in who lives down the block, or what it is his big sister does when she goes to school each day.

Development of the child is multifaceted, and occurs on a number of levels. How his body grows, how he feels about himself within his family, how he learns, and how he relates to others are all important. It is difficult for a child to achieve his full potential without proper growth in all four areas of physical, emotional, intellectual, and social development. You may know a child who has been encouraged toward academic achievement at the expense of other areas of development; he may have difficulty making and keeping friends, or feel his self-worth is only as good as the grades he brings home.

Each child comes into the world with an inborn urge to learn, to become competent, and, ultimately, to achieve independence. The desire to master his body and his environment is inherent and recognizable at every stage of development. The infant who follows you with his eyes is just as determined to grasp the world around him as the three-year-old is to dress himself, by himself.

A child's ability to do what is expected of him is determined by his level of thinking, which proceeds in a sequential way. A child of one, for example, has a year-old brain. Expecting him to put away his toys is unrealistic, no matter how advanced he may seem in moving about. He has only recently come to realize that his toys remain in existence when he can't see them.

It is important for us, as parents, to consider these aspects of growth in light of our son's unique characteristics, and to be accepting of the variabilities he may demonstrate. There is no other boy quite like your little boy, and recognizing what sets him apart from others makes parenting more interesting and enjoyable. Mothers and fathers who are accepting and enjoy youngsters for who they are rear the most competent children.

For a little boy, feeling competent and knowing that the important people in his life think highly of him is essential to his sound development. Competent children are loved and nurtured; they are given training and teaching when they need it; reasonable limits and expectations are set for their behavior; and they are respected for the individuals they are. Of all the gifts parents bestow upon their children, understanding of a child's unique timetable for development may be most important to a boy.

The Gift of Time

Many prominent individuals have been slow to develop, taking their time to achieve. Winston Churchill, whose words inspired half the world, had great difficulty learning as a boy. Albert Einstein's headmaster once said the boy would never succeed at anything. Beatle John Lennon's school experiences were dismal at best, and F. Scott Fitzgerald, in spite of his intelligence and obvious ability, was a poor student. Ronald Clark, in his 1984 biography of Charles Darwin, comments that the naturalist had a childhood "unmarked by the slightest trace of genius." Darwin's father once told him, "You care for nothing but shooting, dogs, and rat-catching, and you will be a disgrace to yourself and the family." Despite such unpromising beginnings, these men made contributions of lasting value to the world. Bertrand Russell once observed that a number of multitalented men of his generation all had in common a period in early childhood when they were free to do more or less as they pleased. Left to their own devices and allowed to pursue their own interests, these individuals, developed, as adults, extraordinary abilities in several fields.

Time, the very currency of childhood, can be well spent or squandered on a child's behalf. The mother who pushes a little boy to unnatural levels of achievement in the preschool years may rue her zeal. The boy who recited the proper sounds in response to flash cards at three may well decide, at thirteen, that the continuing struggle to please his parents isn't worth the price he pays in time, lack of friends, and the neglect of his own interests.

The consequences of pushing children and keeping the pressure on are every day growing more apparent. Fear of failure is cited as one reason for the rise in adolescent suicide, which in less than a decade has jumped more than 40 percent in the 15–24 age group. A Virginia physical education specialist notes that a number of high-school athletes decline to play once they enter college. Others who do enroll in college athletics often play out their scholarships and then leave the sport entirely. After thirteen or more years of pressure, these young men are fed up. And who can blame them?

For little boys, time is a priceless possession. How we help them spend it can bring uncounted dividends later on. Sometimes, though, it is hard to counter pressures for too much too soon, especially when they come from those who are supposed to be "the experts." The appeal of a particular educational method, a new technique, or a book that promises the magic formula for raising or educating children is hard to resist; most of us have given in at one time or another. After all, who doesn't want the best of everything for his child? In choosing methods or techniques we use with our offspring, however, it is important to remember the significance of time to a boy and his development.

Today's boy is growing up in a world that becomes increasingly complex every day, with technological innovation, rapid social change, and shifting moral values. More than ever before, it is essential for parents to help their sons become competent people. The ability to learn at a reasonable pace, apply his knowledge, and recognize when he needs to know more will be vital attributes for the successful man in the year 2000. Adaptational skills, which will enable him to alter his focus or direction. Most important of all, today's boy will need the competence to make right choices among the multiplicity of alternatives that scientific advancement will present to him and his generation.

Knowing some of the characteristics that make little boys so different from girls can be of enormous help in meeting the challenge of raising a son in today's world, and in making our own choices about how to help our boys to become happy, self-assured adults.

Infants and Toddlers

Martha Adams is sitting in a chair beside the window nursing ten-week-old Justin. She gazes down at the baby as his tiny lips move rhythmically against her flesh. He is larger than his sister was, and Martha knows he has an appetite to match.

He is so different from Lisa. Martha recalls that her daughter nursed fitfully—ravenous or fretful in turn. This baby has seemed far more easygoing since the day he was born; unfortunately, he is not so willing to sleep through the night. His daytime naps seem shorter, too, but perhaps it is just that she doesn't remember Lisa's schedule that well. Martha shifts her son to the other breast. After a momentary protest at the interruption, he settles down again.

Justin's dark eyes gaze fixedly at his mother's face as he nurses. A tiny flailing hand jerks outward, then moves toward her breast and makes several patting motions. The toes on his left foot fan out, and then his whole leg quivers. He seems so alert, so aware of everything. A crystal bird hanging in the window catches the sun's light, causing Justin to shift his gaze to its shiny surface. Still sucking, his eyes follow the light for a few seconds.

How beautiful her son is, Martha thinks, and so different from Lisa. They each seem to have such unique personalities: Lisa, screaming her way into the world a short four years ago, so eager to turn over, to crawl, or to talk before hurrying on to the next milestone; and Justin, who takes his time about everything, not rushing himself in the slightest.

When his mother holds him to her shoulder, Justin feels the soft thumps of her hand as she tries to get the bubble up. He can see from here, and his eyes search the room, focusing briefly on objects that are now becoming somewhat familiar. Then he is in his mother's lap, looking up at her. Martha's face is close, and she is making that pleasant sound again. Just as she comes to the part about "Daddy's gonna buy you a diamond ring," Justin pulls back his lips, crinkles his eyes, and tells her how much he likes her song. Martha is unable to continue. He smiled! He really smiled!

Boys Are Bigger but Less Well Developed

"What is it—a boy or a girl?" is usually the first question parents ask. Only the concern that our baby be healthy takes precedence over our interest in its sex. Although important differences begin even before birth, those that are evident in early infancy are often subtle and may require sophisticated testing procedures to determine accurately.

Besides the obvious genital differences, boys are, on the average, longer and heavier than girls at birth. As early as two months of age, they consume more calories than girls. They also have larger hearts and lungs, a higher systolic blood pressure, and a slower resting heart rate than do girls. The male has been compared to "an engine which operates at higher levels of speed and intensity and needs more fuel than the less energetic female organism." A boy's average weight gain is 300 percent in the first year of life. He is likely to gain a pound and a half more and to grow an inch taller than a baby girl before his first birthday, although the female's rate of growth is greater overall in childhood.

Newborn boys have less fat and more muscle than girl babies, and this difference continues throughout life. A male infant demonstrates greater strength in lifting his head as he lies on his stomach. This size and strength advantage may give boys a more robust, mature appearance than is actually the case.

In many unseen, but important aspects of development, a newborn girl is considered by some to be the equal of a four- to six-week-old boy. The female's advantage shows up in her behavior; a boy's relative immaturity may be a factor in the fussiness found in some male babies. If you have an older daughter and a new baby boy, you may notice your son is not as easily quieted as she was. As a rule, it takes a baby boy longer to settle down than it does a girl, and several studies show that male infants sleep less than female infants. For a number of years, it was assumed that baby boys were more active and irritable because they suffered the pains of circumcision, but comparisons of *un*circumcised boys with girls show that even these males are more fretful and somewhat more difficult to calm.

Sex Differences in Hearing and Vision

One reason boys may be harder to calm than girls seems to be that male hearing is less acute. Your daughter is likely to be quieted by the sound of your voice; your infant son may not be. It appears that the auditory system in girls is more sensitive than it is in boys. Newborn girls, hearing another infant cry, are more apt to join in and cry longer than boys.

Not only do girl babies hear different kinds of sounds better than boys, they also seem to make deliberate sounds themselves. Earlier and more often than a boy, a baby girl may use her own voice to get her mother's attention. Hearing in girls and women is more sensitive than it is in men and boys throughout life; females are able to locate the source of sounds more readily than males.

Another difference is pointed up when researchers studying infants record the length of time they look at a particular design or picture. The babies who seem to lose interest and shift their gaze elsewhere are most often boys. It may be that male infants, who until seven months of age lag behind girls in visual maturity, are less likely to respond to visual stimulation than females, or that they simply respond more to novelty even at this young age. From infancy on, boys tend to notice what seems different and are more likely than girls to show interest in the unusual.

Because we humans are such overwhelmingly visual creatures, all babies undoubtedly benefit from a variety of different sights, colors, and patterns. Staring is an active process for infants. Even if your little boy is lying in his crib, he is still busy taking everything in. Very young babies can follow a moving object with their eyes and see objects best if they are placed approximately seven and a half inches from their eyes. They also perceive bright colors, particularly red, and high-contrast patterns like checkerboards.

Similarly, all babies need to hear voices, music, and other sounds. Even before birth, the fetus responds to sound. Talking to your baby from birth on is essential to his development; making eye contact so that he sees your face as you speak encourages his efforts to communicate. Show your approval of his tiny sounds. All babies respond with pleasure to nursery rhymes and poetry. Music, as well, may be soothing, especially classical or country music. Rock music, on the other hand, may cause some babies to seem stressed. Fortunately, infants by and large are able to tune out a variety of bothersome stimuli and select instead the sights and sounds in the environment that meet their needs.

Development Is Strongly Programmed

We humans are programmed to develop in what is called a "species typical" way. Babies in Bangladesh, for example, are very much like babies in Baltimore. The major stages of development are reached in their appropriate order by all normal infants, although there may be differences in timing. Your little boy comes equipped to smile, to become attached to you at a certain point, and also to find pleasure in learning what you teach him. He is, in a very real sense, "prewired" to behave in certain ways that bring about predictable responses in you. If his environment is reasonably normal and caring, your little boy and all other babies will develop in the usual way during the first eighteen to twenty-four months of life.

This strongly programmed behavior of a child's early months is believed by a number of experts to be nature's way of protecting infants and ensuring their survival. There is very little evidence to suggest that accelerating behavior during this period of life has any dramatic effect on subsequent development.

There is, in fact, substantial evidence that a child's environment would have to be extreme in some way for normal development not to take place. All babies "look" closely at their hands at a certain point in development, even if they are blind; babbling occurs on schedule even if a child is deaf. The sucking, swallowing, grasping, and crying of your son's early weeks, followed by the smiling, reaching, and ever more coordinated activity of his first two years, is a behavioral legacy shared by all human babies everywhere.

Very young infants learn about their world through their senses. They have no idea that objects exist unless they can touch, taste, smell, hear, or see them. The newborn will not reach for an object when he sees it, or turn to an object when he touches it; he has not yet learned to touch what he sees or look at what he touches. As a baby matures, he begins to coordinate movement with his sensory impressions. When he hears his mother's voice, he turns his head to look at her. One of the events of your son's infancy that may please you the most comes when he turns his head to the door as you enter his room, and smiles widely when he sees your face.

Underlying a baby boy's growing sensory-motor coordination is an astonishing amount of brain growth. An infant's brain grows rapidly between three and ten months of age. This period is believed by some to be the first of four important brain-growth spurts during childhood; boys may begin brain-growth spurts somewhat later than girls do. The cells of his brain (neurons) multiply in number and size. Nerve fibers (dendrites) and the connections between them (synapses) are being formed, as well. From about six to fifteen months of age, a fatty insulating substance called myelin covers the brain's major fiber tracts. Like insulation on an electric wire, myelin helps transmit impulses and, it is believed, also contributes to the storage of experience, which we call memory.

Many experts believe that certain infant abilities are outward signs of the brain's maturation. For example, between sixteen and twenty-four months of age, but not before, children begin to recognize themselves when they look in a mirror.

A Baby Boy May Well Be What He Eats

The right food is vital to good health, especially in infancy. Not enough, or the wrong kind of food, may well be one environmental extremity that does interfere with normal growth—not only that which is measured in ounces and inches, but the unseen, crucial development of the central nervous system. "The brain is acutely dependent upon adequate nutrition throughout life," writes one neurochemist. Severe malnutrition before birth or during the first two years of life can cause "irreversible loss of brain development needed for 'normal' intellectual and emotional performance." It can also reduce the body's defense against disease. Chronic undernutrition (not having *enough* food) can have other adverse effects —shorter than average height, a small head circumference, and inadequate physical development.

Overwhelming evidence points to the superiority of mother's milk over formula, especially for boys. Mother's milk contains antibodies that protect infants against some respiratory and intestinal infections, as well as certain diseases like meningitis. It also promotes a warm, close relationship between a mother and her baby. More than girls, infant boys are prone to infantile diarrhea, gastrointestinal difficulties, respiratory ailments, and allergies. Unless their diets are carefully monitored, and, in some cases, certain nutrients are added, boys suffering from these problems may be at risk nutritionally.

We know very little about the more subtle effects on behavior or emotional growth that may occur with mild malnutrition or moderate undernutrition. There is, nevertheless, evidence that children with less than adequate nutrition have trouble paying attention, become irritable, are not as active as normal children, and may not respond to others as positively.

Certain youngsters are at risk, including children of the poor, whose families may lack money to buy enough food or lack education to know the right foods; children of women on restrictive diets, such as vegetarians, who often suffer from iron deficiency or may have insufficient reserves of vitamin B-12 to prevent pernicious anemia; children reared as "vegans" (vegetarians who consume no animal products like milk or eggs) who are slow to mature physically and may fall below average in weight and height; children allergic to milk who do not receive special supplements and can suffer calcium deficiency, which is detrimental to bone growth.

Parents' Responsiveness to Boys Is Essential

How we respond to our baby boy—how quickly we come when he cries or feed him when he's hungry, how much we show our pleasure in his accomplishments, how accepting we are of his unique developmental time-table—is nourishment of another but equally important kind. Burton White, who has devoted years to the study of infants and young children, believes that babies need to be "smothered with love and responsiveness" during their first six months. Most experts agree that it is impossible to spoil a baby during this period.

A major element in our responsiveness to any infant is understanding and accepting his temperament. A number of personality traits, some of which were believed to be acquired—adaptability to change, activity level, shyness, attention span, and certain moods—appear to be inherited to some degree. Your baby boy, for example, may be very active but not especially adaptable to new situations or routines, and express his frustrations with intense crying. You may not be able to change these traits directly, but you can manipulate his early environment to some extent so that he is relatively happy. He (and you!) will benefit from a regular routine early on. This is the kind of baby who may be better left at home with a sitter he knows than carried screaming to his stroller or car seat.

How well you adjust to your son's temperament seems to be a factor in his adjustment to the world around him. Alexander Thomas and Stella Chess of New York University Medical Center, who have studied temperament from infancy to adulthood, recognize that a "goodness of fit" between a child's temperament and his parents' reactions is important throughout childhood. Many children are classified from birth as "easy"—they adapt to new situations quickly, fall into a regular routine, and seem, as their description implies, easy to rear.

However, an overly anxious parent, whose own fears interrupt natural routines or prevent a baby's need to explore, may turn an easy baby into a thwarted, "difficult" one.

At birth, only about 4 percent of all babies are considered difficult, and one study found that the number of difficult babies was equally divided between boys and girls in early infancy. However, by two years of age, those toddlers still considered hard to handle were largely boys.

Irregular in sleep and eating patterns, emotionally disorganized and intense, difficult children often seem out of sorts, and it takes them longer than others to adapt to new situations and to warm up to people. Sounds and events that are pleasing to most infants overstimulate or upset these little ones. They may perceive holding and cuddling, which most babies love, as painful; some difficult infants squirm and struggle when their parents try to hold them. However, they do enjoy being touched, kissed, and tickled—apparently restraint is what arouses their resistance.

Difficult babies can be an enormous strain on a parent's patience, sense of perspective, and self-esteem. Those few parents who must deal with a truly difficult baby need all the support they can get. If you have an irritable baby, it may be helpful to keep in mind that your screaming, seemingly unadaptable infant is, if possible, more miserable than you are and certainly is not trying to make a shambles of your life. It also may help to realize that your patience and understanding will pay off in the long run. A study that followed easy and difficult babies into their preschool years showed that some children thought to be difficult early in life were, by two years of age, easy to handle if their parents became adept in meeting their needs. If you have a baby boy who is irritable and hard to adapt to change, or one whose temperament is very different from yours, you may have to work harder than usual to make him happy or to enjoy him.

As Babies Grow, Sex Differences Become More Apparent

At least some of the developmental milestones of infancy seem to produce different behaviors in boys than they do in girls. Because babies do not move about to any great extent in early infancy, sex differences in activity level are difficult to measure. However, as infants become more mobile, boys are much more active and move farther than girls. If you have a boy this age at home, you are probably well aware of this.

Besides moving more, boys show a greater interest in large muscle or gross motor activities than girls do. Boy toddlers enjoy creeping, pulling themselves up, climbing, sliding, and throwing things; they (and their parents) are often happiest when they are playing outdoors or in a large space. While girls the same age do many of these things, too, they may show a preference for fine motor movements—hammering pegs into the correct hole, tearing pages from a magazine, or playing with pots and pans. A boy's enjoyment of whole-body movement continues for much of his life.

From midway through a child's first year, movement is an important outlet. Five- to eight-month-old babies spend a good deal of time mouthing and manipulating objects and repeating the same action over and over again. As they gain control of their bodies, they continue to repeat certain movements—kicking their legs in the air, crawling, walking, climbing, and running. As one researcher said of older toddlers, "Children often become so mesmerized by their own interest in locomotion that their physical activities seem mindless, innervated solely by pleasure seeking."

Many little boys have activity levels that exceed their understanding. One such boy, not realizing that paper lacked the strength of wood, hurt himself by falling when he leaned against an empty grocery bag. Some active toddlers, most often boys, seem unable to pay attention to a parent's attempts to explain why something happens, or the reasons for her demands; training them can be very difficult.

As soon as your little boy begins to crawl, you will want to remove valuables and dangerous objects from his reach. Arranging our homes so that a child can explore safely prevents breakage, hurt feelings, injuries, and confrontations. This means moving furniture against wall outlets so he won't see them, plugging unused ones with plastic covers, finding a temporary home for house plants, and hanging all pictures and wall décor out of your son's reach. As your son's motor coordination grows, so do the behaviors that can hurt him—opening latches, climbing up, falling down, throwing objects, jumping on or off furniture or stairs.

Making Your Home Safe

If you are the mother of an active baby boy (and those of you who are will recognize yourselves immediately), life is very different for you than it is for many other mothers. For one thing, you are likely to be thinner. For another, your level of tension and awareness is higher (it has to be!). Because your son probably walked early and may have a shorter attention span than other babies his age, you may find yourself taking precautions other parents may not need in caring for their offspring, whose abilities at climbing and running usually keep pace with their language development and understanding.

Some children simply tend to be accident prone—it's not their fault or yours. Once you recognize this, you will develop your own sense of how best to protect your son. Do not hesitate to use baby gates at home or well-designed safety harnesses when walking near traffic. Active children may be rapid movers, and injuries can occur in seconds. Help your little boy to understand cause and effect, but remember that he may need extra training.

"BECAUSE SHES AFRAID YOU MIGHT BREAK IT, DEAR."

- *Post numbers of the ambulance service, Poison Control Center,* and *the nearest hospital emergency room* permanently beside your telephone.
- *Use small-mesh fencing to block spaces between railings on decks and porches. Consider barring low windows or large expanses of glass.*
- *Purchase a lock for the medicine cabinet or any kitchen cabinet that contains breakables or poisonous cleansers.*
- *Remove or plug the lock on the bathroom or other interior doors. Boys find locks of all kinds intriguing and like to play with them.*
- *Place electric appliances such as toasters or food processors out of young children's reach. If you have a choice, select a stove with knobs in the back rather than the front. Check your home for exposed wires or cords (toddlers chew on them).*
- *Teach your son early on not to put foreign objects in*

his mouth. Chipping and peeling paint may contain dangerous levels of lead, particularly in old houses. Lead may also be present in colored newsprint and in acidic foods stored in handmade pottery or in cans with lead solder.

- *Pets should be kept away from toddlers unless you are able to supervise your children every single minute. Animals can bite, scratch, or claw your little boy.*

Boys Are Curious Creatures

Just as boys are more active, they are also more curious than girls. Your son will delight in the face-to-face attention he receives from you and other family members. But, unlike a baby girl, he may be equally fascinated by objects, the play of light across his crib, dust motes, or lighting fixtures. From the beginning, boys seem as interested in nonhuman patterns as they are in faces, whereas girls prefer faces to patterns. This greater interest in people on the part of girls may contribute to their later ability to read meaning into facial expressions, a sex difference that increases with age and exists in a wide variety of cultures.

As baby boys become mobile, they explore their surroundings indiscriminately. More so than girls, boys want to taste everything (even if it crawls), touch anything they can get their hands on (even if it's hot), and move things about (even if they're plugged in). They are apt to upturn containers so they can peer into them, jiggle a latch to discover what's on the other side of a door, and move furniture if it's in their way or will help them climb up to see better.

As your little boy grows, starts to walk, and says his first tentative words, he becomes more purposeful in his play, trying out different uses for his toys and observing what happens. Strings and sticks may be used in various ways, especially as tools. Even as babies, boys use their toys in "creative" ways. Your son may turn a drinking cup into a container for tiny cars, or roll the pegs you expected him to hammer into those round holes, while he uses the hammer as a pacifier. Boys' curiosity shows up in the "how" and "why" questions they ask when they begin to talk. From infancy, boys are more interested than girls in events that are unusual or novel.

Attachment Signals Different Strategies in Boys and Girls

An important developmental milestone for all infants is attachment to those who care for them on a regular basis. One way we recognize attachment is when a child, usually about a year old, protests if we leave him.

Harvard's Jerome Kagan sees an interesting difference between boys and girls when they are separated from their mothers: girls show greater fear. This anxiety in girls may come from their understanding of separation before they have developed strategies to deal with it.

Key elements in a child's sense of attachment are the ability to realize something still exists even if he cannot see it, and the memory of people and objects he sees again and again. You may have noticed that hiding a very young baby's rattle does not pique his curiosity (if he doesn't see it, it doesn't exist), but as he matures, he will look for a hidden object (he remembers what he cannot see). Usually between eight and thirteen months, an infant begins to remember those people to whom he feels close; he may experience uncertainty when his mother leaves, or a person he can't remember suddenly appears.

Some researchers suggest that the faster pace at which the myelin covers the nerve tracts in the female brain may speed up message-transmitting capacity. Girls appear to recognize people, objects, and events earlier than boys do, and may pay for this precocity by having more frequent bouts of fear during their first year.

From the time they are approximately six months old, girls and boys will respond differently when they see something unusual, hear a strange noise, or undergo similar new experiences. Girls are likely to be upset, whereas boys may well show great interest. Taken visiting to a neighbor's, or being presented to a stranger in her own living room, a little girl may inhibit her movements and stay close to her mother. Even though he may be just as uncertain as the girl in these circumstances, a little boy will usually do something—walk or crawl away and then back, go behind a chair, or appear to play purposefully with a toy. Activity of some kind may help boys short-circuit their fear.

Research at Stanford University reveals another strategy baby boys may use to deal with fear. Boys around one year of age were shown a mechanical monkey that clapped cymbals together loudly when it was activated. Many one-year-old boys are afraid of this kind of toy and a number of subjects responded with tears and were very fearful. However, the boys who were taught how to control the mechanical monkey, activating it themselves rather than being uncertain when the experimenter might turn it on, did not appear frightened. A sense of control in boys may actually counteract fear.

You may have noticed, as other parents have, that your baby boy can leave you quite easily (he is in control). But it is when you try to leave him (he is no longer in control), that he becomes upset. Manipulating objects or moving them about seems to be a way many year-old boys can gain control. In a series of experiments that separated babies from their mothers by a barrier, one-year-old boys were more likely than girls to jiggle the latch that held the end of the barrier to the wall or try to get around the barrier.

Language Appears to Develop More Slowly in Boys

The same experiment with older children suggests that girls in their second year use language more effectively than boys do to get what they want. By two, girls placed behind a barrier called out to their mothers and asked for help, using more two-word sentences than boys, and they also did a better job of working the latch. Many of the boys did not rely on language but resorted to tears and fretting, using what the researchers regarded as less mature behavior than girls.

From infancy on, girls appear to have a language advantage. They may be more accurate in producing speech sounds and also use more words in phrases than little boys do. Infant girls rely on speech before boy babies do to seek information. Observations suggest that girls may talk more to people and to dolls who represent people, whereas small boys will make random noises almost as often as words and talk both to people and inanimate objects. It is clear that speech problems and language disorders are more often found among boys than girls.

Learning to talk is the most remarkable achievement in a child's second year. From his first to his second birthday, a toddler may begin to understand or use up to approximately three hundred words. A vocabulary of at least fifty words is considered by one expert to be typical of two-year-olds. A child's first efforts to talk are often accompanied by a number of gestures that enhance what he is trying to say. Most of us are familiar with an infant's upraised arms to indicate that he wants to be picked up. "Up" can mean "Pick me up," "Pick up my bottle," "It is time to get up," or "Swing me up and down, Daddy." Being able to use speech gives a little boy power he did not previously possess; it brings the dog, makes siblings notice him, and gets mothers and fathers to do all sorts of things. Infants practice their new speech sounds repeatedly, much the way they practiced their crawling and walking.

Speech, memory, and the ability to process information are all linked to an infant's more mature way of thinking. Between eighteen months and two years of age, toddlers begin to use symbols and learn to think symbolically in a number of ways. Words are symbols for ideas and objects. A block that your son pushes across the floor may be a symbol for a car or a truck. This higher level of thought leads to greater independence, some confusion, and the beginning of conflict. Late in infancy, your son will use the word no, and it is symbolic of many changes he is undergoing.

When a Little Boy Says No

As a toddler grows more independent, he experiences a seesawing of emotions. He may feel compelled to show his independence—walking away when you call him or climbing out of his crib at naptime—yet he knows he still needs you and still feels dependent on his parents. The conflict this causes can lead to negative behavior, which has particular significance for boys.

From a very early age, even as young as ten months, a boy may be less compliant than a girl. He is more likely to ignore what you tell him to do, or to counter your demands in some way. If this behavior is as universal as it appears to be, it seems reasonable to assume that it has some usefulness or value in male development. Perhaps boys' greater activity level and their apparent need to control what happens to them contribute to their lack of compliance.

All children have bouts of anger between eighteen months and two years, but little boys then begin to show more frustration and anger than girls do. At two, boys and girls seem equal in problem-solving abilities, but girls can use their greater language skills to get attention; boys, whose immature language abilities contribute to their frustration, are more likely to use anger. Girls learn to control their frustration and their tempers earlier than boys do.

All children between one and two years of age are limited in their reasoning abilities. Cause-effect, if-then, or means-end logic has little, if any, relevance for toddlers. In his need to satisfy his body, to explore his environment, to exercise control over what happens to him, a little boy between one and two faces inevitable frustration as he meets very real limitations on his movement, his desires, and his time—most often in the form of his parents.

The sense of power and control he experiences as a result of speech and mobility may give a little boy, even more than a girl, an exaggerated sense of his own ability. The same toddler who smilingly helps pick up the blocks can turn, within thirty seconds, into a grimacing, foot-stomping rebel when told it's time for bed. Even if a boy doesn't speak very well, his behavior clearly says, "Maybe you think it's time for bed, but I've got other ideas!"

Few of us are trained to deal effectively with a creature who has little reason, less tact, and loads of resistance, especially when that would-be tyrant barely reaches our knees. From infancy, boys are more defiant than girls.

The Beginning of Discipline

When it first happens to us, our child's defiance comes as quite a shock. Other people's children were supposed to act like this—not ours! Few of us undergo any formal training before becoming parents. We can read books and articles, but many of our ideas about discipline come from how we were treated by our own parents. It is important early in a child's life to recognize certain patterns in the way we respond to our child's no's. Parent-child behavior patterns tend to continue for years. Less effective ones can lead to difficulty for ourselves and our offspring.

A number of parents back away from training toddlers, especially if they are active little boys. These parents may recognize a toddler's needs—allowing him to explore and providing plenty of outdoor play—but fail to realize the importance of patient, consistent behavior training. Mothers of difficult boys have been found to hold and physically comfort their young sons, but some do little to teach them how to act. One such mother, observing her son hit a visiting youngster, may simply call out, "Brian, now you stop that!" She does not get up from her chair, or indicate by her body language that she means what she says. The other child retaliates; Brian comes crying to his mother. She picks him up and holds him, then puts him down and returns to her conversation with the visiting child's mother. Brian has not really gotten the message that his behavior is inappropriate; his mother did not take the time to teach him.

Lacking an inner motivation to comply with parents' requests, and failing to receive an external one in the form of parental firmness, toddlers can be even harder to handle by eighteen months than they are at one year. While difficult children do not seem to initiate more "bad" or negative behavior than other youngsters do, they persist in it once they have started.

Many parents are great believers in the "it's just a phase" approach to child rearing. A natural extension of this line of thinking is, "Why bother doing anything about his behavior? He's only a baby. He'll outgrow it." Unfortunately, without some pretty heroic efforts by their parents, little boys rarely outgrow angry, negative behavior that begins early in life. Another problem that can arise when toddlers are permissively handled is that older siblings, who may be repeatedly coerced into giving in, are likely to resent the younger child. Allowing a toddler with little reasoning ability to dominate family life is absurd. All family members have needs, and toddlers learn this readily, given a little help.

Other parents adopt a drastically different approach to their curious, often resistant little boys. "Do as I say!" probably best sums up their point of view. These parents often feel they need to show a baby who is in control. They rarely hesitate to give their child reprimands, warnings, or spankings to "teach him a lesson," and fail to spend much time in real training. They often believe a toddler understands more than he really does.

Not too surprisingly, these parents have a high number of conflicts with their children, especially boys. If an infant's efforts at exploration and independence are continually blocked by parents determined "not to let him win," everybody winds up a loser. A child who is spanked regularly and often by the adults who are supposed to love him receives a very mixed message.

Harsh methods of discipline can have far-reaching effects, as discussed in Chapter 3. If these contrasting parenting styles are not very effective in training or disciplining a toddler boy, what, then, is a useful approach?

Distraction, Diversion, and Diplomacy Are Best for Toddlers

Tactics of distraction, diversion, and diplomacy work well with all toddlers. A mother might distract a foot-stomping bedtime-hater by saying, "Guess what I saw upstairs? It's got four legs, a tail, and it's soft." Once she has her son upstairs, she gently but firmly gets him undressed. "While we put on your pajamas, let's see if we can find out what it might be." Recognizing her son's need for independence and self-control, the parent's behavior says, "I know you are a big boy. But now it's time for bed." Her pleasant way of diverting his attention to something interesting (his teddy bear) and the diplomatic way she avoids a confrontation, lets her son know that she respects him. And she expects respect from him in return.

Reciprocal respect is a pattern of discipline that works well for boys. The adult, rather than the toddler whose brain and understanding are still developing, is in charge. By helping a boy do as we wish, instead of by ignoring or forcing certain behaviors, parents encourage a toddler to act in a positive way. All children learn by doing. Reinforcing desirable behavior may be the most effective form of training for very young children. Smiling and thanking your little boy when he takes your hand instead of running off down the sidewalk, or telling your spouse in his presence how grown up your son is because he's learned to drink from a cup, will encourage a little boy to continue to comply with your requests.

How a parent treats a child has a direct bearing upon how that child treats others. Most children who are treated kindly are themselves kind. Mothers who use a policy of *explaining why* children should behave in a certain way, and stating the principle behind their rules ("We don't hit other people—hitting hurts!") rear youngsters who are more cooperative or generous than those whose mothers' main method of discipline is hitting their children and saying, "Don't do that!" As simple a technique as introducing positive words such as *nice, kind,* and *helpful* into your toddler's vocabulary may discourage negative behavior. Avoid the use of phrases such as *bad boy,* and offer reasons for your insistence on compliance.

Temper tantrums are normal, if somewhat disturbing, displays of anger in young children. Most child-rearing texts suggest that parents ignore or deal calmly with tantrums. If your son throws himself on the floor in a rage, you may want to disregard his behavior; however, it can be very difficult to use this approach if you are at the supermarket or on a street. Thomas Lickona, an educator and father of boys, recommends the "hold and talk" technique, which has been shown to defuse tantrums. Take your toddler out of the store or away from traffic. Hold him firmly without hurting him—kneeling behind him or if you can sit placing him on your lap. At the same time talk to him firmly and calmly, letting him know that his lack of control is inappropriate.

An important ingredient in successful toddler management is a regular routine. Orderly household environments have been found especially helpful to little boys, and it is far easier to maintain routine in the midst of order. Making a strong effort here may be especially important if we are not, ourselves, orderly people. (It is, however, amazing how much an incentive to order an active toddler can be!) Regular bed and bath times, an easy-to-manage system for storing toys that encourages your son to help clean up, and simple mealtime routines can help create a pleasant home environment. One toddler boy kept his placemat, cup, plate, and spoon in a low drawer and set his own place at the table. In another family, the word "storytime" served to quiet an active little boy who looked forward to this winding-down period each evening.

Little Boys May Be Harder to Toilet Train

Many child-rearing experts recommend that parents begin toilet training a toddler at eighteen months or later, only after he shows some interest in cleanliness, takes pride in his accomplishments, and begins to imitate and identify with others. Girls usually achieve bladder and sphincter control more easily than boys. By school age, those children whose parents are concerned over their bedwetting are mostly male.

There are many reasons a boy may wet his bed at night, ranging from milk allergy to an immature bladder; whatever the cause, almost all children are embarrassed by a bedwetting problem. They may be teased about their lack of control and be reluctant to spend the night at a friend's for fear of letting another child know about what they perceive to be their own failure.

Pediatrician T. Berry Brazelton has developed a system of toilet training based on a young child's own developing sense of control, described in detail in his book To Listen to a Child. *He has found youngsters trained according to their own developmental pace experience an almost perfect success rate. Parents can begin by introducing their toddler to his own "potty chair" and explaining that this is like the toilet they use. At first he sits on his potty fully clothed, while his mother reads to him. Next he becomes accustomed to sitting on the potty*

*without diapers; then, if he soils or wets his pants, he is
brought back to the potty and his pants changed while
he sits on the chair. When the young child shows an
understanding and interest, he can be encouraged to sit
on his potty two or three times a day.* At no stage in this
process is a child pressured to perform; *he moves from
one step to the next only after a week or more of interest
and cooperation in his training routine.*

*Each success is applauded, no matter how small.
Most little boys enjoy learning to stand and urinate, following their fathers' examples. Nap-time and night
training are postponed until after a child begins to stay
clean and dry during the day, sometimes a year or two
after initial training begins. In England, where youngsters are pressured to be trained earlier, twice as many
children are bedwetters.*

The Larger World Beckons
the Two-year-old

As a little boy approaches two, he becomes more interested in other children and in what goes on outside the
family. He may not be ready to venture forth into this
world as of yet, but he is nevertheless interested in it.
Memory improves, vocabularly increases, and play becomes somewhat more sophisticated. Cars are not just
pushed, but turned in the right direction beforehand.
There may be an increase in ritualistic behavior, often
connected with play. The box that holds the cars may
have to be put in a certain place or a specific position
before the cars are removed.

This is a good age to introduce your son to playmates,
even if they see one another only once a week. These
tentative first attempts at play with another child center
around objects rather than ideas, and motor activities
rather than speech. Little boys may say little as they
share cars, but enjoy moving them around and making
random, carlike noises. Children this age play side-by-

side rather than cooperatively. In the presence of older children, toddlers do a great deal of watching.

A little boy plays more vigorously if he has another boy to play with. There seems to be an elusive "something" about the presence of a second male child that is intriguing and exciting to a little boy. If you have had several small boys in your home at one time, you are no doubt familiar with the escalation of voices, rise in emotional intensity, and general exhilaration that characterizes the play of boys in pairs or small groups. By his second birthday, your son will be able to sustain a reasonable period of play, and will begin to cooperate to some degree with a friend.

Much of your son's behavior at two involves movement. A boy's pleasure in movement is greatest around his second birthday. It is still more difficult for most boys than it is for most girls to put on the brakes, but little boys begin to show a measure of self-control. Many two-year-olds are able to wait for a short time and to moderate their behavior somewhat when it is called for.

The ability to invent a means to an end—figuring out a new way of solving a problem—marks a higher level of thinking in a young child. One boy, rolling a rubber ball about in the kitchen, claps delightedly as it bangs against the stove and cabinets. His game is disrupted, however, each time the ball rolls down the small flight of steps to the family room.

Nearby in a corner of the kitchen is his toy chest. The boy looks at the chest, then at the stairs. Pushing the chest across the kitchen floor, he blocks the stairs and prevents the ball from escaping. He has found a means to solve his problem by using an object in a novel way for his own purpose. He is able to plan ahead of time what he is going to do.

As he earlier learned to use his block to represent a toy car, and words to represent his thoughts, he now thinks about an act before he does it. This ability marks a turning point—the end of infancy, and the beginning of childhood.

Learning to Be a Boy

PRESCHOOLERS

From very early on, children learn to act like boys or girls. Parents play a major role in their socialization. We applaud our sons for not crying when they are hurt: "What a big boy you are!" We smile and nod approval as they learn to stack two, then four blocks on top of one another: "We have an architect on our hands!" A sports-loving father glows with pleasure when his son can throw a ball: "Believe it—this is another Hank Aaron!"

Young children also play a part in their own socialization, exaggerating traits they associate with their own sex and imitating behaviors they observe in others. Beginning around three, preschoolers seem to prefer playing with children of their own gender. This "sex cleavage," as psychologists call the phenomenon, extends well into the elementary-school years and crosses cultural barriers. As preschool children become more cooperative with others, peers of the same sex seem to reinforce certain activities. Girls enjoy playing house; boys wrestle happily with one another or work together to build a rocket out of blocks.

The years between two and four are marked by the highest metabolic rate for humans; boys' metabolism runs higher than that of girls. You may notice that your son uses his whole body when he moves; he is often happiest outdoors on his jungle gym or his tricycle. Boys may be less advanced than girls in the fine motor skills important in preschool. How competent a boy becomes at this age and how he feels about himself will affect his success for years to come.

Learning to get along with others is one of the most important tasks to be accomplished during the years between two and five. Boys, more than girls, may need time and often help to develop skills necessary for successful play with their peers. They are likely to be combative with both siblings and friends. It is far more important for preschool boys to acquire the social skills of give-and-take than it is for them to be taught the alphabet or how to write their names. A young boy who gets on well with others and is becoming able to control his impulses will be ready for the academic tasks of elementary school, while a boy who has not had a chance to make friends before starting school may well spend much of his classroom time focusing on other children instead of his work.

What It Means to Be a Boy

As young children learn what their own gender means, society's notions of masculinity and femininity become important to them. Gender *identity* (a child's realization that he is a boy and not a girl) usually develops around the age of three, but the concept of gender *permanence* (the understanding that a boy will always be male and grow up to be a father rather than a mother) does not appear in most children until they are close to seven years old. As a child learns his own sex, he begins to recognize male and female traits in others, largely by the clothes people wear, the length of their hair, and the way they behave.

Little boys adopt a wide variety of male roles and

often depend upon props (a "superhero" cape or an assortment of hats that designate different occupations). As the preschool child learns about and becomes accustomed to his own gender, he is fairly rigid in his definition of acceptable male and female behavior. Your son may suddenly refuse to play with the little girl next door, although she's been his favorite playmate since they were toddlers; if he has an imaginary playmate, it's likely to be a boy. He may be scornful of other boys who act like girls, and afraid he might be teased for acting that way himself. Even if he has "liberated" parents, a little boy may behave like a male chauvinist until he realizes his gender is permanent.

Despite a growing acceptance of equal rights for women in the United States, men continue to be the more powerful sex—at least to young children. They hear their mothers ask their fathers to open a jar for them; they also see fathers, rarely mothers, shoveling off the walk or performing any number of tasks that require greater physical strength. To a preschool child, strength means power. As children learn their own gender, they also come to perceive males as dominant. As they mature, boys and girls today tend to adopt masculine traits.

Parents Socialize Their Sons into Little Boys

By our smiles, our body language, and our tone of voice, we parents let our offspring know which of their behaviors we condone and which we discourage. Because males have been the dominant sex for millennia, both mothers and fathers are reluctant to encourage feminine traits, often perceived as weaknesses, in a little boy. We are less comfortable when our son cries or clings to us than we are when our daughter displays the same behavior. We rationalize this feeling by saying, "We don't want to turn our son into a sissy." Parents may tolerate messiness in boys, or allow a young son to get consider-

"GEE, YOU'RE *LOTS* OF FUN! ARE YOU **SURE** YOU'RE A GIRL?"

ably dirtier than they would a daughter. After all, we think, "Boys will be boys." We are also more likely to encourage independence and competitiveness in our sons than in our daughters.

While a father tends to play more unconventionally than a mother with both boys and girls, and encourages problem-solving in children of either sex, he usually gets more involved with a son than he does with a daughter. Fathers are concerned that their children adopt behaviors appropriate to their gender, and they offer their boys important models for masculinity. Dad plays rougher with a boy, romping or wrestling; he also expects more of him, and punishes him more severely than he does a girl. It seems hard for many fathers to punish their daughters. They would rather protect their little girls and are apt to praise them for how pretty they look or how well they get along with another child. With their sons, fathers often emphasize learning and achievement.

"MOM JUST RAISES HER VOICE BUT MY DAD YELLS."

In most families, fathers are not as available to their children as mothers are. When preschoolers play house, the role of mother is a rich and elaborate one. Little girls draw on their daily experience with mother in their make-believe play. Even though their fantasy may allow them to have jobs outside the home, girls' "mother" roles are invariably nurturant. The role of father, however, is elusive and vague. If a little boy does play "daddy," his activity may be limited to eating dinner or getting ready to go to work. In one rare make-believe scenario where "father" actually took charge of his "children," the little boy playing out this domestic role got it all wrong. He put the "baby" to sleep in a dresser drawer instead of his crib, and was quickly reprimanded by "mother," who is portrayed in most childhood fantasies as the ultimate authority on proper behavior. Away from home during the hours when preschoolers are most alert and active, fathers remain somewhat mysterious to their offspring, no matter how much young children delight in their company.

A preschool boy must do without the same easy access to sex-role models that most girls have in their mothers. Some psychologists suggest that learning to be a boy involves, at least to some extent, learning not to be feminine. It is hardly surprising, given children's relatively limited contact with their fathers, that *many little boys define their masculine identity by what males are not*—they are not mothers or housekeepers in make-believe play, and they do not wear dresses or lots of jewelry in real life. Nor is it unreasonable that preschool boys, still figuring out what it means to be male, show less tolerance than girls of inappropriate sex-role play in other children.

Fathers Make a Difference

In one of the few extensive reviews of the father's role in child development, University of Utah psychologist Michael Lamb suggests that many men today want to be closely involved with their children, especially their sons. Traditionally, dad took over in the evening while mom fixed dinner, and this playtime before supper or bed was treasured by small children. For many fathers, however, commuting or job-related travel makes it difficult for them to spend as much time as they might like with their families. One busy attorney periodically invites his young son down to his office on Saturdays. While he packs his briefcase, his little boy loads up his lunchbox with Legos or action figures. Other fathers, who leave for work before their children are up or who come home after their bedtimes, try to assume child-care duties on the weekends.

Even if most fathers leave the primary responsibility of child care to their wives, the interest and concern they show a young boy is very important. Warm, nurturing fathers seem to encourage strong sex-role development in all their children, and greater competence and generosity in their sons. A mother who enlists her husband's opinions about their son can stimulate his active participation in child rearing. When a father is available to his family and relieves his wife of some child-care responsibilities, a mother seems to respond more positively to her sons than when she is on her own.

Role-reversed families, where the mother goes out to work and the father provides daily child care, are relatively rare. However, studies of this kind of family in Australia, Israel, and the United States point up some positive effects of active fathering. Boys in these families appear more masculine than those in traditional families, and no problems with gender identity have been noted among the children studied. It seems that preschool children reared by their fathers don't need to lose out on traits usually associated with the opposite sex; if boys observe their fathers caring for youngsters on a daily basis, they may learn to associate concern for others with masculinity the way most of us reared by women associate it with femininity. When fathers are the primary caregivers, boys see a strong image of males, not only as powerful, but also as nurturing. One such father was asked if he was concerned about the unusual role model he represented to his young son, and he answered, "Any kid who bombs around the neighborhood on his Big Wheel with his baby doll in the jump seat is probably going to turn out just fine."

Boys and girls in role-reversed families appear well developed, if not more socially active and adaptive than traditionally reared youngsters. Yale University researcher Kyle Pruett suggests that children reared by their fathers have two "stimulating" parents rather than just one. Fathers, as regular caregivers, handle children daily in a "jostling, stimulating way," while working mothers, as the mysterious "coming and going" parent, pique their offspring's curiosity. It appears that these mothers, even though they spend much of the day away from their children, continue to be nurturant, and are perhaps more interested in their sons and daughters than conventional working fathers are. Their children may benefit from the strong role models of two actively involved parents.

But What if Dad's not Around?

In 1980, nearly two million children were living in single-parent families, usually headed by women. Fortunately, most boys develop masculine traits even if there is no man around the house. A preschool boy will take a lively interest in any and all men—a repairman fixing the washer, as well as a character on television. But single mothers need to make a special effort to encourage independence and assertiveness in their sons.

Parenting is not easy for two adults. For one alone, the burden of everyday decisions and discipline can sometimes feel too heavy to bear. Single mothers of active, often aggressive little boys face a double-barreled problem—a child who is frequently defiant, and one whose interests (toy guns, earthworms, metal soldiers, and machines that convert into robots) can seem quite alien to her own memories of childhood.

Nevertheless, many single mothers do an excellent job of rearing little boys, especially if they are able to build a stable base of support for themselves and their children. Friends and extended family become particularly important in these households. Sharing a home with another single mother or senior citizen can cut expenses, and also provide companionship for a mother and her children. In one long-term study of inner-city children, those youngsters growing up in single-parent households where the mother lived with her own mother adapted as well to school and appeared as socially well adjusted as children in their community who lived with both parents. Groups like Parents Without Partners can be very helpful to single mothers, and child-rearing books and parenting courses may offer much-needed practical advice.

Aggressiveness May Be Biologically Based

One of the clearest differences between preschool boys and girls is combativeness. Little boys who tentatively push or poke another boy usually get poked or pushed in return; little girls are less likely to initiate aggression or to counterattack. Several little boys playing together will act out sequences from their favorite television shows, often taking on violent, aggressive roles that little girls rarely assume. From infancy on, boys stimulate other boys to be more active and combative.

Cross-cultural and animal studies suggest that this male combativeness is universal and innate. Most young males, animal and human, join together in good-natured wrestling and romping—what experts call rough-and-tumble play. Females rarely do. In human societies and many animal groups, such as the primates, who most closely resemble humans, males use aggression—behavior that seems intended to threaten or harm—to settle disputes or to express anger and emotional upset. Females are likely to rely on other strategies.

Body chemistry in both animals and humans fluctuates according to a male's level of aggression. Androgens, like testosterone, and neurotransmitters found in the brain, such as serotonin, appear to play some role in combative behavior. Although the findings are clearer and easier to test in animals, a few human studies link testosterone to aggressive behavior in adolescent and adult males. In experiments with monkeys, whole blood serotonin levels appear to be affected by the male's rank in a group; more dominant monkeys have high serotonin levels, and serotonin increases after an individual assumes a leadership role. In a 1984 study, Michael McGuire of UCLA's Neuropsychiatric Institute found similar whole blood serotonin differences in college-age males. "The social feedback a male receives from other males seems significant here," McGuire says. How other males react to expressions of dominance appears to influence certain physiological mechanisms. The connection of neurochemical substances with aggression in males seems to underscore a biological level of combativeness.

In group situations, such as preschool or a day-care center, young boys' aggressiveness is obvious. It may serve a certain function much the way similar behavior in animal groups does, as children sort themselves out into a ranking or dominance hierarchy. In the innumerable property squabbles of early childhood, little boys who are "tough" and able to hold on to their possessions gain respect from other children. For most boys, the "if-you-don't-give-me-that-toy-I'll-hit-you" approach is at its height at around four years of age when they begin to assert their rights verbally instead of using physical aggression. Knowing which boy is liable to fight or stand up effectively for his rights helps youngsters avoid trouble. Dominance rankings in boys' groups seem to reduce aggression once they stabilize, usually at the end of the preschool period.

As young children mature, boys tend to play in groups, while girls prefer one or two close friends. Dominance rankings remain important for boys, but girls' relationships seem more affiliative than hierarchical. As early as two, little girls begin to compliment each other. Throughout childhood, girls ask favors and advice of their friends, while teasing and rough-and-tumble play are typical behaviors among boys who are friends.

Although boys who are close to kindergarten age may hit others less often than they did previously, aggressiveness is a part of the make-believe play of many young boys. Often to their parents' dismay, toy weapons and aggressive action figures are favorite toys for preschool boys. Even in homes where such toys are banned, boys will create guns out of sticks, clay, or their index fingers. Talking to your son about why you disapprove of toy guns or knives, and discouraging play with violent toys can be an effective way to inhibit his interest in them.

Strict banning of such toys, especially if coupled with severe threats, may actually encourage a little boy's interest in aggressive play.

Some Aggressiveness Is also Learned

While a certain level of combativeness is basic to most little boys, aggressive behavior can also be a response to situations and society's expectations. Children will usually strike out in anger at others, if they, themselves, have been hit. Frustration is a factor in aggressiveness, and it is clear that preschool boys become frustrated more often than little girls. After the age of two, boys are twice as likely to explode in anger as girls are; they are also likely to cry when they are frustrated. Preschool boys are more likely to cry than girls, and to show emotional distress in strange situations. As they grow older, however, boys are socialized out of crying, although they continue to express irritability, fear of the dark, and worries as frequently as girls do.

Big Boys Don't Cry

It is hard for some little boys not to cry when they are hurt, or when it is just their feelings that are ruffled. Being taunted for crying by other boys can be even harder. If you have a sensitive son, help him to see that his feelings are nothing to be ashamed of ("We all feel like crying when we hurt."). At the same time, foster more mature responses to stress ("It's not easy to stand up to a bigger boy like Max." "You were right to tell John to give back Mary's doll; I was proud of you.") Reinforce behavior that indicates your son is trying to overcome his propensity to cry easily. Brad will see that what he did represents a milestone if he hears you tell his dad at the supper table, "Brad had to sit in the dentist's chair for almost forty-five minutes this afternoon and he didn't cry once!"

There are some little boys who may refuse to cry even if they are in pain or bleeding. More than sensitive boys, these "tough" little guys need to know that sometimes crying is not only okay, it is also appropriate. Dad can be a big help to a noncrying youngster ("The time I got my bike stolen when I was five, I must have cried for almost an hour!").

As certain ways of emotional expression, like crying, are cut off to boys, other outlets will be more frequently used. Beginning in the preschool period, boys may learn that anger and aggressiveness are acceptable for expressions of their feelings.

Boys, more than girls, appear to imitate aggressive behavior. Unfortunately, there is a great deal of male aggression to imitate—in cartoons, fairy tales, on the playground; even in the news it is usually males who behave in violent ways. Little boys are also born mimics of male gestures. They swagger and ape macho gestures they have seen on television, or will start up a toy lawn mower just like dad, even repeating his oaths if the engine doesn't kick on.

Sexuality in Little Boys

Another aspect of rearing a preschool child that raises questions among many parents is how to deal with a little boy's interest in sex. Boys are more sexually active than girls at all ages and their interest begins early in life.

All children become actively interested in bathroom functions and the facts of life during the preschool years. They ask questions about how babies are made, but despite parents' often clinically thorough answers, many young children are unable to grasp the concept that they did not always exist. An Israeli study turned up some sex differences in young children's ideas about how babies get into their mothers' bodies. Most boys thought the baby was formed from food eaten by the mother, while most girls believed the baby had always been inside the mother. Few preschoolers seem to understand the father's role in reproduction.

A child's level of thinking seems to be reflected in his understanding of sex. Only with abstract thought in adolescence do most youngsters fully come to realize the facts of life. While preschool children are interested in sex, their ability to understand and their concept of sexuality remain childlike and distinctly immature.

Preschoolers are sexually active within the limits of their understanding and emotional development. Half of all young children indulge in some kind of exploratory sex play, either by themselves or with other children. Because a boy's genitals are external, his curiosity about his own body may be far more obvious than a little girl's.

Your son probably discovered his penis in infancy and became accustomed to handling his genitals when he was toilet trained; and, much to his parents' embarrassment, he is apt to clutch them in public. You may also notice that he plays with himself at nap time—rubbing or pulling his penis can give a pleasurable sensation to a little boy. However, what is a mildly erotic activity in a young child takes on a completely different meaning in adolescence, when a boy is capable of fantasizing sexually and ejaculating while he masturbates.

For the most part, preschool sex play with other children involves undressing and showing and seeing each others' bottoms, and may simply be evidence of curiosity about how another child goes to the bathroom. Preschoolers still associate their genitals with urination. Sex drive, as we know it, does not appear until adolescence.

Parents of a little boy are sometimes concerned about his obvious sexuality. We don't want our sons forcing themselves on little girls, and if two little boys undress each other in an exploratory sex game, we worry in quite a different way. However, a few incidences of sex play between boys does not mean our sons are homosexual. Sexuality for young children, boys and girls, involves a

2483670

Dennis the Menace[R] used by permission of Hank Ketcham and copyright by News America Syndicate.

"NOW CALM DOWN, MRS. WADE, AND SAY THAT AGAIN. MARGARET WANTS TO JOIN DENNIS' NUDIST COLONY? *WHAT* NUDIST COLONY?..."

degree of pleasure and a great deal of curiosity. Parents who recognize the innocence of a young child's interest in sex can help him learn self-control.

More active and curious than a little girl, a preschool boy needs to understand the importance of individual privacy. One mother found her son's questions about sex and her simple answers a good way to teach the concept of privacy—telling this little boy that his body belongs to him and no one should force him to let them touch his private parts. Another mother whose young son had instigated sex games on several occasions with the little girl next door talked with him about the importance of respecting other people's privacy. Parents of preschool boys may want to supervise their play with any child, and train their sons not to handle their genitals in public. But there is no need to make children feel guilty as we teach them about sex.

Masculinity and Sexual Preference

Regardless of sex, those individuals with the highest self-esteem and the greatest achievement motivation seem to possess a mixture of positive male and female qualities—they are both effective and expressive. Many adult women tell of having been tomboys in their youth; few men are comfortable, even in retrospect, with suggestions that they were once considered wimps or sissies. Our language does not even have a term for this type of behavior in boys that is not pejorative.

Gender deviance, a child's persistent confusion over his own sex, receives far more clinical attention in boys than it does in girls. Little boys who fail to develop traditional masculine characteristics and who also prefer girls' games, toys, clothing, or gestures are often rejected by others. Many feminine boys become homosexuals as they mature.

No one really knows what causes gender deviance or preference for one's own sex, but popular theories look to the family. Recently, research has begun to point to biological factors. Some males who have an extra sex chromosome, either XYY or XXY, are homosexual. Fetal androgens have also been shown to affect a child's later psychosexual behavior.

Berlin endocrinologist Günter Dörner has found that androgen deficiencies in male fetal rats produce a predominantly female brain and homosexual behavior in adult males; these animals appear more receptive to female hormones than do male fetal rats with normal levels of androgens. Human studies show that homosexual males respond to the female hormone estrogen more than heterosexual males do. Since both male and female hormones are found in all humans, with the levels varying according to one's sex, some male homosexuals may be more responsive to the female hormones that are present in their bodies than heterosexual men are. Dörner suspects that males will be sexually attracted to other men if their brains follow the typical female pattern of development.

Homosexuals are often uncomfortable with stereotypical masculine behavior, and many report that they
feel no particular attachment to their fathers. Male homosexuals have also been found to have fewer positive
masculine traits than heterosexual males do. For some
men, being "gay" appears to run in the family. It may be
that sexual preference, and even some sex-related traits,
are established before a child is born.

Parenting Styles, from Controlling and Permissive to Firm

Training of all sorts becomes important during the preschool years, especially for boys. How we socialize
young children is influenced by their own personalities
and needs, some of which differ in boys and girls. Research suggests that mothers of boys may be more tolerant of resistant, sometimes "fresh" behavior in boys than
in girls, and that both parents are more likely to use
physical punishment with boys than with girls.

If a boy fails to comply with our requests, if he responds to other children aggressively, if he is slow to
develop impulse control, his behavior will influence the
kind of discipline we use. Likewise, the kinds of discipline patterns that parents rely on late in infancy are
likely to have a different effect on different children,
especially when they are used, more or less consistently,
year after year. Parents' influence on a young child is
considerably stronger than the child's effect on the parent. We are, after all, more powerful and have greater
reasoning ability; we need to be in charge for our children's sakes.

As with toddlers, many parents respond to a preschool boy's resistance by stepping up their efforts to
control him ("I'll show him who's boss!"). Some boys
respond to their parents' rigid standards and stern punishment by becoming even more angry, hostile, and defiant. If their parents persist in their use of harsh

measures to control them, these boys behave more aggressively than other children.

Other boys reared by *controlling parents* may become dependent on adults, withdraw from boys who are impulsive and rough and exhibit characteristics associated with shyness. Regardless of their sex, shy children are described as feminine, in conformance with the traditional image of girls as more compliant and passive. Shy boys can eventually become overcontrolled emotionally and fail to show the spontaneity so delightful in young children. Regardless of the high standards controlling authoritarian parents set for their sons, many of these boys show little motivation for intellectual or academic achievement.

Other parents may go too far in the opposite direction. While *permissive parents* consider freedom all important and stress creativity rather than training, their offspring are rarely self-reliant and often act impulsively. For preschool boys especially, training in impulse control is very important.

Permissiveness in parents is often interpreted by a young child as indifference or neglect, and can have significant long-term effects on a boy's aggressiveness. Consistently ignoring a little boy's aggressive behavior, either physical or verbal, encourages him to continue acting this way. Lack of rules or failure to train a boy how to act with others may be a form of silent violence more corrosive to his development than even harsh, physical punishment.

The style of discipline that works best for boys from infancy on is a loving pattern of firmness based on reciprocal respect between parent and child. *Firm parents* set clear rules while offering warm, caring concern for their children. Boys who have been trained patiently and consistently to behave in age-appropriate ways rarely need scolding or harsh punishment; they grow up to have internal self-control and independence. Firm guidelines, such as telling a boy that hitting is unacceptable, and consistently separating him from any child he does hit helps enforce alternatives to aggression. For boys espe-

"WHO *SAYS* I GOTTA STAY IN BED?"   "JUST CHECKIN'."

cially, this firm, authoritative pattern of discipline has long-term positive effects on their friendliness to others, their willingness to cooperate, and their motivation to achieve.

Children reared firmly do not fear punishment, nor do they seem especially resentful when they are punished. Parents who respect their children are able to reestablish affectionate ties quickly after meting out punishments; their children learn to respect and trust adults. A close look at this firm, reciprocal style of parenting suggests that techniques these parents use pay off—if not immediately, certainly over the long haul.

Qualities of Firm, Loving Parents

Responsiveness to a child's needs from infancy helps any preschooler feel at ease with himself. Boys will imitate nurturing adults and learn to help others. Unselfish, nonaggressive schoolboys tend to have parents who consistently responded to their needs as young children.

Respecting your son's point of view, while insisting at the same time on firm guidelines for his behavior, sets an example of reasoning ("I know you don't like picking up, but if we put your toys away, they won't get lost or broken"). Age-appropriate expectations increase a boy's sense of competence and self-worth. A little boy who assists his parents will accept regular chores and responsibilities as he matures. A three-year-old boy is old enough to pick up his toys and clothes, although you may need to help him. A four-year-old can clear the table. Responsible behavior should grow as a boy does.

Encouraging problem-solving helps all children develop independence. Asking, "What might happen next?" instead of telling a boy the consequences of his actions prompts him to think for himself, and helps him to understand why he needs to control his impulses. Monitoring your son's play with another child allows him to practice problem-solving, but intervention may be necessary with combative preschool boys. The astute parent who prevents a fight by separating two boys who are beginning to fuss may be training them more effectively than one who harshly punishes them for fighting. Giving a boy some voice in family decision making ("We have to go shopping now. Would you like to stop at the playground on our way home?") encourages his cooperation. Parents who make suggestions, rather than overtly direct a child's action, can help preserve the sense of control that many boys find important. Wise parents limit the choices they offer young children, asking questions like, "Which sweater would you like to wear— your green or blue one?" rather than "It's cold outside. Don't you want to wear a sweater?"

Family values provide a yardstick against which we measure behavior. Discipline that focuses on "right" versus "wrong" helps children learn what is expected of them even if adults are not around, and encourages greater self-control. Offering your values and a statement of principle seems to help children tell right from wrong. "You will have to return Bobby's car. It's wrong to take things from other people."

Boys Need Special Help Learning Not to Be Aggressive

Since boys are naturally more combative than girls, they need extra training. One psychologist believes young boys may be preoccupied with guns, aggressive make-believe, and rough-and-tumble play because they make him feel more powerful—at least briefly. Compared to far larger and stronger masculine role models, a pre-school boy recognizes his own relative weakness. He lacks the muscles, beard, and deep voice of adult males. Given the stereotyped view of masculinity many young-sters have, a little boy may believe that by acting tough he is displaying appropriately male behavior even if his appearance belies the comparison. This exaggerated preschool machismo often fades as a boy matures.

Some aggression seems almost inevitable in little boys, but preventive tactics as well as strategies to en-courage self-control can help parents teach their sons to keep this emotion within reasonable bounds. Recogniz-ing your son's anger or frustration, and allowing him to talk it out instead of acting aggressively lets him know that his feelings are acceptable, even if his actions are not. "Active listening" techniques that echo a child's feelings and encourage him to express them verbally teach a boy to air his thoughts, rather than bare his fists. Encouraging your son to recognize his own feelings is a first step in developing concern for others; boys seem to need extra guidance in developing empathy with other children. While we might simply tell a toddler that hitting hurts, a preschool boy is mature enough to see for him-self the consequences of his actions if we encourage him to think about them. Active listening techniques are de-scribed in greater detail in Thomas Gordon's PET, Par-ent Effectiveness Training: The Tested New Way to Raise Children *and problem-solving dialogues in Myrna Shure and George Spivack's* Problem-Solving Techniques in Childrearing. *Both are included in the list of recommended books on page 289.*

Active Listening

Active-listening techniques are based on the principle that when a child feels truly accepted as he is, *not as he should be, he can begin to think about change and decide how he might want to be different.*

Acceptance can be communicated nonverbally through facial expressions, posture, gestures, and even silence. Active listening combines feedback (telling the child what you understand his words to mean) with acceptance (empathizing with the child's feelings).

For example, a young boy comes home, obviously upset:

CHILD: *I hate Billy.*
MOTHER: *You and Billy had a fight.*
CHILD: *He's not my friend anymore.*
MOTHER: *You're really angry.*
CHILD: *He won't let me play with his truck.*
MOTHER: *Billy doesn't want to share.*
CHILD: *I'd give it back to him. I just want to play with it, too.*
MOTHER: *He doesn't trust you to share.*
CHILD: *I let him play with my toys.*
MOTHER: *You share with Billy.*
CHILD: *Maybe he'd like to play with my tank.*
MOTHER: *If you give him a toy of yours to play with, he might let you play with his toy.*

This parent's active listening defused her son's anger and allowed him to try a new approach in a property rights squabble—to change. *Had his mother criticized him ("You and Billy are too friendly to fight!"), offered advice ("See if you can take turns."), or tried to make him feel better by denying his anger ("You'll feel differently about Billy tomorrow."), this young boy might have sensed that she was rejecting him and stubbornly clung to his anger.*

Problem-Solving Dialogues

Teaching a child to think for himself takes extra steps. A problem-solving dialogue might combine the acceptance and feedback of active listening with a series of questions that help a preschooler figure out what is happening and what he should do about it. One mother, in her effort to master this technique, found the following dialogue very effective:

A young boy comes in the door, crying.

MOTHER: *Justin, what happened?*
CHILD: *Billy (a friend) hit me.*
MOTHER: *Why did he hit you?*
CHILD: *He just hit me.*
MOTHER: *You mean he hit you for no reason?*
CHILD: *I hit him.*
MOTHER: *Why?*
CHILD: *He wouldn't let me play with his truck.*
MOTHER: *How do you think Billy felt when you hit him?*
CHILD: *Mad.*
MOTHER: *Do you know why he doesn't want you to play with his truck?*
CHILD: *No!*
MOTHER: *How can you find out?*
CHILD: *I could ask him.*
MOTHER: *See if you can find out why.*

Later the child returns.

CHILD: *Billy says I never let him play with my toys.*
MOTHER: *Now you know why he won't let you play with his. Can you think of something you could do, so he'd want to let you play with his truck?*
CHILD: *I can stop playing with him, if he won't let me.*
MOTHER: *What might happen then?*
CHILD: *Billy might not be my friend?*
MOTHER: *Can you think of something different to do, so he'll still be your friend?*

CHILD: *I could let him play with one of my trucks.*
MOTHER: *That's a different idea.*

Through this kind of dialogue, a parent can encourage causal thinking (why the child was hit) and sensitivity to others' feelings (being hit makes people mad). Rather than lecturing the boy or offering him advice, the parent directs the child's thoughts to the original problem (two boys want to play with one toy) and to alternative ways of solving it. Instead of criticizing his judgment, the parent helps the preschooler to go further in his thinking—to realize the consequences of his action (if I don't play with Billy, he may not want to be my friend when I want to play with him). The child reasons on his own intellectual level, learning how to solve his problems in a way that is appropriate to his age.

Learning to cooperate with others in early childhood can reduce a boy's level of competitiveness. Little boys are likely to look for distinctions between their efforts and those of their peers, while preschool girls seek similarities rather than differences between themselves and other children. In boys, competition and concern for others are incompatible; their competitiveness seems to heighten their concern for themselves instead of empathy for others. Highly competitive girls, on the other hand, appear as empathic as less competitive ones. In one interesting experiment with young boys, researchers attributed qualities of "cooperativeness" or "wanting to win" to certain boys, then asked pairs of boys to build together with blocks. Boys who had been labeled cooperative did, in fact, work better and more cooperatively with their partners than those given competitive attributes.

Learning self-control is an important task for all children during the years from two to five; however, boys seem to need more training than girls. Consistent handling and a "cooling off" period instead of yelling at a preschooler or spanking him helps both parents and children hold their tempers. A three-minute "time out" in a safe place, like a special chair, can defuse a lot of anger. Teach your son to recognize those times when he's likely to lose control—when he's tired, excited, or hungry.

Preschoolers find it very difficult to wait; their sense of time is not yet well developed. Help your little boy avoid unnecessary frustration by using strategies that take his immaturity into account. Put off telling a three-year-old about grandmother's visit until shortly before her arrival. Avoid the use of long-term rewards. "If you pick up your toys every day this week, we'll go to the park on Saturday," is less effective for a preschooler than, "If you pick up your toys now, we'll have time for a story." Waiting for a holiday such as Christmas can seem impossible to small children. Focusing your son's attention on specific preparations (making ornaments or baking cookies) can ease some of his intense anticipation.

Many of us are familiar with the grumpiness, occasional frenzied behavior, and lack of control some children exhibit when they are required to wait a long time between meals. One nutritionist emphasized the importance of making sure a preschooler does not have to wait too long to be fed. Four small meals, carefully balanced, may be preferable to three large servings daily; most young children can learn to wait for regular feedings if they occur often enough.

Getting Along with Your Preschool Boy

The preschool boy can be very trying to a busy mother. He seems to move about constantly, even when he's sick; he has definite ideas about what he wants to do, which often conflict with our own desires or schedules; and he seldom takes kindly to correction. Raising a little boy can be particularly nerveracking if you have been an only child, you had no brothers yourself, or you are by nature a neat and tidy person.

Nevertheless, boys of preschool age do respond positively to the same three approaches we all do—helpful-

ness, praise, and respect. By putting techniques to work that incorporate these attributes and paying some special attention to your household environment, you may not turn Attila the Hun into Little Lord Fauntleroy, but you will see better behavior.

Helpfulness

Faced with a sinkful of dishes, two baskets of laundry to sort and fold, and a meeting to attend in forty-five minutes, most of us want just one thing—help. The three-year-old who must cope with picking up forty-five small metal cars, twenty-three pieces of plastic track, and six action figures feels the same way. An all-too-typical parental stance at such a time is, "Pick it all up—now!"

Instead, try being helpful. Say something like, "You've really got a lot of work to do there, don't you? Here, let me help." Begin picking up the cars and dismantling the track. Keep at it, with your little boy, until everything is put away. When the job is done, acknowledge what has happened. "There! It's all finished. Now let's read a story."

Young children need lots of help. In teaching your child something brand new, it is not enough simply to show him how. Show him, then stay with him until he completes the task. This tells him, "I'm really interested in seeing that you have learned this, and I care about how you do it." In cleanup tasks, helping our children models the kind of behavior we would like to see them display. Tell anybody who will listen whenever your son has been helpful. Don't forget to tell him, too.

Praise

There is probably nothing that works so well as praise, given in an appropriate way. It is human nature to want others to think well of us. It is not necessary, however, to use words like good, terrific, marvelous, wonderful, *or* great *when we praise a preschool child. A simple acknowledgment is usually all that is needed.*

Phrases such as, "You did it!" "You're finished!" or "What a scrubber you are!" suffice, and let a child know we are aware of what he has done. Young children know if praise is honest or affected. In a preschool class, an aide once told a little boy that his painting was beautiful. "I don't think it's beautiful," he told her, matter-of-factly. "I think it's purple."

Acknowledging your little boy's achievements tells him that you are proud of him and what he does; it builds his self-esteem. "Billy knows how to tie his shoes now," said to a neighbor who drops by for coffee, is music to a boy's ears. The opposite side of this coin is that hearing his faults declaimed to others engenders bitterness and anger. If someone has a complaint about us, we like to be told it ourselves instead of having others told about it. Children feel the same way. Make it a point to mention your child's positive qualities outside the family—not his negative ones.

Respect

Because the parent-child relationship is inherently one of greater knowledge and power versus lesser, it is sometimes easy to get into the habit of command, forcing our authority willy-nilly in a variety of ways. To see if this is happening in your house, try to recall a number of directives given to your child during one morning or afternoon recently. Then pretend you are in the workplace and the identical instructions are given to you by your supervisor. Ask yourself how you might feel.

Children deserve the same respect we afford other people. They have legitimate likes and dislikes (including food); they have good days and bad days; and they have their own distinct personalities. We all have friends or relatives about whom we say such things as, "You know Harold—he's never been on time for anything." We are willing to accept eccentricities in adults that we sometimes refuse to countenance in children, primarily because we believe we stand a chance of altering them. Some kinds of behavior should change, of course, and it is the job of parents to help children adjust their behavior when it is necessary; but these may exist because of personality factors and need to be approached in a spirit of compensation. If you have a child who is a slow starter, for example, it is essential to work out a way to get him up and going early enough to arrive at school at a reasonable time without driving everyone crazy. It is not necessary, and can cause conflict, to insist that he maintain a fast pace in everything he does.

Respect your little boy's needs and desires, especially where other children are concerned. One little boy, visiting at the home of a friend, spied his host's brand new toy car right away and asked to play with it. The boy's mother replied, "Patrick will hold it for you. He's only had it for a little while, and he's not ready to share it yet." This mother respected her son's need to savor his new toy instead of insisting that he part with it. The other child accepted the woman's explanation without protest. It made sense to him. He would have felt the same way, himself.

Avoiding Conflicts

Any number of conflicts occur between parents and preschool boys because they want to do something one way and you want them to do it another way. Issues of time or preference are often involved. Typical are the following:

- You want him ready now, but he wants to take the time to put on his coat by himself.
- He is wearing his blue pants and you want him to wear the matching blue shirt; he insists on the purple one.
- It's time for lunch, but he doesn't want to move his cars off the table until he's moved the rest of them into the garage.

Each of these situations has the built-in potential for confrontation. Most of us have been there. In taking a second look, however, it is possible to see that each can be either prevented or resolved peaceably.

Clothing and food are matters about which most of us have some pretty strong preferences, and children are no exception. At a certain point in every little boy's life, he wants to have some control over what he wears. If he has just started preschool where everybody else puts on his own coat, a boy is even more likely to want to do it his own way. Respect this need, and allow time for it. If you have a real emergency and can't wait, tell him: "I know you want to put on your own coat, and you really do a good job; but the nurse called and your sister is sick at school. We have to go and get her right away. This time I have to help."

You may still have an occasional argument over clothing, but giving your son enough time and being flexible about his choices can reduce their frequency. The type of clothing he wears is less important to a little boy than the fact that he gets to choose it (mothers care about type and appearance). If your son wishes to wear an odd combination of colors or patterns, wear his clothes inside out or backwards, what difference does it really make? Neither of you will remember by next week what shirt the argument was all about—but your little boy will remember your anger. In one family, such conflicts about clothes were avoided entirely when a boy was allowed to choose his school clothes, but mom chose outfits for church and visiting. This same flexibility with regard to what a boy eats can avoid a lot of problems at mealtime. Any dietary behavior that is extreme in some way should be called to the attention of your physician; however, with most normal children, being offered reasonable choices and having some control over what happens prevents major problems.

Allowing a similar latitude in terms of your son's schedule will go a long way toward preserving a peaceful household. If we are in the middle of an interesting activity, most of us resent being made to stop or rushed in some way; it causes a sense of incompleteness with which we are very uncomfortable. Nevertheless, adults do this with children all the time and think nothing of it. Respect your little boy enough to allow him to complete what he has begun—a very important element in learning of many kinds. For the boy who is moving his cars into the garage, being allowed to carry out the activity is very important; lunch should wait. Giving "advance warning" about what is to come helps small children schedule their activities and can prevent misunderstandings. "We're going to be eating lunch in about fifteen minutes, Mark; try to get all the cars into the garage pretty soon."

The Telephone

When mothers spend a long time talking on the telephone, small children resent it very much. Our attention is diverted to someone else; we often ignore our child's behavior or needs while we are talking; and we sometimes spend more time with our caller than we do with our child. This sends a strong message.

Many children misbehave while we are on the phone, and it may well be nothing more than a bid for the time we are giving to someone else. If a child interrupts when we are in the middle of a call, most of us have little problem saying, "Wait a minute—I'm on the phone." How often do we tell a caller, "You'll have to call back —I'm in the middle of a game with Tommy"? Telephone calls during your child's active hours should be brief. Spending half the morning on the phone is asking for trouble.

Structuring the Environment for Positive Behavior

How we arrange the household environment can make a positive difference in a little boy's behavior. Whenever possible, organize your home in such a way that your son can do things for himself:

- *Proper storage keeps toys and supplies neater and makes cleaning up easier. A set of low shelves that hold plastic bins for different toys, labeled on their fronts with pictures of what goes inside, helps a boy remember where his toys should go. Bins can be re-*

moved while he plays; at cleanup time, toys can be replaced and the bins taken back to the shelf. Containers can be made from cardboard boxes.

- *While toy chests are popular items, they seldom encourage neatness or respect for one's belongings. Plowing through a jumbled mass of metal and plastic to find something is a poor way to learn to care for toys. Large items like stuffed animals are suitably stored in toy chests, but a different kind of storage, such as bins or canisters, works better for smaller items.*

- *Several small bathroom rugs with rubber backing can serve as a play area and can be rolled up for storage. These rugs contain the items a child is playing with in a defined space, and eliminate a floor strewn with small objects. Trained early on not to walk on the rugs when they are being used in this way, and to refrain from bothering a sibling's or friend's toys while they are on the rugs, children learn tolerance and respect for others and their property. These rugs are commonly used in Montessori classrooms.*

- *Investing in a sturdy child-size table-and-chair set is well worth the money. First of all, it prevents accidents; many children fall while climbing on adult-size furniture. Second, it gives a boy more control over what he does; he doesn't have to ask you to help him as often, because he can take care of himself. You may want to place the table and chair near the kitchen or family room, close to the center of activity in your house, because that is where your son is most likely to spend his time. His own table and chair combined with a nearby set of shelves on which favorite play items are stored makes it possible for a little boy to choose his activities, learn to care for his belongings in a suitable way, and be close to you.*

- *Lowering the clothes pole in your son's closet will enable him to begin taking care of his wearing apparel. Labeling the drawer fronts on his dresser with pictures of the items stored inside reminds him where to find*

things; if he likes to put away the laundry, he can identify the right drawer easily.

- The purchase of a set of serviceable cleaning tools is
also a good investment. A dustpan and floor brush encourage a boy to clean up his own messes; some will
even do the whole kitchen floor! As some dustpans
have sharp corners, be sure to buy one with rounded
edges, or cover pointed edges with cloth or plastic
tape. A small, light-weight basin and a sponge are
helpful for cleaning up spills, and boys love to use
them. The basin can also be used for washing plastic
dishes when he plays house, and for other kinds of
water play, which boys find very soothing. Children
should be closely supervised when playing with water.

- Mealtime can become more enjoyable (and less
messy) if you provide a placemat on which you have
drawn outlines for your little boy's plate, cup, spoon,
and fork. An inexpensive placemat can be made from
poster-board covered with Con·tact paper. Outlines
should be drawn with broad-tipped markers. Small
boys enjoy setting the table, washing up the placemat
afterward, and storing it in its proper place.

The Importance of Routine

It is hard to overemphasize the importance of a sensible routine in helping a little boy to good behavior. If
you establish a routine from your son's earliest months,
he will become accustomed to behaving in certain ways
at specific times each day. One reason routines are so
helpful is that preschoolers like predictability. They want
to be sure what will happen next. They like sameness in
the environment, too; some two-and-a-half-year-olds
may protest, for example, if you decide to change
around the living-room furniture.

Routines encourage good health habits. The baby
who is put to bed at seven every night is less likely to
complain about this bedtime when he is a toddler than
the child whose schedule has been erratic. Children
served nourishing meals at the same hour each day will

be less likely to crave junk food than those who are fed when their mothers get around to it.

Bedtime routines, if turned into rituals, can be soothing to a young child and help him adjust to the nightly separation from his parents. Knowing that the bath comes first, then the story, then the drink of water, and then the song as he is tucked under the covers provides a consistent and pleasant framework for this every-night event. Children benefit from a sensible routine throughout the childhood years.

Siblings Are Important in Family Life

While parents exert an enormous influence on a little boy, siblings are very important to his socialization. Much like his relationship with his parents, a child's attachment to his brothers and sisters lasts a lifetime, and can provide an important sense of continuity during childhood and adult life. For many children, siblings are their first playmates. They affect one another's personalities, and play a large role in a young child's developing social understanding. Young brothers and sisters may spend far more of their time with one another than with their parents.

Overall, boys seem to be less influenced by their siblings than girls are; they are also less likely to consider themselves to be the caretakers of younger brothers or sisters. Boy siblings seem to fight more than sisters do, and the preschool years show the greatest rates of conflict between siblings. Although fighting is frequent between brothers and/or sisters, it is rarely physically harmful, even when children actually hit one another.

Younger siblings often imitate older ones, especially if they are of the same sex. By the second year, a younger boy may imitate the behavior of an older brother more than the actions of an older sister. By the age of three, this tendency is strong. Younger children often seek out an older brother or sister for comfort if they are hurt or distressed. A boy who is encouraged to help a younger sibling learns nurturance and tolerance. If you have several children, you may have noticed that the older one will modify his speech when he talks with a younger sister or brother; he uses fewer words, shorter sentences, and may even raise the pitch of his voice. One researcher calls this type of speech "motherese" and in children it seems a natural response to younger siblings.

One of the most important lessons for any child to learn is that other people matter. Preschoolers usually absorb this lesson quickly, but for a firstborn child, who has grown accustomed to having mom and dad all to himself, adjusting to a new baby may take special effort. In most families, the arrival of a brother or sister means parents have less time to spend with a preschooler. Some young children will respond by making greater demands on their parents, and confrontations often increase between adult and child. Other children seem to withdraw into themselves as their parents spend less time with them. One study showed that preschoolers whose mothers had been relatively playful and permissive with them before the birth of a sibling spent a good deal of time wandering aimlessly or just sitting without playing, unless their mothers continued to make time for them. A little boy, with his built-in combativeness and delayed impulse control, may respond aggressively to a new baby.

Many parents, concerned about potential rivalry between a firstborn child and a new baby, wisely prepare a preschooler for the new arrival. One sensitive mother included her young son in her anticipation of another child, telling him what it would be like to have a brother or sister, while urging him to share his feelings or concerns about the new baby with her. With his mother's assistance, he purchased a present to give to the new baby when she came home from the hospital. Efforts such as these to encourage affection between siblings may stimulate nurturing feelings in little boys.

Stuttering

A small percentage of preschool children repeat single sounds, whole words, or phrases when they speak. Stuttering, which may be a form of incoordination in young children, affects three times as many boys as girls. Adult stutterers are five times as likely to be male as female. While early theories emphasized family tension as a cause of stuttering, this speech dysfunction is now regarded as a neurophysiological difficulty, with genetic components in some cases. One expert states, however, that tension cannot be altogether discounted as a factor.

Advice you may receive to "relax" and "don't worry about it" if your child stutters more than likely falls on deaf ears; but try your best. As much as possible reduce sources of tension or frustration. An excellent suggestion by pediatrician Benjamin Spock is to "Play with him by doing *things instead of by always* talking *things." Avoid interrupting your little boy when he speaks, and bend down so that you make eye contact. Two developmental experts caution against discussing his problem with others in his hearing or using rewards or punishments in connection with speech production.*

If you are concerned about your son's stuttering, it may be helpful to consult with a speech pathologist. George Washington University speech and hearing specialist James Hillis recommends that a child begin speech therapy, if needed, when he becomes aware of his problem himself. A number of preschool-age children see speech therapists regularly.

The Value of Play

In the preschool years, nature seems to have programmed children to reach out to others, to mingle and play with children their age, and to hone the give-and-take skills essential to sound social relationships. This behavior takes place worldwide.

The preschool child enjoys experimenting with words. Your little boy may like to rhyme or use words to tease; four-year-olds enjoy coining new words. In preschool classrooms, children often do invent nonsense words and syllables, exchanging and elaborating on them with each other, almost as if they had a language of their own. There is even some evidence that this interaction among young children is a factor in the generation of new language forms. At the turn of the century, diverse ethnic groups were brought to the islands of Hawaii to work in the sugarcane fields. The adults among these groups communicated with great difficulty. Within one generation, however, their children, who had played together at very early ages, developed what amounted to a new language that made use of linguistic forms derived from each tongue represented. These children communicated despite their basic language differences; the biological program of children this age seems to facilitate this kind of interaction.

For much of childhood, boys tend to spend more time with other boys than girls do with their friends. A little boy may be popular with other boys for a number of reasons. Size seems to be one factor important to acceptance. A solid build, physical strength, and motor dexterity help a preschool boy win approval from his peers, while facial attractiveness seems less important. Obesity, however, is a definite liability for any child.

Friendship skills—beginning to share and cooperate as boys play together again and again—take time to learn. Young boys who have frequent opportunities to watch and play alongside other children at playgrounds seem to play with their own peers longer and more frequently than do boys without early exposure to other children. Even in group situations, most preschool children play best in pairs; introducing any young child to one other playmate, and giving him a chance to learn to play successfully with one young friend may help him learn to seek out a compatible playmate in a larger group.

Playgroups, where mothers bring together a few pre-school children for an hour or so a day, are excellent ways for young children to become accustomed to peers. Little boys who learn to play together in pairs in a playgroup seem to talk more often to other children and have a more mature understanding of sharing and cooperative play. Youngsters who take an active interest in what's going on around them are more likely to make and keep friends in early childhood.

Some boys have trouble playing successfully with others their own age; they may fight over the same toys and compete rather than cooperate with one another. Playing on a one-to-one basis with someone younger than themselves and therefore less threatening than a peer has been found to help withdrawn, isolated preschoolers cope with group play. Similarly, an aggressive boy may not feel so competitive toward a younger child and may learn to play without hitting; he may even nurture a young friend. A boisterous five-year-old from a troubled family who used aggression to solve his problems became more willing to talk out his differences with others after he was placed "in charge of" an entering three-year-old in a Montessori class. Having to explain the workings of the classroom, be responsible for seeing that the younger child was occupied, and living up to the teacher's expectation focused this child's interests in a more positive direction.

Sharing is particularly hard for many children. If you find this is so for your little boy, try preparing him in advance to share with a visiting friend, and help him decide which toys his friend may use to prevent squabbles later. You may want to mark these "guest toys" with colored tape; areas where preschoolers play can be divided by using strips of masking tape. Having one's own space sometimes makes sharing toys easier for young children. Putting your son's name on toys to be shared can help him and his playmate understand that the car that says BILLY still belongs to him, even if Jack is playing with it.

A child's responsiveness to other children outside his own family is voluntary. He can withdraw from a peer group whose company he doesn't enjoy. Peer play does not involve the same kind of obligation that preschoolers may feel toward their parents or siblings. Other little boys give your son a chance to experiment, testing out behaviors that may or may not be acceptable to his peers.

Whether they play by themselves or with another little boy, preschool boys spend considerably more time than little girls do in constructive or building play. They make cars or spaceships from whatever materials are available. These manipulative, three-dimensional activities may teach boys spatial skills that males find useful later in life. Not only are boys more likely than girls to use toys in unconventional, novel ways, they may also take them apart to find out how they were made or what makes them work. For boys, the characteristics of playfulness—imagination, curiosity, humor, and novelty seeking—appear linked to creativity.

Play is the day-to-day business of all young children. In itself, it may have no obvious objective and may shift direction on a whim; but play serves serious functions. Through play a child develops problem-solving skills, imagination, tolerance, and respect for others. He practices new language forms (some we wish he wouldn't!), learns how other people live, and acquires practical skills of various kinds. Good relationships with parents and other children also seem to encourage play among preschoolers. A young child's attention span may be twice as long if his mother joins in his symbolic play—encouraging him to load "bricks" (in reality, blocks that he's scattered all over the floor) into his wagon—and preschoolers seem to become more exploratory in their play when their parents pay attention to what they are doing. Although the home has long been the traditional playground for young children, more and more preschoolers are leaving home for nursery school, preschools that offer extended care, or day-care centers.

Boys and Preschools

Many parents send their sons to preschool to get them out of the house, to give them an opportunity to learn in a structured setting, to play with their peers, or to allow them physical outlets that won't damage the living-room furniture. While preschool and nursery schools traditionally take children only part of the day, a number of them now offer day care in combination with a developmental program, an alternative chosen by many of today's working mothers.

A boy's personality, degree of maturity, place in the family, and willingness to leave home all influence his response to preschool. In general, boys are more likely than girls the same age to cry when their mothers first leave them at nursery school, and they tend to cry when frustrated or angry with a teacher or an aide (young girls are more likely to cry if they are injured or hurt). Shy boys may need to become gradually accustomed to a nursery-school situation, while outgoing youngsters often forget to say good-bye to their mothers on the very first day of preschool.

Structured classes are better suited to the needs of small boys than permissive ones. Florida researcher Diane McGuinness indicates that chaotic preschool environments may lead boys into behavior that some teachers characterize as hyperactive. Structure varies in preschool. Traditional nursery schools often carry out certain activities at the same time each day. Montessori schools are organized around an orderly, child-size environment and specific behavioral guidelines ("We always put our work away when we're finished").

Your son may enjoy being with other children, especially other boys, as much as he does anything else about preschool. It is not unusual for two little boys to rush eagerly toward each other, touching in some way, as they meet on a schoolday morning. As a rule, boys are more task-oriented in their nursery-school play, while little girls talk about more social aspects of being together (recognizing similarities in one another, admiring one an-others' clothes, discussing who is friends with whom). Boys play together in the block corner ("We're building together, right?") and two of them may integrate their play with trucks—one driving to the building site to dump logs, while another carries sand in his truck to make cement. Observers who recorded children in nursery-school classrooms found that the boys per-formed more individual acts of work or play in a speci-fied period of time than girls, and they interrupted what they were doing three times as often.

Humor, in the form of laughing and teasing, seems more a part of boys' play than girls' in preschool situa-tions. Boys laugh a good deal among themselves; they are more often the initiators of humor, while girls may often bear the brunt of their teasing or become a willing audience for their jokes. Boys also differ from girls in their response to newcomers in the classroom. While lit-tle girls, frequently welcome a new child to the group and go out of their way to be friendly, little boys are more likely to ignore a new child for a while. This same equivocal approach to people is seen in preschool art-work; drawings by boys contain figures representing people less often than pictures drawn by girls.

The dominance and aggressive behaviors of little boys are very much in evidence in preschool settings. Intelli-gence and a child's ability to get along with others are as important to dominance rankings in preschools as a boy's size or physical prowess. Popularity fluctuates from day to day.

Hitting is a common form of aggressiveness in pre-school groups. A few girls strike out at other girls, but their hitting is usually ineffective and seems almost sym-bolic. Boys take longer to learn not to hit others. Obser-vations of children in nursery schools show that boys make unprovoked, if rather mild, attacks on girls; they will, for example, push little girls out of the block corner or gesture menacingly at them. Most girls in preschool classes will back off from more aggressive children, even when little boys do not overtly threaten them.

Choosing a Preschool

What is the best type of preschool for little boys? There is no one correct answer. Evaluations of early childhood programs, many associated with all-day care, showed mixed results. One long-term assessment of low-income children assigned to four different types of preschool programs when they were four years old showed that boys in Montessori programs sustained gains in reading and math achievement through the tenth grade, the last year the children were evaluated. It is clear from other research that intellectual gains are found in all but the poorest of programs, but there are questions about how long they last. Evaluations of Head Start, for example, show that apparent IQ differences between children in these programs and those without preschool experience diminish over time.

Achievement-test scores and measures of intelligence are but one way to evaluate a program's effectiveness. Preschool shows clear effects in other important ways. Of obvious benefit to any little boy is his sense of greater competence, which allows him more control. Having to share, take turns, and be concerned for the needs of others have positive benefits for all boys, but especially those who are firstborn or only children. The opportunity for fantasy play in groups seems to help youngsters improve their skills in planning, cooperation, and being able to detect similarities and differences in quantity. Play opportunities in preschool may enhance a child's divergent thinking abilities—thinking that demands speculation, imagination, and invention—characteristics often found in intellectually and creatively gifted children. A number of preschool programs are designed to help disadvantaged children by increasing their competence in various ways. In one study, children who had gone through such a program were less likely than their peers who did not attend preschool to repeat a grade, enroll in special education, or show delinquent behavior in adolescence.

In choosing a school for your son, take into account

his temperament and his approach to other children. The little boy who is task-oriented and has an abundance of friends in the neighborhood may find a Montessori school very comfortable. A child who has few playmates and is intrigued by the social interaction of groups may enjoy a more traditional preschool. Some boys may be better off waiting until four to attend preschool, especially if they have problems controlling their behavior, cry frequently, or seem inordinately distressed at separation from their mothers.

Your community has a lot to do with whether or not you choose to send your son to preschool. If you live in a relatively high-pressure locale with "academic" kindergarten programs and schools that emphasize achievement, you may feel your son will be at a disadvantage when he enters kindergarten if he has not been to preschool. If attendance is a common experience among your son's peers, sending him several mornings a week might be a suitable compromise between a five-day program and no preschool at all.

Are there risks to little boys as well as benefits in preschools? Teaching that forces or coerces boys into learning for which they are not ready is one risk and should be actively discouraged by parents. In some preschools that stress academics, little children are expected to sit and write letters, numbers, or small stories. These kinds of activities may be fine for children who enjoy them, are interested, and able to perform the tasks required, but academic programs can be educationally unsound for those who are not. Overzealous teachers can coerce young children into performing an activity, and even into believing that they like it, with relatively little difficulty. Fortunately for little boys, this is much easier to do with girls, who are more tractable and concerned about adult approval.

Many other risks come into play when your son ventures outside his family; preschool means a child is likely to encounter them sooner rather than later. Boys are more vulnerable to environmental factors than girls, and a little boy has increased exposure to communicable diseases in preschools. In addition to health problems, preschool may expose your son to behaviors you find objectionable such as swearing and rude noises, and he may discover that other children enjoy privileges he does not, such as being allowed to watch television shows forbidden to him. However, the overall benefits of a good preschool program far outweigh the possible risks, provided your son enjoys going to school, looks forward to it, and has a teacher who helps him feel good about himself.

What if you are ambivalent about sending your little boy off to preschool? Will he miss out in some way if he doesn't go? Many parents can empathize with the suburban mother who said, "I guess I'm going to have to send my son to preschool. There's not one other child in this neighborhood who's at home every day."

It may be comforting to know that people used to wonder if their child would be harmed if he did go to preschool. There are still those who believe that children are better off at home until they are six or seven. If your little boy gets along well at home and in his neighborhood, has no obvious problems, and appears to be developing well, there is no reason to think that preschool is an experience he cannot do without. Besieged as we are by books and articles pointing out all the benefits of early education, we sometimes lose our sense of perspective.

No single method of educating young children has been shown to be significantly better for every child. When and if this happens, you can be sure you will hear about it! Also, no preschool is ever an adequate substitute for a caring family environment. You will not harm your son permanently by refraining from sending him to preschool as long as he has opportunities to play with other children and you stimulate his interests. Reading to your son daily, encouraging his persistence at simple tasks, and letting him know you find intellectual competence rewarding, satisfying, and interesting are ways you can help your little boy to sound development—with or without preschool.

Alternative Care for Sons of Working Mothers

For an increasing number of families in America, Canada, and Europe, there is simply no choice about whether to keep the preschool child at home. Approximately half of all preschoolers today have working mothers, and receive alternative care for a good part of every weekday; by 1990, it is estimated that approximately 60 percent of American mothers with infants and young children will be employed; two million preschoolers will need alternative care for all or part of each day. Unfortunately, it is far from clear just what effect this unprecedented, widespread change in child-rearing patterns will have on our children as youngsters and as adults.

The studies that have been made on long-term effects of day care suggest some differences for boys and girls. Sons of mothers from lower social and economic groups seem to benefit from their mothers' working; these mothers probably have the greatest financial need to work, and their employment may raise their families' standards of living and educational expectations. According to some researchers, boys from intact middle-class homes, where mothers probably are better educated and may have more options available to them (part-time work while their children are young), have been found to adjust more poorly to school if their mothers worked full time while they were small. Their math and language scores in elementary school were lower than those of middle-class boys whose mothers did not work. A separate study found that boys whose mothers were at home while they were preschoolers appeared more intellectually successful than boys whose mothers worked out of the house, but they were also likely to be conforming and inhibited as adolescents. Daughters of working mothers seem to benefit regardless of their family's economic or educational backgrounds. A working mother can be a strong, competent role model for a daughter. Combining a full-time job with childcare responsibilities can be something of a strain, even to a very energetic young woman. After a hard day at the office, it may be easier to come home to a talkative, but generally compliant little girl than to a messy, active little boy.

From the standpoint of physical health, alternative care lowers the age of primary exposure to communicable disease from five or six years to infancy and early childhood. Males have lower levels of blood proteins needed to make antibodies, and young boys are more prone than girls to a number of childhood infections. "Glue ear," a middle-ear infection that appears to be brought on by viruses, can make young children bad tempered and inattentive. For boys who seem to have some sex-related speech delays, chronic ear infections may further retard their language development. Parents of preschoolers may also notice that their children pick up viruses and infections more readily, but the risk of exposure to communicable diseases appears less in preschool than day care. Children in alternative care spend long hours with other children, often eating and napping away from home.

While it is important to recognize how working may affect a little boy, any mother has to balance a number of diverse factors in deciding whether to combine a career with child rearing. For a growing number of women, work is a financial necessity rather than a matter of choice. Other women, who lack the monetary incentives, may find it extremely hard to stay at home, leaving behind a career they worked on for years or failing to apply training they took great pains to acquire in school. Among the most unhappy women of all are mothers at home who wish they were working, and, by and large, unhappy mothers make for unhappy children. Family discord, whether the mother works or not, is associated with behavior problems in boys, and being overprotected by a stay-at-home mom may be as detrimental to their development as the independence a working mother might encourage too soon. More recent studies of children in exceptionally well-run day-care centers indicate that good alternative care can meet the developmental needs of most young children.

Parents of a little boy will want to look closely at their son's temperament, age, and developmental needs in considering alternative care. One psychologist who has studied day care extensively suggests that many boys may benefit from an extra year of one-on-one interaction, whether with their own mother or a sitter hired just to care for the children in the family. An approximation of this one-on-one interaction can be found in day-care homes, where a mother takes in a few children to play with her own offspring. Infants and toddlers seem to do best with a substitute mother, someone who will pick them up when they cry, cuddle them, and get to know them well enough to understand them. Boys, especially, need someone to monitor their behavior and help them learn to get along with other children. An orderly environment in your home or someone else's, a fairly specific routine, and limit-setting by a caregiver who can be kindly as well as firm, are particularly important for young boys.

If your son is slow to warm up to strangers or new situations, a day-care home or a sitter in your own home may be best for him. Adjusting to one or two new faces is less intimidating than being placed in a classroom or day-care center full of strangers. Difficult children often behave better with this kind of alternative care when they are young. An additional benefit for preschool boys with one-on-one care is that it gives them greater opportunity than they might have as one among many children to feel in control of their own lives.

Boys in Day-Care Centers

Older preschoolers appear to benefit from center-based programs, especially if they are educational in nature, for a part of each day. A mix of ages, personalities, and a larger number of children of each sex gives a boy four or older a good chance to get along with a variety of children. Even difficult boys do well in centers, if the care is first rate and they are not immature when they enter. Boys who play with other children daily in centers seem to play in more creative and complex ways; their greater social interaction may increase their skill in getting along with other children.

Children of both sexes in well-run day-care centers have been found socially competent and self-confident. They seem helpful to other children and cooperative with adults. Verbally expressive, these youngsters often adjust quickly to the routines of school. The trade-off is that many children who attend centers are less compliant than those reared in smaller settings. Center-reared youngsters may, on occasion, seem impolite or disagreeable; they may also be louder, more aggressive, or bossier than other children. Since many four- and five-year-olds show these behaviors at one time or another, some researchers are reluctant to blame center-based care solely. It is possible that this combination of somewhat unpleasant behaviors simply reflects the greater overall maturity of children in day-care centers.

If children in centers seem more intellectually and socially advanced, part of the reason may be their exposure to trained teachers. Unlike mothers (their own or someone else's in a day-care home) who give directions and focus on socialization, teachers in centers encourage children to be self-directed and independent. They show them how to solve problems, use interesting materials, and provide for guided activities that help preschoolers develop cognitive and social skills.

Mothers at home or in day-care homes spend a fair portion of each day cleaning the house, preparing meals, or watching television. While they provide children in their care with toys or books, they are usually not as actively involved in teaching specific skills or concepts as teachers in centers.

Whatever your son's age or the kind of alternative care you choose, the quality of that care is of overriding importance. High-quality centers and home caregivers who join supportive, supervisory networks in their communities provide the best care possible. In choosing alternative care for any child, it is also important to try to match your philosophy with that of the caregiver. Ask the director of any center or a day-care mother you are considering for your son how they might handle certain specific situations. "If my little boy hits another child, what would you do?" "How would you help my son if he seems upset when I leave him with you?" It's important to share your understanding of your child's personality and needs with an alternative caregiver, and if your preschooler spends his days with that individual, you will want to communicate openly and often about how he is doing. It may, as well, be helpful to talk with parents whose children are cared for by the person you are considering.

Whether a young boy spends most of his waking day in a center, day-care home, preschool, or his own home, how he spends his time during the years from two to five is important. Those children who learn to give and take by playing with others develop invaluable social skills. Those who feel competent by five—able to dress themselves, to draw a simple picture, and to control their feelings to some degree—may be ready for the next developmental step: learning as part of a group. It is this competence in social and emotional development, coupled with a child's sex and age, that will play an essential role in his academic career.

When Is a Boy Ready to Start School?

The level of maturity a boy has attained when he begins formal schooling can make an enormous difference in his achievement, self-perception, and relationships with others. In the United States, children generally begin kindergarten at five and first grade at six. The attendance cut-off date established in his community largely determines when a boy begins his educational journey. If the date is November 1, for example, children with prior birthdays are allowed to enter kindergarten or first grade in September of that school year, but those whose birthdays fall after this time are not.

Learning in groups begins for all children when they enter kindergarten, and is far different from the one-on-one instruction typical of preschools. In many elementary classrooms, children are assigned to reading or arithmetic groups based on their ability. In one school, children who were in the highest reading group were called the Bluebirds. The middle group was known as the

Cardinals and the lowest as the Sparrows. In this chapter, we use the term Bluebirds to refer to children who are mature enough to learn well and be comfortable with their friends. Generally, children who are older and more mature when they start school make higher grades and test scores. Fewer of them are retained or enroll in remedial classes. Even children regarded as gifted achieve on a higher level if they are more mature when they enter school. More important than grades or test scores is the effect of maturity on a child's self-esteem. Older children are more competent, have more experience relating to others, and feel that they control what happens to them; older children become Bluebirds more often than younger ones do.

The Importance of Being a Bluebird

For boys, with their built-in need to feel competent and achieve a satisfactory place in the group, being a Bluebird is all important. Children wish to play with Bluebirds at recess, sit beside them at lunch, and have them for friends. While they are not all high achievers, Bluebirds, for the most part, are adequate achievers—children who have the ability to do what is expected of them and relate to others without stress. They make acceptable grades, have a number of friends and interests, and generally feel good about themselves. The parents of Bluebirds are pleased with their children's accomplishments. "He's really doing well this year," or "He's holding his own," are typical comments.

Status positions in elementary classrooms, labeled or not, are established early on and may be difficult to alter. The inability to change his position may heighten a boy's sense that he lacks control over what happens in his life. *Feeling competent, having suitable rank among his peers, and being in control are building blocks to self-esteem in boys* and contribute to Bluebird status. A little boy's failure to measure up socially or academically early in his school career—knowing that he has little chance to become a Bluebird—can have profound and lasting effects on his future. Research conducted in the past decade shows that *failure early in their school years has greater effects on boys than it does on girls*.

Early Failure Linked to Adolescent Problems

A long-term study conducted in the Chicago area followed first-grade inner-city children through high school. Researchers led by psychiatrist Sheppard Kellam found that first-grade failure was associated with a number of problems that appeared when the students reached adolescence.

Begun in 1961, this study indicates that "Almost fifty percent of the males rated as moderately or severely underachieving in first grade reported a high level of depressed symptoms ten years later." Females were not affected in this way. The Chicago team concluded that this finding "... appears to be an important difference for males compared to females in the meaning of failure to master first grade learning tasks."

A second finding of Kellam's team linked aggressive behavior in first grade with drug and alcohol abuse in adolescence. Boys who were both shy and aggressive (the "angry loners") were the heaviest abusers of all. Noting that both behaviors in first-grade boys are often related to classroom difficulties, the Chicago team suggests that greater competence "might reduce the stress and therefore reduce the concurrent aggression and/or the shyness in some male children." Their work underscores the importance of ensuring that a little boy is mature enough for the demands of first-grade tasks.

Kellam also points out that parents and teachers need to pay close attention to developmental markers in boys, because what is true of first grade is true of second and subsequent grades. The boy who finds it impossible to sit still in kindergarten, for example, may be easily distracted in first grade. A partnership between parents and teachers to follow a child's progress closely is essential.

Later Entry Age for Boys?

The Gesell Institute in New Haven, Connecticut, has also been investigating school problems. According to their researchers, at least one child out of three may be in a grade too high for his ability level. The researchers use the term "overplaced" to describe these children. Again, more boys than girls are affected. Louise Bates Ames of the Gesell Institute suggests that boys should be fully six-and-a-half before they start first grade. It would be even better, she says, to base school entrance on a behavior test rather than on the paper-and-pencil tests administered in many school systems. Gesell researchers believe that children who fall behind do not catch up. Instead, they tend to fall further and further behind. The notion that a child is "going through a phase" or will "grow out of it" is false.

The lasting difference immaturity can make in a child's educational performance was underlined by a 1983 survey of over four hundred fifty junior-high-school students in Fairfax County, Virginia, a relatively affluent suburb of our nation's capital, which assessed school performance based on the age children entered kindergarten. The results paint a grim picture. Not only did younger children (those with birthdays from September to December) experience disproportionately more failure, they also had lower test scores in both fourth and sixth grades. Even more significant, a staggering 44.3 percent of the younger boys had received some form of remedial help during the years from kindergarten to junior high school. Dr. Sammie Campbell, author of the study, and currently assistant superintendent of Georgia's Savannah-Chatham County schools, found that her results parallel those of Kellam and Gesell: Children do not catch up as they go through the grades.

In terms of academic performance, his place in the group, and long-term success, the younger child is at a disadvantage from the beginning. He may well need remedial services and has a fair chance of being retained in the same grade. Almost one-quarter of the younger entrants in the Fairfax study were retained, compared to an average of 6.8 percent of the older entrants. Younger children were more than three times as likely to fail a grade.

Why Does Early School Entry Continue?

Educators, especially elementary-school teachers and principals, are well aware of the greater need for maturity in boys. Personnel in both public and private schools increasingly advise parents to hold back their sons if tests indicate they need extra time. Principals and teachers want children to succeed; they know the connection between maturity, performance, and self-esteem.

Unfortunately, educators do not establish policies that determine school entry ages; state legislatures do. In the United States the age at which a child may begin school currently varies from September 1 to January 1. While teachers' organizations lobby for early cut-off dates, many parents pressure legislators for late ones. A major, though unacknowledged, reason for this parental pressure has to do with the schools' function as a babysitter; an all-day kindergarten often is a day-care alternative many parents feel they can't refuse.

Some parents simply cannot accept that their child is too immature for kindergarten, even if child care is not an issue. Test results, persuasion, or logic fail to move them as they insist doggedly upon their child's "rights."

Another reason parents persist in sending immature children to school is that they have been oversold on the "earlier is better" philosophy. Having spent thousands of dollars on expensive preschools for their youngsters in the belief that this preparation is superior (if not, why spend the money?) parents cannot accept the premise that their efforts have not "paid off" in readiness. It is especially difficult for parents to believe their child is immature if a teacher at the expensive preschool has assured them their child is gifted, highly verbal, creative, or already knows how to read.

Popularized versions of early-childhood research have convinced many adults, including some teachers, that the remarkable achievements of preschool children in individualized, one-on-one classrooms and laboratories can translate into superior performance in elementary classrooms, regardless of a child's age and maturity. Unfortunately, this is not the case.

Biology—Not the Calendar— Determines a Boy's Readiness

A little boy's performance in school is influenced by the genetic characteristics he inherits from his parents, which include a degree of his intellectual ability; by the environment his parents provide for him; by his own unique personality and pattern of timing; and by the slower developmental pace of males in general.

Central nervous system growth is the unseen but essential component in school success. Even before your little boy was born, his central nervous system was developing in a characteristically male fashion, beginning with the basic organization of his brain cells. Even at very young ages, boys are better than girls at some mechanical tasks and other activities that require them to manipulate objects mentally. In later years, this right hemisphere advantage translates into superior mathematical ability.

Most girls speak earlier and use longer sentences than boys do, performing much better in beginning reading. Neurologist Richard Restak finds that girls appear to make more "social sense" out of the sounds they hear than their male peers do. In kindergarten or first grade, girls are more likely than boys to understand conversational overtones such as innuendo, sarcasm, tone of voice, and implied ideas. It is precisely these left-hemisphere skills that are important in the primary grades. "For school-related functions," one prominent neurologist says, "sex differences favor girls. Thus, being a boy is a risk factor, because both the timing of maturation and the ultimate mature organization of the male brain seem better suited to life beyond school."

These differences in central nervous system maturity and linguistic ability, as well as others in fine motor control and impulsivity, cause girls, on the average, to be ready for the demands of school at an earlier age than boys. Studies of attention, memory, recognition, and reasoning ability show that the performance of older children is consistently superior to that of younger ones. *A child's sex and age are powerful determinants of his success in school.*

Mature Children Learn Easily

Teachers have long been aware of the differences in performance between younger and older learners. One particularly striking example is attention span. Even moderate distractions interfere with the ability of five-year-olds to do some kinds of school work, whereas the same level of distraction poses no problem for seven-year-olds. Younger children are able to pay attention for remarkably long periods of time provided they are working on an activity of their own choosing. It is when they must perform a task imposed by adults, as they are required to do in school, that they find it hard to concentrate.

Researchers consistently find that older children have a far easier time remembering learned material than younger children do. Experimenters who were testing memory ability in children showed them pairs of cards on which common objects were pictured, asking the children to name the objects. Then, one card from each pair was shown to them, and they were asked to recall the item that had been paired with the one being presented. Five-year-olds required many more presentations of the cards than seven-year-olds before all items were recalled. The experimenters next asked the children to construct sentences that linked the pictured objects in some way. This strategy was very successful if the children were over five. Seven-year-olds, in fact, performed almost as well as fourteen-year-olds. Older children are more likely to recall information and to transfer strategies learned to new material than younger ones. If asked by a teacher to remember how to spell a list of words, for example, the more mature student who underwent this experiment or who had been taught such a strategy might very well link his spelling words in some way. It is characteristic of children who are around seven years of age to begin using learning strategies spontaneously; it is not usual in five-year-olds.

Psychologists have discovered that the speed with which a child recognizes objects increases with age. If you show a dot-to-dot drawing to children five and seven, the five-year-old has to complete far more of it than the seven-year-old before being able to tell what the picture represents. Older children need less information than younger ones to arrive at the same perceptual conclusion. In learning letters, numbers, or sight words, which require rapid recognition and response, older children have the advantage over younger ones.

Differences between boys and girls, and younger and older children, become paramount when parents must decide when a boy should start school. The almost-five-year-old who still finds it hard to sit through a story, dress himself completely, or wait his turn without frustration may find the demands of a kindergarten class impossible to meet. The youngish six-year-old who dislikes using pencils, markers, or scissors, who shows little interest in printed material, and cannot remember directions even though he tries, may well face serious problems in a first-grade classroom.

Readiness for Kindergarten

Children who are ready for kindergarten are not afraid to be away from home for a portion of each day. Capable of taking care of their bodily needs, such youngsters know their full names, are able to ask questions to obtain information, and have a degree of self-control. Certain physical skills are usually in evidence, such as being able to catch a large ball, run and stop on signal, and hop several times on one foot. Although these motor abilities are not, of themselves, necessary for school, they are accepted markers of central-nervous-system maturity important to school success.

While a five-year-old boy who is ready for the work of kindergarten will not ordinarily display great skill at writing, drawing, or cutting, he will generally know how to hold a pencil and use scissors, be interested in drawing and writing (especially his name), or enjoy making three-dimensional figures out of paper. He may on occasion find it hard to wait, and every now and then his temper may get the best of him, but he demonstrates his maturity by making solid efforts to keep himself in control. He will be able to fix his attention for a considerable period of time on tasks that interest him. He will have a harder time paying attention to those he finds boring, but he will try. If a group of boys is building an intriguing block skyscraper, or the teacher is reading an exciting story to a small group of his classmates, he may be somewhat distracted from the task at hand.

Five-year-old kindergarten boys enjoy learning numbers, and many of them are proud of their ability to count. A few children begin skip counting (counting by twos or fives) at this age. They find riddles, "knock-knock" jokes, and stories that feature incongruities of various kinds hilarious.

Developmental tests, which are sometimes given before or at the beginning of the kindergarten year, contain other measures by which a child's readiness can be determined. These tests, one of which has been designed by the Gesell Institute, are a combination of hand-eye coordination and verbal answers to questions. A child might be asked to copy certain simple drawings, add the proper parts to a partially completed human figure, or tell all the animals he knows in a specific number of seconds. Trained examiners determine what the Gesell researchers call a child's "behavior age" from such tests, and it may or may not correspond to his chronological age.

What Kindergartens Teach

The specific skills children learn in kindergarten classes vary from state to state, but most have similar goals. At the end of his nine months in a kindergarten class, some of the things a little boy will be expected to have mastered include being able to tell an experience or story in sequence, knowing the names and/or sounds of the letters of the alphabet, understanding one-to-one relationships, counting to ten, realizing that books and words have meaning, and showing respect for the rights and feelings of others.

Kindergarten teachers emphasize the importance of consideration for others, politeness, taking care of one's belongings, putting things away properly, learning to share and take turns, and cooperating with other people. All of these behaviors are important if one is to get along in groups, which is what children will be doing for the next twelve years. Because the five-year-old is eager to please and to be praised for his efforts, these simple lessons are readily absorbed by most children.

Some are even learned too well. One kindergarten teacher received a note from a mother which read: "Please tell Brendan there is more than one way to put on a coat. I know that you have shown the children how to lay out their coats on the table, stand behind them, place their arms in the sleeves, and flip them over their heads. However, there is a better way to do it when you are thirty-one and pregnant. Thank you."

Almost all children enjoy kindergarten. Both boys and girls are naturally responsive and outgoing at five, and take real pleasure in being with others; school is often one of their favorite places. Few students are as eager to learn and have such a wish to please as the five-year-old. If your son is fortunate enough to spend his kindergarten year with an experienced, pleasant teacher who likes and understands little boys, his first school experience will be a positive and happy one.

Although in many schools kindergarten children receive report cards, grading is far more informal than it is in subsequent years. Conferences may substitute for report cards in some cases, and teachers usually keep in close touch with parents if there are problems of any kind. Because growth is so variable during this year, especially in boys, more latitude in performance may be allowed than in later years. Five-year-olds can change in dramatic ways from September to June. Boys of this age can differ greatly.

A description of several boys in one kindergarten class illustrates this very well. Throughout the year there were noticeable variations in the boys' fine motor control, and reading readiness scores at the end of the year showed remarkable differences. An exceptionally able youngster, midway through the year, could snip away at a piece of construction paper with scissors for several minutes and come up with an airplane, a man, or a dog. Another child, however, could barely cut across a piece of paper only one and one-half inches in width by mid-April. One boy could read a primer. Another, who could name few of the letters, was nevertheless able to form graphically correct numbers and letters out of clay.

The Little Boy Who Is Unready for Kindergarten

How can you tell if a little boy is not ready for kindergarten? One indicator is his chronological age. Boys with birthdays in the last three or four months of the year may be better off waiting until the following September. They may be competing with peers who are as much as 364 days older. Throughout the country, kindergarten teachers attest to the difficulty such younger boys have in school. NIH neurologist Martha Denckla has for a number of years worked with children who have learning problems. Herself the mother of sons, Dr. Denckla writes forcefully with regard to readiness in younger boys: "Boys with birthdays in the months of September through December, brilliance notwithstanding, are at risk in elementary school."

A second sign of unreadiness is a little boy's distress at going to school, and his unwillingness to remain there. While a few tears and statements of "I don't want to go" are not all that uncommon early on, a child who persists in his protests is giving parents and teachers a strong message.

A third and excellent way to tell if your child is unready is to believe his teacher. Many kindergarten teachers are remarkably accurate in being able to predict whether or not a child will do well in school. A teacher with ten years of experience in instructing both morning and afternoon kindergarten classes has taught approximately five hundred children. If such a teacher indicates that your son is not ready for kindergarten or first grade, do not treat her advice lightly.

Parents are often terribly distressed to discover that their little boy is not ready for school, especially if they both work. Child-care expenses are no small matter, and the prospect of diminishing costs for time spent in kindergarten is difficult to pass up. Full-time monthly charges at one nationwide day-care chain in suburban

Virginia amount to $240. A half-day kindergarten program reduces this amount by half. Nevertheless, economics should not overrule developmental factors and needs at this time in your little boy's life. The one-time savings of slightly more than a thousand dollars (half-day tuition of $120 per month at a day-care center for ten months) is a terribly high price to pay for what could become twelve years of frustration, possible school failure, and a lifetime of lowered self-esteem.

Maturity Is Especially Important in First Grade

It is in the first-grade classroom, at the age of six or younger, that a child is judged in a formal way by an adult other than his parents. It is here that he is rated for the first time—by his teacher, by his peers, and ultimately by his parents. First grade is *real* school. Even if a child has attended preschool and kindergarten, he knows—and his parents know—that these experiences have been only a preparation. *First grade is the first grade that counts.*

A child who is ready for first grade should be able to do most of the following tasks:

- follow simple spoken directions
- sit still and pay attention in a group
- express his needs and ideas clearly to others
- be physically independent—go to the bathroom by himself, tie his own shoes, button his coat, and so on
- hop, skip, and jump
- recognize basic colors and shapes
- recognize similarities and differences in sounds
- listen to a story and retell events in sequence
- identify and count numbers from 1 to 10
- use a pencil and cut with scissors
- copy simple figures, including a circle, square, and triangle

- know how to write his name and the numbers from 1 to 10
- follow a classroom activity to its proper conclusion

Even though they are ready to sit at their desks for longer periods of time than in kindergarten, six-year-olds are often in motion, and boys are more so than girls. Because nature is urging them to move about and exercise their large muscles, boys find it harder to be still. Well-developed first-grade boys, however, are able to restrain some of this overflow motor activity in order to pay attention to the tasks at hand.

A boy who is ready for a full day of school has the ability to control his impulses most of the time, even though it may still be difficult on occasion. First graders display a number of tensional outlets like nail-biting, pencil-chewing, facial tics, and twitching. Studies have found that animals may also display tics when they are somehow restrained. Nervous behaviors in first-grade children could very well reflect attempts to control their impulses to move about. If so, it is also a sign of an increasing maturity—a realization of the need for self-restraint in order to attend to tasks at hand.

While it is not always easy for a six-year-old boy to pay attention in a first-grade class, he will make an effort to understand directions and do as he is asked. "Not paying attention" is a common complaint on report cards written by first-grade teachers. Because they are still somewhat distractible (a road crew observed through the classroom window wins hands-down over vowels), paying attention is one of the more difficult challenges faced by first-grade boys.

The mature first-grade boy will probably display a toothless smile. Teething is an intriguing sign of readiness theorized by Gesell researchers, who find a connection here between physiological and behavioral maturity. In one group of eighty school children, only 4 percent of those who were advanced in teething were doing poorly; of those who were behind in teething, 54 percent either repeated a grade or, in the estimation of Gesell personnel, should have repeated.

Even though the first-grade boy may not write as precisely or as neatly as the little girl who sits beside him, he enjoys learning to compose words, sentences, and picture stories on large paper. He is likely to spend far more time on the picture than the story, but he is nonetheless pleased with his efforts. Some exceptionally mature boys of six-and-a-half spontaneously decide upon lengthy projects involving a great deal of writing and copying. "Books" about dinosaurs or space travel may be assembled over a period of days, complete with illustrations and fancy covers.

While more girls than boys in a given class may achieve high scores on reading tests, most well-developed first-grade boys do learn to read without undue difficulty, provided they have a competent teacher and a sound reading program. In the beginning phases of reading instruction, they will be able to hear the separate sounds in words, tell the difference between similar sounding words, and be able to discriminate visually between letters and words. From their kindergarten lessons, they will know the letters of the alphabet and a fair proportion of their sounds.

The recognition and reasoning skills of older first graders make reading and arithmetic easier for them than for younger classmates. "I know that word—it's *cake!*" such a boy may say. I learned it yesterday." The ability to generalize goes along with an increasing ability to reason. "The *a* in that word can't sound like the *a* in *cat* because there is an *e* on the end." In arithmetic, greater reasoning ability makes the learning of some concepts far less difficult. Understanding that only ten numerals are needed to write all numbers seems a simple concept; yet many immature first graders are unaware of it because this concept may not be directly taught. This, and other concepts which may be learned as much by inference as by direct teaching, are far more easily learned by older students.

Six-year-old boys are often very proud of their ability to remember all sorts of things—oddball facts about dinosaurs or sea shells, the words to songs and television commercials, the numbers to one hundred—and many of them seem to memorize new material with relatively little difficulty. Mature first graders begin to use effective learning strategies to help them remember, without prompting from a teacher or a parent. "If I spell the word three times and run my finger under it, then I remember it," one proud boy told his mother.

The boy who is ready for first-grade work will find a measure of satisfaction each day as he becomes more competent. Not only does he find the work challenging and interesting, he also enjoys the entire process of school itself. The performance of mundane activities like remembering to put his name on the top right-hand side of the paper with the day's date below may be executed with great care and seriousness of purpose. "Oh, that's really neat!" he may say to himself, as he works out an addition table and observes the pattern the numbers make. The intricacies of school procedures and social relationships provide learning of a different sort, and he partakes eagerly.

First Grade Brings New Expectations and New Tasks

Unless a little boy has attended an all-day kindergarten or a day-care center, first grade will be the first time he is expected to go to school for an entire day, usually between six and a half and seven hours. It may also be the first time he rides a school or commercial bus, or walks to school by himself.

Two topics of conversation that appear with regularity at the dinner table in the homes of first graders are what happened on the way to school and what took place in the cafeteria. Both are situations in which much social learning occurs and new skills are demanded.

For little boys, a major worry is getting "picked on" by bigger boys on the way to school—a practice that does not appear to have diminished over time. It helps a little boy enormously to have had prior experience with older children, or to have older siblings to accompany him. The boy who is able to handle a certain amount of teasing with equanimity is able to buffer himself against further onslaughts.

Eating lunch with twenty-five other six-year-olds for the first time has to be, in addition to a gastronomic miracle, an eye-opening experience. A little boy may learn, for example, that other mothers are less concerned about nutrition, or more so, than his own (a friend's bag of potato chips and packaged cupcake compared to the thermos of soup and the carrot sticks his mom packs); that some children have all the money they want (enough to buy two chocolate milks and an ice cream); and that some people will eat anything (including peanut butter, mayonnaise, and baloney sandwiches). The cafeteria line is a big worry for incoming first graders. What if they lose their lunch money? What will happen if they drop their tray? Will the pizza really taste like cardboard?

Another initiation for little boys which mothers rarely hear about is the one that occurs in the boys' restroom. Bathroom functions, which until now have taken place in privacy, become a group process. Many six-year-old boys are unfamiliar with urinals, not to mention relieving themselves in the presence of others. And there may not be any doors on the stalls. Not a few primary children make a mad dash to the bathroom as soon as they reach home for the first few weeks of school.

Assuming responsibility for his belongings and his behavior are major new tasks for a first-grade boy. Each child has his own desk, books, pencils, notebook, and art supplies, most of which are expected to be kept neatly at hand in a space that is little bigger than a breadbox. As boys of six are seldom neat by nature, disorganization can cause a few problems in the beginning.

First-Grade Friends Are Important for Boys

Almost everyone can remember that special friend we had in first grade. It may have been someone to whom we were attracted because she smiled at us when nobody else did (the others were all scared to death, too), or because he was different from us in a way that seemed mysterious or intriguing. First graders often form fond attachments with another child in the beginning weeks of school, usually with a member of their own sex. A red-haired, freckle-faced youngster proudly walked up to his teacher one morning, arms wrapped about the shoulders of a smiling classmate whose dark straight hair contrasted sharply with that of his buddy. "Me 'n Kim are best pals," the redhead announced. "I'm learnin' him American and he's learnin' me Kolean."

Dominance behaviors of the other boys in his class are especially relevant to the first grader. He is acting and responding in ways that help him to find his place in the scheme of things, and this may well be of greater importance to him in the early weeks than schoolwork. If you listen carefully to your first-grade son's after-school and dinner conversations, you will probably find that it is the relationships in his classroom he speaks of more often—not how many new words or vowels he learned. How to deal with other boys, especially aggressive ones, can be an issue of major concern.

Young schoolboys have a particular need to learn to handle the aggression in themselves and in other boys. A small percentage of children fall into two categories in schools—bullies and whipping boys. Bullies, who appear to be more self-assertive than other boys, sometimes find it difficult to control their impulses and may deliberately pick on other students. Whipping boys are often their victims. As endearing as the perfectly behaved and passive little boy may be to adults, he may well be fair game to a bully. More anxious and apprehensive about what might happen to them in groups, these youngsters are sometimes described by teachers as over-protected. Boys who are uncertain of their place in the group may align themselves with a bully when he is ha-rassing a whipping boy and help him out. Most children will, on occasion, both witness and participate in aggres-sive encounters, and these can begin on the first day of school.

The more mature boy can turn aside occasional ag-gression by being assertive rather than returning the ag-gression in kind. "That's not fair," he can say, or "I don't think you ought to push Jimmy around." Among six-year-old boys, aggression can take the form of staring, pushing and shoving, name-calling, occasional real fights, and taunting. "He stared at me!" is a common complaint of this age. More mature students may short-circuit aggression in other boys by approaching them in a friendly way.

What Happens Every Day

A first-grade boy will find his day highly organized from beginning to end. Reading is most often done in the morning, but there may be a second reading period in the afternoon. In many schools, children are ability-grouped for reading. Children learn the difference between groups very quickly, favoring membership in those that denote high status. A Scottish study found that boys be-tween five and seven were well aware of classroom dif-ferences in ability, and displayed a "readiness to classify and even reject peers in these terms."

In his reading group, a little boy will usually sit with six to eight other children in one area of the room, most often at a large table with the teacher. When he works by himself, he may be assigned what is called "seat work" or other appropriately quiet activities. Seat work often consists of single worksheets with letters to be matched with pictures. Instructions may require the child to write short words demonstrating a phonetic principle, solve math problems, or complete workbook pages that correspond to the reading program.

During a given day a little boy may come together with other children for group instruction in subjects like reading and arithmetic. He may also work at a learning center—a special table or desk furnished with materials to learn about a specified topic, which may serve one or several children at a time. In addition to reading and arithmetic, social studies and science are subjects usually included in a boy's first-grade curriculum. Health, physical education, art, and music may be taught from one to three times per week, as well.

The First-Grade Teacher Is Important

A little boy's first-grade teacher may well have an effect on his life that persists into adulthood. Her experience, expectations for each child, and her skill in teaching and managing her class can make a difference in a little boy's performance.

In a study at Canada's McGill University, the effects of one remarkable inner-city first-grade teacher on the adult lives of the children she taught showed that her pupils experienced far more success in adulthood than those taught in two other first-grade classrooms in the same school. This woman's secret was to have high expectations of every child. "If children are fortunate enough to begin their schooling with an optimistic teacher who expects them to do well and who teaches them the basic skills needed for further academic success," the researchers concluded, "they are likely to perform better than those exposed to a teacher who conveys a discouraging, self-defeating outlook." Unfortunately, the opposite may be true, as well. In one assessment of the reading performance of New York primary-age children, teachers characterized as poor by their principals had higher failure rates among their students than teachers regarded as more competent.

Boys need a first grade teacher who has high expectations for them. Because teachers are so aware of developmental delays in boys, expectations for them may be lower than those for girls. The effect of teacher expectations on a child's performance can make a difference. Harvard psychologist Robert Rosenthal has studied the effects of teacher expectations on performance for over two decades. When asked what advice he would give to the parents of a first-grade boy, Dr. Rosenthal said, "Do not let a teacher teach your child who doesn't think your child can learn." Teachers who have high expectations for their students get better results than those whose expectations are lower.

It is also important that a child's first-grade teacher be an effective classroom manager. Competent, well-organized teachers plan ahead, use effective techniques of group instruction that minimize discipline problems, and respect their students. Teachers who rely on benign methods of discipline have students who are more eager to learn and have fewer behavior problems.

Good communication is essential. Let your son's first-grade teacher know that she can expect your help and support. She needs to feel that she can tell you about problems she may have with your son in an objective way, and count on your assistance in solving them. She needs to know that you have prepared your little boy to be as well behaved and polite as possible. Many first-grade teachers welcome parents as room mothers or aides, or may need help with holiday celebrations in the classroom. A competent, caring first-grade teacher and sensible, helping parents can make a little boy's initial school experience a productive and happy one. However, if you have serious concerns about your son's teacher, air them with her or ask her how she deals with the class and your little boy. Try to keep a balanced perspective, but if problems persist, make the principal aware of them, as well.

However competent and caring his teacher may be, the boy who is too young or immature when he begins school can face enormous difficulties. More than his parents, a good teacher recognizes the traits that set a Bluebird apart from a Sparrow. But it is the first grader, himself, who feels his success or failure most keenly.

The Tale of a Sparrow

Last fall Justin Adams was sent to first grade. With his mid-December birthday, Justin fell just two weeks within the cut-off date of January 1 in his school district.

Justin had enjoyed his kindergarten year, especially getting to know so many new children. He liked snack and storytime best, and the days when he got a turn in the block corner. They really had neat blocks in Miss Farmer's kindergarten room. Justin was not as fond of the writing, coloring and painting he was required to do, and still has a hard time cutting straight. Even though kindergarten was fun most of the time, Justin preferred being home and playing with his friend, Billy. They both had sets of action figures, and spent hours making the small people perform heroic feats, sprinkling their play with the strange-sounding noises of their imaginary landscapes.

Only three weeks after Justin entered first grade, his parents received a note about their son's first-grade progress. "Justin is having trouble keeping his mind on his work," the message said. "We are having a slight problem with reading, as well." Miss Smith didn't mention that Justin's handwriting was poor and he had trouble keeping his letters on the line.

His mother, Martha, notices that Justin seems very tired when he comes home from school; often he is irritable, and there are those arguments with his sister, Lisa. Justin also wants to watch more TV than usual; she has to keep an eye on that, as she realizes too much TV sometimes makes him fidgety.

At this point, Justin himself is a very bewildered little boy. He knew that first grade was "big school," and that he would be working harder than he did in kindergarten. But never before has he been forced to do so many things that are so difficult every single day! He has learned to read a number of words from memory, even hard ones like *said*, but many of his classmates are able to read phrases and short sentences, while he stumbles along word by word. Do they know some kind of secret he doesn't know?

By the end of the second marking period, Miss Smith asks Justin's parents to work at home with their son. "His lack of concentration makes it difficult for him to get through all his work at school," she writes in her report, adding that homework may help reinforce what he learns in the classroom. Martha makes a diligent effort to help, setting aside a quiet time after Justin's snack to do the homework each afternoon. Justin tries to please his mother, but he wishes he had more time to ride his bike or play with his friends. During the week, it seems as though he never can do the things he likes.

The Christmas holiday and Justin's sixth birthday provide a period of relaxation. Despite the hectic nature of the season, his parents see a noticeable change for the better in their son's behavior as soon as school is out. He and his father have a fine time building all sorts of things with his new Lincoln Logs. But then January comes. Justin balks at returning to school.

By March, Justin is no longer as eager to please Martha during the homework sessions after school; often there is a scene. Martha wonders what she might have done wrong. Maybe she shoud have helped Justin with his letters in kindergarten. His father cannot understand why it is so difficult for his son to read, and he knows that reading is vital to getting ahead. And then there's his behavior—perhaps they need to be more strict.

These very real parental concerns are minor compared to those Justin is experiencing. Almost everybody else in his class is reading—but he isn't. Most of them can write a legible sentence—but he can't. His teacher gets mad at him sometimes when he doesn't finish his work; his mother gets mad at him when he doesn't want to do the assignments at home; and his father gets mad at him, too. All the other kids in his class are good at things. Why isn't he? Is he just bad? Is that why they are mad at him all the time?

The other day Lisa called him a "dummy," and his friend, Susan—the pretty one with the long straight hair—hasn't sat next to him at lunch for a whole week now. Even if she is a Bluebird, she doesn't have to act that way. Why couldn't he be in the Bluebirds, anyway? He has to stay with the Sparrows. It's just because of dumb old reading. Boy, if they had Bluebirds and Sparrows for other things—like Lincoln Logs, maybe—he'd be a Bluebird, for sure.

Maturity Can Make All the Difference

Placing a child in first grade before he is ready ultimately risks the sum total of a boy's knowledge, his level of achievement, and, most of all, his self-esteem. Immature youngsters find their schoolwork difficult. Because it is hard for them, they often prepare or retain less of it than other children do. Thus, their level of achievement is seldom as high as that of their more mature classmates. If he is unable to find a measure of success in academic work, a child like Justin may look for other areas in which he can succeed and feel the approval of the important people in his life. Learning to get along with the children in his class can be very difficult for a little boy if, at the same time, the school tasks he faces are hard for him.

Some little boys react to this double pressure—difficulty in learning and the challenge of dealing with others—by behaving in inappropriate ways. Children who are naturally shy may withdraw still further, making their social problems even worse. More outgoing youngsters can turn frustration into aggression or boastful behavior. Becoming the class clown or developing an "I don't care" attitude is another avenue to relief. Because each child is different, each responds to this kind of school stress and social pressure in his own way. A little boy who does not have a real problem, but who is simply too young for first-grade work, can change from a confident, eager child to one who is hesitant, doubtful of his ability, resentful, and afraid to try.

It is the older and more mature children in a first-grade class who often assume leadership roles and become the Bluebirds. They come to school confident, like most children, but with the social and behavioral advantages that extra time confers. The Justins of the world must shuffle for a position in the first-grade hierarchy, unable to achieve what their more mature classmates accomplish with ease. Developmental delays can deny them success; a year of continuing failure can erode their self-esteem.

Popular Myths Perpetuate the Problem

A first step in the making of more Bluebirds is ridding ourselves of some of the myths that we have come to believe about school achievement.

- "If a boy is five, he's ready for kindergarten." It follows, of course, that if he's six, a boy is ready for first grade. Many parents cannot accept that this is simply not true. We are so accustomed to thinking of age as the only criterion for school entry that we balk at holding a child back, even if we doubt his maturity. What if he has a growth spurt? What will the neighbors think? How can we keep him out of kindergarten when all his friends are going? These are some of the questions that trouble many parents. One way to ease your mind about a child's readiness is to ask a competent first-grade teacher what her experience has been with older and younger students. It is also helpful to ask relatives, friends, or neighbors whose children have been sent to school early or given extra time to mature, what the effects of this placement have been. A third way to settle your doubts is to request that your little boy be given a developmental test. You may find that he is more than ready for the grade under consideration.

- "If he's big enough, he's old enough." For some reason, size looms very large in the minds of many parents and some teachers as more important than other components of readiness. Size can be a significant factor in the rankings boys make in their groups, if it is coupled with maturity. A somewhat larger, more mature boy is often a leader in elementary-school groups; however, the bigger, but immature boy may not be. Being immature and large could well exacerbate a boy's problems. Because of his size, people will expect more mature behavior from him. If he is unable to deliver, adults may lose patience, peers may begin to avoid him, and loneliness and resentment may result. "A little boy who is larger than average can usually handle this extra pressure if he has an additional year to mature," one principal says.

- "His sister was ready when she was six; he should be ready, too." Each child in a family has his own developmental timetable, and girls, on the average, show readiness for school at earlier ages than boys. Comparing a little boy to an older sibling, especially a sister, overlooks the very real differences that boys and girls, and siblings in general, demonstrate in development.

- "My son is bright, and probably gifted. He can handle it." There is something so tantalizing about having a gifted child that some parents will go to almost any lengths to prove they have one. Children who learn to read, play a musical instrument, or master a second language in their early years may, or may not, be gifted. But these achievements, by themselves, do not mean a child is ready for a particular grade in school. Test scores are one of the criteria by which schools make initial selections to screen students for gifted/talented programs. Older children, as a general rule, make higher test scores.

A second way to help more children to proper placement is to consider options that are currently available in many communities, and others that could be put in place. Enrolling an immature six-year-old in an all-day kindergarten class, if one exists, is a good alternative to first grade. Similarly, a half-day kindergarten, half-day first-grade arrangement is a suitable way to address the needs of a child who is ready for a full day of school but not for the full academic load of first grade. Some children spend two years in kindergarten. A readiness or transition class between kindergarten and first grade is offered in some communities; during the year, children have an opportunity to mature and improve in a number of skill areas. An ungraded primary, which groups children of various ages in a single class, is another option more popular in the sixties and seventies than it is today.

Midyear entry of first-grade children was a practice in some communities in the past, although largely abandoned by school systems today; Gesell experts recommend that schools space grades at half-year intervals at least up to the third grade. "Just that half year would make a great deal of difference, say, for a child who is not ready for first grade but is beyond kindergarten level." Often we fail to comprehend the full significance of time in the life of a young child. "You have to realize," one psychiatrist said, "that in first grade, half a year of age is roughly ten percent of a life span . . . six months is a big difference in age."

Whatever the options schools and parents might select, it is especially important for little boys that they be in a learning situation in which they feel competent to do the work required of them. The child who feels competent believes he is in control of what happens to him.

Competence and control are essential for the self-esteem a little boy needs to interact well with his peers and feel that he is a significant member of his group. It is abundantly clear that early school difficulty, especially first-grade failure, is not good for little boys. Parents and schools have a obligation to reduce this failure by recognizing unreadiness and making use of preventive techniques that help boys to achieve success.

What of the Little Boy Who Must Repeat?

It is fortunate that nature has endowed children with the wonderful quality of resiliency. The child who needs a second year of kindergarten or first grade can be made to feel that the experience is a perfectly normal one, and many schools make a point of instilling this attitude.

One Virginia principal begins educating parents about the great differences between children when kindergarten begins. They are told that some children may need three years of preparation for second-grade work. Teachers in the kindergarten and first grade classrooms carefully monitor each child throughout this period, and recommendations for promotion are based on the child's progress and maturity. Because the entire community has been made aware of developmental differences, attitudes toward retention are positive; this good feeling is transmitted to the children.

"The sense of relief some children experience after retention is overwhelming," one specialist says. "They are grateful for the opportunity to be able to perform well and not to have to continue to struggle in school." Researchers find that the students who benefit the most from retention are "normal but immature students in the early grades."

Gesell's Louise Bates Ames believes that being in the wrong grade is worse than the one-time damage to his self-esteem retention might represent to a little boy. If his placement remains uncorrected, his self-esteem suffers repeatedly—year after year. One educator proposes that retained students receive special treatment, including an individualized educational program and the services of learning disability resource teachers, if necessary.

Some researchers emphasize that there are students who are not helped by waiting *or* retention, but who need special attention. If there is reason to suspect that a child has a specific developmental delay or a learning disability, he should be in a school where his needs can be adequately addressed.

How a child is rated and judged by the important peo-ple in his life affects his image of himself and his abili-ties, and may often be reflected in his behavior. The importance of the parents' attitude toward retention can-not be emphasized too strongly.

Fathers, especially, sometimes have a difficult time with the notion that their son has "flunked" a grade in school. It is human nature to deny the existence of prob-lems we do not like to face, and after denial comes ratio-nalization. Fathers often think, "If he'd worked harder, he'd have passed." Mothers are more likely to wonder, "Where did I go wrong?" It may help to remember that no child deliberately sets out to fail, especially first grade. *If a little boy has had to face failure, he needs the support of his father and mother more than ever.* One family, confronted with this situation, told their son how proud they were of his efforts when the work had ob-viously been so hard for him. They assured their little boy that his second year in first grade was going to be better, and that they would be right there beside him. They tried even harder to encourage his success at sports during this period, and never once let him feel that he had done less than his best. This fortuante little boy became a competent student, achieved high grades, and, in addition, assumed a position of leadership among his new classmates.

What if *Your* Little Boy Must Repeat First Grade?

If you can greet the notion of his repeating a grade positively ("Now you'll have the time you should have had to enjoy first grade." "It'll be more fun because you'll be ready."), retention will not seem a disaster to your child. For the boy whose only problem is immaturity, repeating first grade is far better than continuing a struggle for which he's not ready. You will want to pay attention to his self-esteem, and here are some suggestions to help bolster children who repeat (and those who don't):

- Tell him—every single day—how wonderful he is.
- Share with him an interest in something other than school, and help him as much as possible to be successful at it.
- Let him hear you tell other people how great your little boy is.
- Express honest pleasure at his achievements—no matter how small they may be.
- Read with him and read to him every day to help him learn that reading is enjoyable.
- Display his schoolwork and other written material in a prominent place, so he knows that you are proud of his accomplishments.
- Help him put together a scrapbook or photo album showing all the progress he has made over the years. Most six-year-olds love to hear their own "history." Remember when you first climbed that big tree?
- If possible, contribute time at school as a volunteer. If you are employed full time, help with an evening project such as a book fair or banquet. In this way, your son will feel that you are involved more closely in what he does all day.
- Keep in close touch with his teacher—weekly, if need be—to see how things are going.
- Listen to him. Look at him when he is speaking to

you, and take the time to make sure you understand what he is really saying.

• Most important of all, remember that *grades and school achievement are not a measure of your child's value.*

Every child deserves the opportunity to start off right in school. For the child who is fully ready, first grade can be one of the most exciting experiences of his life.

Learning to read introduces a boy to new ideas, far-away places, and different people. It gives a boy an independence that he welcomes eagerly. Library books reveal intriguing facts about magic, Zanzibar, reptiles, or secret codes. Dictionaries, encyclopedias, and almanacs become resources he can turn to when his curiosity needs to be satisfied.

Knowing how to manipulate numbers to his own advantage will open up new dimensions for him in calendars, clocks, and money. He can tell when it is time for his favorite TV show, or pay for purchases at the store by himself. He can count how many days it is until Christmas or his birthday.

For the successful, ready first grader, the entire world is an immense, exciting laboratory—awaiting his eager exploration.

The Primary
School Years

GRADES ONE THROUGH THREE

The typical American child goes to school for thirteen years, beginning with kindergarten at five and ending with graduation from high school at eighteen. During these years, he spends approximately fifteen thousand hours in the classroom, encountering close to forty teachers on his educational journey. In the primary grades, a child becomes part of a larger society separate from that of his family; adults other than his parents make the rules, and his needs often must be subordinated by those of the group. The society is not the same for boys as it is for girls.

Teachers respond to children differently, depending on their sex. Boys are apt to receive almost as much feedback about their behavior as their work; girls hear more about the work itself. Girls act in ways that make it easy for teachers to like them, maintain group control, and keep the classroom neat and orderly. Boys, on the other hand, wiggle, get out of their seats, fiddle with whatever they can get their hands on, and may have trouble staying on task. Neatness and order are relatively unimportant to boys, as is the teacher's opinion of

116

what they do. The natural behavior of young human males is less conducive to established classroom norms than is that of females. As one neurologist, possibly remembering his own childhood experiences, put it:

> The male brain learns by manipulating its environment, yet the typical student is forced to sit still for long hours in the classroom. The male brain is primarily visual, while classroom instruction demands attentive listening. Boys are clumsy in fine hand coordination, yet are forced at an early age to express themselves in writing...there is little opportunity in most schools, other than during recess periods for gross motor movements or rapid muscular responses.

It is hardly surprising that boys are usually the students who sit out in the hall, stay in at recess, and fill the after-school detention rooms. Very few teachers value the ability to run fast, turn on a dime, put mechanical gizmos together right, construct a miniature spaceship out of discarded lumber, or spend the entire afternoon in a ditch to find just the right-size frog—skills boys are good at. Instead, they value a number of things that are difficult for small boys: writing neatly, keeping quiet, sitting still, reading, and remembering what they were just told to do.

What a child learns in school is not limited to the information he reads in books or hears from the teacher—the manifest curriculum. He learns as much, if not more, from the latent curriculum—the subtle, unspoken lessons he absorbs about himself in relation to others. "Nowhere else will he be judged so frequently by others and, it is possible, judged by himself," says education specialist Benjamin Bloom.

The relative size of the school and community have an important effect on a child's performance, which Harvard psychologist Jerome Kagan illustrated with his hypothetical boy, Paul. Reasonably intelligent and self-sufficient, Paul grows up in an Oregon town of four thousand people. There is only one class for each grade in his elementary school, which includes perhaps fifteen other boys his age. In this environment, it is relatively easy for Paul to become a leader and to feel good about himself. If he lives in Los Angeles, however, his school might have six classes for each grade. During recess Paul sees that at least twenty other boys are better at sports than he is. A similar number, which includes lots of girls, outperform him academically. Winning an adequate place in his group in Los Angeles is more difficult than it is in the small Oregon town. How Paul comes to feel about himself in relation to his peers will probably be very different depending on his environment.

Where we live, the kind of school system available to our children, and the classmates and teachers our boys will come to know are factors over which most of us have little or no control. We can, however, take steps to give our son the maximum possible advantage as he embarks on his educational journey. We can make sure he is mature enough when he begins. We can become acquainted with his teachers and keep up with what is demanded of him each year. And we can follow his progress closely, letting him know we value each new accomplishment.

How Boys Behave in School

If you were to ask a first-, second-, or third-grade teacher to describe the ideal student, she would probably tell you about a child like Karen. One of the older children in her class, Karen is able to do whatever is asked of her. She listens attentively when the teacher gives directions, remembers them, and carries them out faithfully. He work is always handed in on time and is neat enough to read easily. On the playground or in group projects, Karen rarely argues, tries to change anybody's mind, or objects loudly to what others wish to do. Dependable, responsible, and cooperative, Karen is a real joy to have in the classroom. If you were a teacher of twenty-five young children for six and a half hours every day, wouldn't you want a lot of Karens?

Instead, teachers in public schools get a relatively even mix of boys and girls whose test scores and behavior vary widely, all of whom are expected to learn the same things at the same time and arrive at the same place in the curriculum at the end of nine months. Unlike Karen, the boys will generally display few of the characteristics of the ideal student.

- Boys are more active than girls. They need to move about and exercise their large muscles. They require opportunities for blowing off steam.
- Boys are more exploratory than girls. After a week or less in a classroom, boys can tell you where you keep the cleanser to scrub the sink, which of the window latches has a piece broken off, and how many of the desks are for lefties. They will already have examined the pencil sharpener and may inform you that it is different from the one in the classroom down the hall (they took that one apart last year). Part of this exploratory drive is a need to do things with their hands—to manipulate objects.
- Boys are more competitive than girls. The presence of other boys stimulates them to greater achievement. They are also more peer-oriented than girls and may even ignore adult standards to gain the approval of their friends.
- Young elementary-school pupils of both sexes believe in stereotypes. For boys, this means they value, and will display, behavior they consider appropriate to their sex. Masculine qualities—being tough, assertive, competent, and approved by others for behaving this way—matter greatly to boys.
- Boys need to feel they are in control of what happens to them. This sense of power, or potency, is far more

important to boys in the early years of school than is commonly realized.

In general, boys have a positive outlook at the beginning of school. They believe that, if they work hard enough, they can do what is necessary to succeed. When asked to rank themselves and others in their classes, both boys and girls who are starting school are more than likely to place themselves at or near the top. Below the age of seven, children look at ability in terms of specific skills. A child might be good at puzzles, but not a fast runner. Around seven, however, as the child moves into an "all or nothing" frame of reference, he begins to look at ability as a generalized quality. If he, or someone else, is good at the things parents and teachers (his adult raters) encourage and approve, then he perceives himself or the other as good in a number of ways.

Until he starts primary school, what the child has been asked to do has been tangible and observable. A tower is made from blocks. Shoelaces are crossed, then tied. Forks and spoons are placed on the table just so. The child, himself, can judge whether or not he has been successful. On intellectual, school-related tasks, however, children "may be less likely to know what they are aiming for, why they are aiming for it, how to get there, and when they have gotten there," two researchers say. This uncertainty about their performance arises at the same time a child is placed in the position of being judged (and judging others) on a daily basis. The result is that first-grade children, over time, become less certain of their ability or that they will have success. From second grade on, children's rankings of themselves are far more likely to be in line with those of their teachers. A child's image of himself in school gradually becomes less positive.

How Teachers Treat Boys

In general, teachers reward behavior that is considered by some to be feminine—following directions, sitting still, and keeping quiet are examples. Boys are reprimanded far more often than girls (one study found this to happen on the order of five to one) and the reprimands are louder. When boys are doing what the teacher asks them to do, they may be given more positive attention than girls who are doing the same thing. Girls, it seems, are expected to behave. When boys behave, teachers actively encourage them.

For a number of years, critics of schools have believed that boys are discriminated against because of the feminine environment. Primary teachers are typically female, and male role models are seldom available in elementary schools. However, a study that focused on male teachers found that their behavior toward boys differed little from that of their female counterparts. Male teachers scolded boys more than girls, too.

Boys appear to receive more overall attention of every kind from their teachers. More often than girls, though, they are given negative feedback about their behavior, their motivation, *and* their work. Harvard's Carol Dweck found that when told by teachers that their work is poor because they "haven't tried," boys reason that if they just try a little harder, they will be successful. Girls are more apt to believe that failure in school is due to a lack of ability, and thus are less likely to believe that greater effort will produce positive results. In spite of the higher degree of negative attention they receive, most boys who do not have major school problems such as immaturity or learning disabilities, continue to remain confident. Dweck suggests that because boys sometimes believe their poor grades are the fault of the teacher, and that if they try harder they will be successful, a change in the teacher or the situation can motivate them to renew their efforts to achieve. Having a new teacher, starting another school year, or going to a different school may cause a boy to try harder.

Teachers have different expectations for their students based on their ability, and their behavior toward them differs. Children thought to be high achievers receive more praise and less criticism than low achievers; teachers give good students more opportunities to respond, and wait longer for them to offer answers. They like youngsters who conform to what is expected of them and make an effort to achieve. Teachers are rarely fond of children considered to be behavior problems, and may be more or less indifferent to those who make few demands and blend into the background. Unfortunately, it is also true that teachers sometimes respond negatively to children whose racial or economic characteristics are other than white and middle class.

An exceptional teacher can influence his pupils in remarkable ways. Charles Darwin's botany instructor, Professor Henslow, encouraged Darwin's interest in geology and also recommended him as ship's naturalist aboard *The Beagle* for the journey that was to change Darwin's life and the way we look at the history of man.

Parents' Help with Reading Begins Early

Most of us believe that a child learns to read when he goes to school. But reading really begins long before, in the interaction between parents and child that starts in infancy. How pleasurable we make the back-and-forth coos and pat-a-cakes of the early months, how often we encourage a toddler to initiate conversation or praise him for his responses all influence the young child's attitude toward verbal interaction and language itself. Born with a readiness to communicate, girls almost demand conversational give and take from late infancy on. Frequently less motivated than girls to converse with other people, little boys may have to be encouraged to "be verbal" to the same extent girls are.

One of the questions often asked of teachers is, "What can I do to help my child with reading?" A more appropriate question might be, "How can I help prepare my preschool child to be responsive to reading later on?" and the time to ask it is well before first grade. Columbia University reading expert Jeannette Jansky had some excellent suggestions for what parents of children three and older should be told in response to this question.

- Observe your little boy carefully to find out how he amuses himself, and what he is interested in. Talk to him about these activities, and listen to what he has to say.
- Pay attention to whether or not a preschooler is naming things. If he is having more difficulty than his siblings did, or his friends do now, work systematically to help him acquire new vocabulary. Begin with words that remind him of something he is very much interested in (cars, for example); slowly increase his exposure to words associated with this topic (shiny, door, exhaust, bumper).
- Read to your little boy often. Take care, however, not to read beyond the point at which he listens attentively. Because it is sometimes hard for parents to know which books may be appropriate for specific ages, Jansky suggests that a good reading level for a child is one where the material does not have to be paraphrased in order for him to understand the story.
- Be a model for good language usage. Speak clearly and distinctly. On occasion, repeat what your son has just said when you begin a response. This lets him know you understood what he said, and that you are a good listener.
- Talk about the past and the future, not just the present. If you are planning an event, talk to your little boy about it and encourage his participation. Review what took place when the event is over, helping your son to talk about his experiences.
- Be aware of the importance of helping a child relate on

a verbal level. Preschool children, especially boys, often respond through their motor system; encourage them to express themselves through language, moving from a motor to a verbal level of communication.

- Encourage the notion of one-to-one correspondence. Help your son to see that the word he is saying corresponds to something visible. It is important for a child to recognize that concrete objects can be represented by spoken words, pictures, and, later, by written words. The spoken word "box," for example, comes to mean a real cardboard box, a picture of a box, or the written sequence of letters, "b-o-x."
- Show your little boy how to use pencils, so that he is comfortable with them by the time he gets to school.

Approximately one child in a hundred learns to read before he starts school, and researchers find that his parents contribute to his early ability. With very small children of eighteen months or two years, simply having them point to known objects in picture books or magazines shows that we value the reading process. "Let's play a game," a mother might suggest. "I'll find something red (pointing to a red flower in the child's picture book) and you find something...blue. Do you see anything blue in the picture? It's little." When reading an exciting story for the first time, asking your little boy, "What do you think will happen next?" lets him see that he can be a participant as well as a listener.

Parents of early readers model reading—they are readers themselves. They not only read to their children, but also provide supplies (paper, crayons, pencils) for their youngsters to create their own reading materials. When their children begin to read and write, these parents accept their invented spellings and tentative first efforts with pleasure and praise, and do not overcorrect them. The preschooler whose parents make an effort to encourage communication from infancy onward will regard reading as an extension of skills he already has.

"You corrected my English so much I
forgot what I was goin' to say!"

Let's Make a Book About...

*Preschool children enjoy making their own books. Boys
who are old enough to handle scissors like to cut pictures from a magazine and paste them onto the pages.
Books about their favorite things or special family events
can be embellished with photographs as well. Help them
to write words on the pages they wish, or have them
dictate the words to you.*

*Boys of kindergarten age who are learning to write
letters and numbers like to make their own alphabet
books, writing the letters themselves at the top of each
page. Drawing the correct number of objects on a page
with each numeral reinforces learning.*

*First and second graders who know how to print
sometimes make elaborate books about space, dinosaurs, vehicles, or their own superheroes. Be sure to give
them plenty of help with hard-to-spell words.*

Provide your little boy with an abundance of paper, markers and pencils, seals of various kinds, tape, glue, and string. Keep these supplies in or near the kitchen, and watch what happens!

Parents, teachers, and reading experts all have strong opinions about which reading method is the best one to use. Children have learned to read, however, as the result of any number of approaches ranging from phonics to specialized alphabets. A child needs to learn a certain amount of letter-sound correspondence in order to decode words, and should also have a sight vocabulary for immediate recognition of others; he comes to understand that what is written down has meaning. As important as any single method for teaching a child to read is the ability to synchronize these elements at the appropriate stage in the learning process.

Teachers rely on a variety of methods to do this. Basal reading programs (graded reading series) are widely used in our nation's schools, and incorporate activities that help a child learn the combination of skills essential to becoming a good reader. Despite the criticism heaped upon these programs in recent years, many little boys find them enjoyable and look forward to finding out what happens next in the small stories. Teachers in most elementary-school classrooms also use experience charts; a story is produced by the teacher and the children together, then is written down on large paper by the teacher as the children watch. Phonics charts, which teach the sounds of letters or combination of letters and often have pictures to illustrate them, are another tool, as are workbooks or worksheets; these often accompany the child's basal reading series and give children practice in applying new skills that are reinforced in the stories. If your little boy is in the primary grades, his school probably uses a reading program that incorporates most of these methods.

Reading Can Be Hard for Boys

One of the more perplexing problems of researchers is that, while few differences are found between boys' and girls' achievement test scores, boys are less successful in beginning reading and more likely than girls to be referred for special help.

A possible reason for this greater vulnerability of boys to reading deficits is offered by psychologist Sandra Scarr, who suggests that the tasks we humans find easiest to do are those "most rooted in our biology," and thus are least likely to be influenced by the environment. Tasks that are less biologically determined are more easily influenced by environmental factors. Because girls appear to have a linguistic advantage from a very early age that has some biological components, environmental factors are less relevant to their progress in reading.

Researchers have found a number of factors to influence the reading of children under study. It should be emphasized that this does not mean that *all* children are similarly affected, only that these factors have shown up in some studies and indicate possible differences between the responses of boys and girls. A factor as seemingly inconsequential as the sex of a little boy's siblings made a difference in reading performance in one group of subjects from families with two to four children. The performance of boys increased noticeably if they had at least one sister. Emotional problems can also have a dramatic effect on a boy's reading achievement. One experienced elementary-school principal notes that reading problems often occur when a first-grade boy's parents divorce, and studies support her observation by underscoring the fact that boys in such families frequently have more trouble in school.

How appealing a boy finds the material he is to read sometimes makes a difference in his performance. One investigation of fifth-grade students found that boys asked to read about high-interest subjects performed better than a control group reading books with little relevance to their lives. Immaturity, which makes learning of all kinds difficult, has also been found to be a factor in reading performance for boys. The fact that most primary teachers are women is frequently cited as another reason for the lower reading achievement of boys; girls, some suggest, find it easier to identify with the teacher and her goals. One expert notes that the differences in reading progress between boys and girls is sometimes not as great when measured by achievement tests as it is when measured by grades. A child's motivation, behavior, and attitude may influence a classroom grade; an achievement test measures performance only.

For children of either sex, family stability, socioeconomic factors, personality characteristics, and intellectual ability have an effect on many aspects of school performance. The little boy whose family is plagued by personal or financial problems may use up much of his energy coping with what happens at home, leaving little left over to devote to schoolwork. Poverty exacerbates problems of every sort for children. The child who is extremely gregarious may so enjoy being with his friends that he finds it hard to focus his attention on academic tasks. Boys and girls of moderate ability may take a longer time to learn certain tasks than will many of their classmates.

Reading Is a Life-Long Venture

It is important to remember that learning to read is a process that extends over a period of years. Providing support for a little boy undertaking this basic and continuing task of the primary grades is all important. Encourage your son to read to you if he chooses, and praise him for every small achievement. Share information you read in newspapers and books with him, or point out a particularly amusing cartoon from the funny papers. One mother sends jokes, cartoons, or silly notes to her children in their lunch bags. In another family, a father continues to read to his children in the evening, even though they are both avid readers themselves. Sharing exciting stories not only provides enjoyment for all of them, but also may well foster a relationship that encourages other kinds of communication.

Educator Thomas Lickona says that reading can be a way of helping a child learn values. Reading about a youngster who is like himself in some way can help a boy learn how to cope with problems or understand his own special qualities. Positive values that some parents find hard to teach can often be transmitted to a child if he reads about them in a well-written and appealing story.

Make reading accessible to your little boy. Take him to the library on a regular basis, and help him to select books that are appropriate to his reading level. Provide him with his own library. The price of books is often high, but used ones from yard sales or thrift shops can be had at a fraction of the cost. Children who love to read have parents who see to it that they have books *to read*.

Boys Respond Positively to Math

Boys and girls in the primary grades seem equal in computational skills. Sex differences in mathematical ability are not found until the end of the elementary-school years. One interesting difference, though, is that boys, more often than girls, spend their leisure time in pursuit of mathematical interests. In general, boys like arithmetic, and many of them have little trouble mastering this subject. If your son is in first or second grade, he may comment to you that math is "cinchy" or easy. Some children of this age are proficient at counting by ones, twos, fives, or tens. Simple addition and subtraction problems can be done in their heads, but they are easier to do if the counting procedures have been routinized by practice.

Children in the primary grades are very interested in

time and money. Because the skills they involve are both practical and useful, children often master them very quickly. One group of disadvantaged first-grade boys was asked what they most needed to know about numbers. A consensus was quickly reached. They wanted to be able to tell time in order to understand the TV schedule, and to make change for a dollar to be sure the convenience-store clerk was giving them the correct change. They learned both skills within two weeks' time.

Some children may have problems learning mathematics. One type of learner may concern himself with detail and solve problems step by step. Another may grasp the larger picture, and come up with the right answer even though he has a hard time explaining precisely how he got it. A teacher's approach can make a real difference in how a child feels about arithmetic, and in how much of it he learns.

Five teaching practices that have been found to contribute to math anxiety are an emphasis on memorization, speed, and doing one's own work; authoritarian methods; and a lack of variety in teaching or learning processes. If your little boy is beginning to learn addition or multiplication tables, help him to make the chore less odious by being willing to call out problems to him while you are doing the dishes or driving in the car. The child who is reflective and works more deliberately than others may have trouble taking daily timed drills in school and find tests frustrating. If your little boy is like this, you might practice such activities with him at home in a more relaxed setting where he is competing only against himself. The emphasis on doing one's own work is sometimes misplaced in elementary school, particularly in mathematics. Young children gain enormously from talking about numbers, figuring out problem-solving techniques together, and comparing quantities and measurements. Teachers might do well to promote games and activities that involve more group participation in mathematics.

Deciding that there is only one way to teach, one way

to learn, and one right answer is another means by which teachers help to create math-anxious individuals. In *Overcoming Math Anxiety* (New York: W. W. Norton, Co., 1978), Sheila Tobias says that boys' tendency to believe that if they work hard they will succeed helps them to persist in learning arithmetic they find difficult, even if teachers do use some of these less effective methods. If your little boy has trouble with math, certain materials that appear to be toys can be quite helpful. Tobias suggests a geoboard, which can be made from a piece of plywood or cork. Pegs or nails are placed on the board in ordered lines, and rubber bands stretched between them to make various geometric shapes. Montessori-type math materials, many of which are well-illustrated in Elizabeth Hainstock's book, *Teaching Montessori in the Home* (New York: Random House, 1971), are attractive teaching tools for boys and can be made at almost no cost.

Being able to orient oneself in space, or figure out mentally how objects look or move about is called spatial visualization. This ability is measured by many intelligence tests; males consistently score higher in this area than females, and the differences appear to be innate. Spatial ability seems more concentrated in the right hemisphere of the male brain than in the female brain. Sex differences have been found in the ability of four- and five-year-olds to build three-dimensional models out of blocks. In a number of cultures, boys are more advanced than girls in these skills. In one experiment where electroencephalograms were taken of children engaged in spatial tasks of various kinds (such as figuring out which folded shapes could be made from flat, irregularly-shaped pieces of paper), the right hemisphere of boys appeared consistently activated. In girls, both hemispheres were more apt to be activated.

Young children show a progression of skill in their acquisition of spatial information. Your two-and-a-half-year-old, if taught to recognize a cube and a sphere (a block and a ball), will easily learn to identify each by touch, even if he can't see them. Somewhat more time will go by before he can build an accurate replica of a cube from blocks or Legos. And he will be close to ten before he can reproduce with clarity a face-on cube by drawing it. When he does, however, he may create a better reproduction than will a female classmate.

The extent to which spatial ability is linked to mathematical ability is a subject of much debate. Males achieve at higher levels in many forms of advanced and theoretical mathematics than females do.

One intriguing hypothesis is that late maturers of both sexes have greater spatial ability. An investigation of eleven-year-old girls found that many of the later-maturing females chose recreational activities having to do with their their spatial talents, which are often regarded as masculine. They built models and go-carts, enjoyed carpentry and mechanical drawing, and repaired electrical equipment.

A majority of learners like mathematics less with time; this seems to be true of both males and females. The difference may be that males, believing they will ultimately be successful at math, stick with it longer than females do. Boys have a distinct advantage over girls in that they receive more out-of-school experience with mathematics. Scout programs teach mathematical skills for badges like orienteering, and more boys than girls work with computers or go to computer camps. Boys who traditionally spend far more time than girls in physical activities that involve manipulating their bodies in space—namely, sports—have more opportunities to enhance these kinds of spatial skills. There was evidence in one study that spatial ability in some female athletes was greater than that of the average men who were compared with them.

Computers and Little Boys

At almost every age, a majority of computer users are males. Students with home computers are more often boys than girls, and those enrolled in more advanced classes at summer computer camps are males, as well. More than girls, boys use computers on their own time. They also show greater interest in video games, and much of the software available for home computers is considered masculine. For instance, a popular math game involves the comic strip character Snoopy shooting down the Red Baron when the child's answer is correct.

Computers are probably very much overrated as learning tools for children below the high-school level. Students, in general, make minimal use of computers in elementary schools, even though a lot of money is spent on them and there is little thus far to indicate that they do a better job of teaching than is accomplished by traditional classroom methods. However, a number of enthusiastic educators disagree with this point of view and believe them to be excellent teaching tools.

At the high-school level, courses are designed to teach job-related computer skills, and this seems an appropriate time to learn them. For elementary-school children, home computers can probably be fun and educational to a limited extent. If you have preschoolers, your money would be more wisely spent on a good set of blocks.

Single-Sex Classes—
Are They Better for Boys?

If boys are slower than girls to develop important skills in the early school years, if they respond more positively when there is another little boy to stimulate them, and if environmental factors make a greater difference in their performance, it is logical to ask if they might be better off in single-sex (all boy) classes. Such an arrangement would eliminate the presence of the highly verbal girls, provide plenty of other boys for company, and allow for classrooms to be structured in ways that would be maximally conducive for boys to learn. Some people suggest that boys in all-male classes might make better progress.

As a ripple effect of the women's movement, the notion of separating the sexes has become almost taboo as a subject of serious inquiry. For refusing to allow girls to play on the varsity football team, one high-school principal was taken to task, and community sports leagues frequently face the issue of single- versus mixed-sex teams. School personnel in this country are justifiably concerned about the repercussions of instituting programs that appear to discriminate, especially against females. However, as Jerre Levy of the University of Chicago states, "In a completely sex-blind meritocracy, biological differences would still appear between men and women. There would continue to be more male engineers, but there might well be more women psychiatrists." Males and females are more alike than they are different, but, as Levy points out, differences that do exist make an impact on how we think, learn, and ultimately fulfill our goals. Despite the emphasis in favor of coeducation, there are valid reasons to ask if single-sex options might have value.

While the research is sparse, results that are available appear positive—not only for boys, but for girls, as well. Studies have shown the academic progress of boys in single-sex classes to improve in comparison to boys in mixed-sex groups in some subject areas. In one experimental Virginia program, boys taught in single-sex classes had higher morale, were more interested in their schoolwork, participated more freely in music and art, and showed greater achievement overall. More boys than girls wished to continue in the program. Even though the classes were noisier and the boys less inhibited than those in mixed-sex classes, researchers felt that the teachers were accepting of males' active behavior without the continual contrast provided by female students. One significant result of the experiment was a drop in the school's retention rate from 10 to 3 percent. In another study that assessed the progress of students from twelve countries, boys from single-sex schools were found to have higher scores in mathematics than those for mixed-sex schools.

At least one group of researchers suggests that teachers may prefer to teach one sex over the other and that they may, in fact, do a better job if allowed to teach the preferred sex. Comparisons of children in mixed- and single-sex classes revealed in the Virginia study that stereotypical behaviors such as girls' tendency to be passive and boys' reluctance to participate in music or art were not always found.

This raises the question of whether our beliefs about coeducation may be tenuous. Some people believe that boys will be too rough if they do not have the "leavening" influence of girls in their school classes. Others feel that females are insufficiently challenged by teachers unless their classes contain an equal number of males. However, it was found that gifted high-school girls were more likely to achieve as well as or better than gifted boys in special mathematics classes if they were taught by a woman and the classes enrolled either all girls or a sizable number of girls compared to the number of boys. In our haste to equalize everything, we may well be overlooking some important ways of enhancing the abilities of children of both sexes.

What Makes a Boy a Successful Learner?

Children who are successful learners have usually been successful before they came to school. Parents especially, but also preschool teachers, day-care workers, and other important adults in their lives have encouraged them to achieve. When they begin formal schooling, these students expect to do well. Moreover, they have already learned a lot about how to go about it.

The successful schoolchild comes equipped with a fund of information that he will be able to tap. Adults not only have helped to motivate him; they have also provided him with toys and books that interest and challenge him. They have answered his questions and given him explanations; in short, they have provided this child with a knowledge base. He can draw upon a store of information like money in the bank that will help him learn even more.

Mature, able learners use specific strategies to acquire new information. They "rehearse"—perform an activity of some sort that helps them to retain information. Their practicing may consist of simply looking at a list of words a number of times in succession—rote repetition of single items; which is a tactic used by many younger students. Another rehearsal strategy is to spell out a series of words letter by letter, look at each, close one's eyes, and try to spell them. Touching and labeling of objects to be remembered is yet another, as is associating objects or words in some way. Older children begin to organize information to be learned in order to make their efforts more effective; outlines are an example.

In recent years, psychologists have found that children recall more information if they generate some of the data they are to learn themselves. An example might be the memorization of vocabulary words. Teachers often suggest students first write a new word, then write the definition, as a way of learning its meaning. However, if a student writes the word and then traces an image pro-

vided by the teacher (TEPEE—), his recall is better. The most effective technique, though, occurs when a child writes the word and then draws his own picture to represent the definition, generating the image himself. Combining new information with one's previous knowledge or experience appears, in some way, to make remembering far easier. Successful students become able to extend information they already possess. They know "what to do with what they've got." As one researcher said, "It is the efficiency with which a learner uses whatever is available that defines intelligence."

Little boys can become very successful students in the primary years, especially if they are mature and ready for the work required. Because they sometimes have trouble with organization, however, their parents may want to help them pay close attention to their own learning and monitor its progress. Just talking about learning strategies helps a child to understand that they are useful. A simple procedure that can help a boy stay focused on a task involves a series of five questions that he can learn to ask himself as he approaches a specific assignment.

1. What is the task? (Learning to spell ten words correctly.)
2. How should I do it? (Spell each word, write each word, spell each a second time, close your eyes, spell it again, then write it down.)
3. Am I doing it right? (If you are learning to spell the words correctly, yes.)
4. Did I do it? (Ask someone to test you and see.)
5. If not, what can I do to fix it? (In this case, try the same procedure a second time for misspelled words, or ask a teacher or parent to suggest a more effective strategy.)

Because it is important for a boy to feel that he is in control of himself and what is happening, this approach has great appeal. It can also be a motivator; because it does help him stay focused, tasks he prefers not to do (like homework) may get done more quickly. For boys who have an especially hard time getting organized, writing down the answers to the first two questions can help in getting started.

Successful learners usually have a high degree of self-esteem. They are willing to take risks. Jack Canfield and Harold Wells, educators who have developed a number of techniques for helping children feel better about themselves, liken self-esteem in school to a stack of poker chips. When they begin the learning game, some children have a great many chips, others only a few. Those with the most chips have the advantage; they can afford to risk more successes or sustain more failures than students with fewer successes behind them. The child who is ill equipped to begin with, or who has experienced failure in the past and lost some of his chips, has a lower opinion of himself and does not dare risk very much. Parents and teachers need to help children by building up their self-esteem. As Canfield and Wells put it, "Self-concept building can be seen as making sure that every student has enough chips to stay in the game." More able, successful learners, with their greater self-esteem, stay in the game and win. This is easier for any child to do if he also goes to a good school.

Boys Like Good Schools

A good school for boys is one in which there is a caring, effective principal who likes children and is visible to them on a daily basis. He or she gets involved. This leader is a sound manager who knows that in order to be productive, people must feel that they have some control over what goes on, that their ideas are considered and appreciated, and that school is a positive place. The principal sees to it that the teachers make children feel this way, too. The rules are firm, but fair. Moreover, teachers and students feel that they have had a hand in establishing the rules; they have "bought in" to the system.

Even though boys, in general, are less enamored of school than girls, they generally like to go to good schools. They are not afraid to take some risks there, and know that if they fail at a task, someone will help them find out why. Teachers in good schools have high expectations for boys, and give them abundant amounts of praise for achievement. Public, school-wide recognition is systematically practiced. Students who do something special are made to feel that it is a "big deal"—that *they* are something special. In the hall near her office, one excellent school principal posts reading and math achievement charts, which publicize the names of children who have learned their multiplication tables or read a certain number of library books. Another principal makes a practice of naming a "special person" of the day whose achievements are extolled to everyone. A third sends home, on a monthly basis, letters of commendation about specific students' achievements. Parents of children who go to good schools hear good news about their youngsters.

Ideal schools use benign methods of discipline. There is clear and unmistakable evidence that schools using harsh techniques, either with individual students or on a school-wide basis, are less effective than others. They end up promoting the behavior they are trying to stop. Schools that use corporal or formal punishment programs that feature paddling and demerits may see worse behavior in their students over time—not better. Dr. Irwin Hyman, professor of school psychology at Temple University, who monitors corporal punishment throughout the country, says that approximately 90 percent of the corporal punishment administered in the schools is directed at boys, frequently by hitting them on the buttocks with wooden paddles. Corporal punishment occurs most often in schools in southern and southwestern states, and is often used in religious schools of various persuasions. However, harsh disciplinary methods are not more effective in school than they are at home. The same characteristics that typify the most competent parents—firmness, fairness, and reason—are found in good schools.

Student participation is important in good schools, and many students participate. Opportunities are given to encourage children to accept responsibility and be of service. Club offices, helping out the school secretary or the cafeteria manager, musical or dramatic events, and sports are all ways in which schools make it possible for students to feel that they are an important part of what is going on. Students in good schools not only like to go there, but they also want to participate and learn. Their achievement is higher.

Parents' Help Is Important in the Primary Years

The primary years, grades one through three, are those in which the basic skills are taught. Compared to later school years, teachers proceed more slowly, monitor students' progress more carefully, and may keep in closer touch with parents. It is during these years that children establish work habits, attitudes toward formal learning, and a basic belief about themselves that says either, "I can do it," or "I can't." Regardless of the school or teachers a little boy has, his parents play a major role in what happens during the first three grades.

Too many of us subscribe to the philosophy, "once he's in first grade, it's up to the school. My job is finished." Such an attitude is not solely due to reluctance on the part of parents to share responsibility for a child's education; schools sometimes foster these beliefs by promoting a "hands off" policy with regard to help in or out of class.

Other parents may become too involved in a boy's academic progress for their son's own good. Occasionally, adults have been known to attack a teacher verbally over their child's poor grades. Some parents routinely tutor their children, whether or not they need it. Overinvolvement in a child's schoolwork often reflects our own competitiveness. However, little boys are competitive enough without any help from us.

Homework Is for Kids—Not Their Parents

Most teachers, school principals, and parents approve of homework. "It develops children's initiative and responsibility," one recent poll reported. Assigning homework for children in the elementary grades, however, can pose some problems. Teachers should allow for big differences among their young students, not only in ability, but in their stamina, as well. A third grader who struggles for an hour on a homework assignment may be putting in an eight-hour day on school-related activities, considering class time, transportation, and homework. This is the equivalent of an adult work day.

The response of many parents to a primary-school boy's complaints about homework is to help him. A recent Gallup poll showed that almost half the parents of elementary-school children regularly help their offspring with schoolwork. Parents of one New York first grader felt the need to give up their own weeknight activities to supervise their child's homework. If parents can support a child's homework efforts without robbing him of the opportunity to learn on his own, they can make a real contribution.

When homework becomes a part of your son's routine (usually around third grade), set a time agreeable with him to work and provide an adequate place for him to do so, furnished with sufficient material (pencils, a pencil sharpener, paper, ruler, reference books, crayons, markers, poster paper). Be willing to keep television sets, radios, and stereos turned off during his study time.

If your son complains that his homework is too hard, make sure he understands the directions, help him get started, but let him do his own work. Calling out a list of spelling words he needs to memorize or drilling him on his multiplication tables can be helpful as long as you can also be tactful about his mistakes. "I always had trouble learning the sevens table; why don't you look those over again before I call them out to you."

Elementary-school-age children need the chance to puzzle over some work alone, but may benefit most when they do their hard work at school where there are trained, objective teachers to answer their questions. It is important that parents refrain from actually doing a child's homework for him.

Educating a child to the fullest extent of his capability requires cooperation by schools *and* parents, especially in the primary years. There are a number of steps parents can take to foster effective learning in the first three years that will make those to come far easier:

- Maintain a positive attitude about school and learning. Let your little boy know that school is important not only to him but to you as well.
- Try to put business and career events second on your list when it comes to your son's school events. This is difficult for many people to do, especially if they are in relatively high-powered positions at work. However, a business meeting can usually be rescheduled; you will probably only get to see your little boy be Robin Hood once. Sons and daughters of the rich and famous frequently point to the absence of their parents during significant childhood events as one of the prices they were forced to pay for their parents' prominence, and this sense of neglect can linger on into adulthood, even when youngsters are successful themselves.
- If you have complaints about the school or your son's teacher, take them up with the school or the teacher—not with your little boy.
- Display your son's schoolwork in your home. This says, "My parents are proud of what I do."
- Be interested in what your son is learning, and think up ways to extend school lessons. "We never did know how big this house really is," one mother told a visitor. "Now, thanks to Mark, we have it down to the inch!" This family found a unique way to challenge

their third grader's measurement skills.

- Encourage his efforts and praise him for his work, not just his good grades.
- Play games. Games of every sort promote togetherness, are a terrific TV substitute, and help a child practice turn-taking, winning, and losing. They can also enhance cognitive ability. Although you are no doubt familiar with these games, you may not be aware of the concepts they teach:

Go Fish, Old Maid	Visual matching
War	Greater than, less than
Blackjack	Mental addition
Checkers, chess	Spatial skills and strategies
Clue	Logical deduction
Monopoly	Estimation, arithmetic operations
Scrabble, Probe, and other word games	Spelling, phonics skills

If they are mature enough and have the help of concerned parents in getting off to a good start, most little boys will be prepared to deal with the far more rigorous academic requirements that begin in the fourth grade. Students of this age are expected to be independent learners and to have mastered the fundamental skills of reading, writing, and arithmetic. "Fourth graders have it all together," one teacher said. "They read well on their own; they are curious and want to learn; and, what's more, most of them like to be here."

Help your son to become enthusiastic about school by giving him all the support you can during the first three grades. A good start in his early years of school will encourage academic success as your little boy grows into a big one.

6

Boys with Special Learning Needs

THE LEARNING DISABLED AND THE GIFTED

Although every child is born with an innate desire to learn, some youngsters—a majority of them boys— seem unable to learn at the same pace or in the same way most children do. If he were a schoolboy today, Thomas Edison might be considered hyperactive or learning disabled. When the world's most productive inventor started school over a century ago, his teachers dismissed his insatiable curiosity as "addled behavior" and punished his less than exemplary classroom deportment. Fortunately, Mrs. Edison removed her son from school and taught him at home. Albert Einstein, despite a measured IQ of 200, failed math; if he were a student today, he might be diagnosed as dyslexic, but once he learned to compensate for his language disability, he might also be placed in a program for mathematically gifted students. Men like da Vinci, Rodin, Flaubert, and Mozart showed learning leaps and delays that would probably make them candidates today for special-education programs that address the needs of both learning disabled and gifted children.

The predominance of boys among children with learning disabilities, as well as those who are mathematically gifted, has led some researchers to suspect that testosterone may set the stage for subtle variations in the brain's ability to process information at the same time it creates a male brain. If a boy has high levels of testosterone and high sensitivity to this androgen, fetal hormones may interfere to some extent with the organization of cells in the brain. These abnormalities may bring about deviations from the way the brain typically processes information, leading to behavioral results as varied as learning disabilities and mathematical precocity. Of the two million children currently being served in learning-disability programs, boys outnumber girls at least three to one. Children who are highly gifted in mathematics are also largely boys.

Norman Geschwind theorized that testosterone may be responsible for left-handedness in males, who are almost twice as likely to be left-handed as females. Geschwind also found that left-handed individuals appear ten times more likely to have learning disabilities than those who are right-handed. Researchers at Johns Hopkins have extended Geschwind's theories to their studies of mathematically gifted youth. These children are twice as likely to be left-handed as the general population. Several other studies show that left-handed people may excel in creative endeavors or fields such as architecture and engineering that make use of spatial skills.

The school success of learning-disabled and gifted children may depend on patience and flexiblity on the part of their parents and teachers. Children with exceptional talent need to be challenged, and their abilities must be fostered both at home and at school. Boys with difficulty in learning often need to be taught compensatory techniques at school, and parents are encouraged to find unusual ways of dealing with their disabilities at home that take advantage of their strengths. Some boys will be in special classes for a number of years; others may benefit from a special school. But for all children with learning problems, the greatest need is to have parents who accept the fact that they cannot be patched up, fixed, healed, or tutored out of their disabilities; parents who are willing to try and try again; and parents who take pride in their child's forward steps, no matter how short or halting they may seem.

THE LEARNING DISABLED

Many boys and some girls show repeated and consistent difficulty learning in regular classroom settings, although they are bright or average in intelligence. If testing finds their intelligence to be higher than their school performance would indicate, these youngsters may be considered learning disabled. According to guidelines established by the U.S. Office of Education, a child is learning disabled if he shows a "disorder in processes involved in understanding or in using language. It may manifest itself in an imperfect ability to listen, think, speak, read, write, spell, or do mathematics." Furthermore, a learning disability or a child's inability to succeed in his schoolwork must not be due to visual, hearing, or motor handicaps, mental retardations, emotional disturbances, or environmental disadvantages. Some factors beyond the obvious ones make conventional learning difficult for these children.

It should be emphasized that learning-disabled children, as a group, are not retarded, poorly behaved, or destined for a low-status future. Many of us live every day with disabilities similar to those now being picked up by more sophisticated diagnostic techniques than were available when we were in school, and may have difficulty performing certain tasks other people accomplish with ease. If you had trouble with reading when you were a child, and had today's methods of diagnosis and remediation been used in your school, you may have been found learning disabled and given special help.

Hereditary factors play a part in some kinds of learning disabilities, as they do in normal reading abilities. It may be that inherited traits do not actually become problems for some children without the added influence of stress before or after birth. Several studies link alcohol use by pregnant women to problems in their offspring, some involving the learning process. There also appears to be a higher rate of hyperactivity among children whose mothers smoked while pregnant. Emotional stress during pregnancy is believed to be partially responsible for some learning disabilities. If prolonged, such stress can bring about chemical imbalances in pregnant women, and may account for a somewhat higher rate of learning handicaps among adopted children.

Problems at the time a child is born, or in the first eighteen months of life while the central nervous system is undergoing rapid growth, have also been linked to learning disabilities. Long or difficult delivery that reduces oxygen to the fetus, premature birth, dry birth (where the water breaks prematurely), breach or rapid delivery, intracranial pressure on the fetus either from forceps or a narrow pelvic arch in the mother, all are possible causes of learning problems. After a child is born, any oxygen deprivation, such as a delay in producing an infant's first breath, or severe respiratory distress, may lead to learning disabilities for some children, as can a high fever at an early age, a sharp blow to the head, lead poisoning, meningitis or encephalitis, and severe nutritional deficiencies.

Symptoms of Learning Disabilities

A number of behaviors are commonly used to identify youngsters at risk for learning disabilities. A boy who shows several of these signs, and who is also having trouble in school (or preschool) should be considered for testing. In looking at any child's behavior, however, it is always important to keep his age in mind; behaviors that are prevalent among your son's well-developing peers do not necessarily signal a learning disability. Some of the symptoms that learning-disabled youngsters repeatedly exhibit include:

- poor motor control
- impulsivity or distractibility
- difficulty getting organized
- short attention span
- reluctance to try new things
- confusion over direction (inability to recognize left from right quickly)
- trouble understanding time relationships
- inability to copy
- poor reading or handwriting
- reversal of letters and numbers
- difficulty putting ideas on paper

A bright preschooler who has trouble distinguishing between shapes, or whose poor motor control does not allow him to put puzzle pieces together even though he knows exactly how they should go, may be at risk for a learning disability. A kindergarten student unable to cut with scissors, a first grader using either hand when he prints, a third grader still reversing letters and unwilling to read aloud—all these children deserve careful attention and evaluation.

No two children will display exactly the same learning deficits, but certain clusters of symptoms are similar for some LD youngsters. Since children with similar symptoms may respond to the same treatment, it is helpful to adults working with learning disabled children to know about them.

Specific language disability (dyslexia) makes reading, writing, and spelling difficult for many children. Dyslexics are predominantly male. In private schools that offer instruction for severe language disability, there may be fifteen boys to every girl, although in public and parochial schools the sex ratio is closer to two dyslexic boys for every dyslexic girl. Researchers Joan Finucci and

Barton Childs explain the difference in sex ratios as a factor of severity; the more severely affected children (usually male) go to special schools. "Evidently, females tolerate deficits in reading and spelling skills more easily than males," they conclude. Boys are also more likely than girls to be disruptive in class if they have trouble learning; teachers notice them more and may call attention to their problems with greater frequency.

Parents may be unaware of learning problems until a child starts school. As the mother of one dyslexic boy said, "He was such a happy little boy, until he had to learn to read." Children with a specific language disability may do well on three-dimensional spatial tasks (working with puzzles, building with blocks, sculpting with clay), but they tend to have trouble with pencil and paper or other two-dimensional tasks (their handwriting is irregular and cramped, or they seem to read as well upside down as right side up). Dyslexic youngsters may also be slow in verbal memorization and arithmetic computation. These are the children most likely to reverse words like *was* for *saw* and confuse the letters *b* and *d* or *p* and *q*. A ten-year-old dyslexic boy described his condition succinctly: "I can think okay. What's wrong with me is just my words."

Academic remediation for these children often favors a phonetic approach to reading and techniques like repeating the word aloud as they write, or using sandpaper letters as tactile reinforcement. Often dyslexics can succeed with language tasks if allowed "secretarial help"—taping assignments on a recorder in lieu of writing them, or having someone else read lengthy passages of text to them.

Attention deficit disorder (hyperactivity) is usually apparent early in a child's life and is the most common disorder seen by child psychiatrists. Most children with attention deficits and those who are overactive from birth are boys. One study of suburban schools found eight times as many boys as girls were hyperactive, and rarely is the ratio less than four boys for every one girl.

As in dyslexia, both genetic and environmental factors appear to cause hyperactivity in males.

Attention deficits seem to have more serious, long-term consequences for boys than for girls. Some parents tend to be critical, unaffectionate, and disapproving of hyperactive sons, which may only add to these youngsters' problems. Longitudinal research shows that by adolescence hyperactive girls are more achievement-oriented and social than hyperactive boys. Girls who are overactive place high estimates on their own intellectual abilities, while boys suffering the same symptoms often lack self-esteem and downgrade their academic ability and intelligence.

Hyperactivity was originally believed to be a behavior problem, but is now considered a cognitive disability. Often overactive from birth, hyperactive youngsters are impulsive and highly distractable. They have trouble separating relevant from irrelevant information; however, they can often work well if an adult helps them to get started. At school, a boy with attention deficits may be unable to follow his teacher's directions, and his performance is often uneven—one day he finishes his math quickly and correctly, another day he can't sit still long enough to complete one row of problems. His impulsive nature, coupled with a short attention span and lack of confidence, may contribute to lower IQ scores and classroom grades. A typical report card might read, "If only your son were more responsible...careful... organized...motivated."

More than other LD children, a boy with attention deficits benefits from orderly, structured environments, both at home and at school. Because these youngsters have significant problems with self-control, they may have low self-esteem even before they start school. For boys especially, disruptive, unpredictable behavior makes their relationships with other children and adults difficult. Behavior-modification techniques are often effective with hyperactive children.

Stimulant medication, such as Ritalin or other amphetamines, may be prescribed for hyperactive children as short-term therapy. Fidgeting seems to decrease and fine motor dexterity improves for some children on medication. Classroom learning that involves the lengthy processing of information and a sustained attention span may also be enhanced by stimulant drugs. However, this medication does appear to have some negative physical effects as well—loss of appetite or sleeplessness may occur unless dosage is carefully monitored; heart rate may increase and blood pressure be elevated. Stimulants should *never* be used as a diagnostic tool to determine whether or not a child has an attention deficit; even youngsters with no learning problems whatever demonstrate increased attentiveness and diminished motor restlessness when given stimulant medication. Most learning-disability experts recommend medication only:

- for children seven and older
- when a child's behavior is clearly a problem both at home and at school
- after behaviors that are troublesome have been observed and recorded on a daily, continuing basis (a baseline established)
- when a child's needs are addressed by an individualized academic program

Administered carefully and reevaluated frequently, stimulant medication can be an effective means of relief for some of the symptoms that accompany learning disabilities; however, they will not cure attention deficits.

Developmental dysfunction (neurodevelopmental lag) is the name given to deficits for which immaturity is the major symptom. As one researcher puts it, an LD diagnosis for a youngster is based on findings that are abnormal only in regard to his age. If the child were younger, an examination might well find him normal.

Although there are few studies of LD children whose only symptoms are delays, those affected appear to be mostly boys. Certainly the description fits—these children are slow in controlling their attention and aggression. Lags in their neural development also appear to affect their motor, perceptual, and cognitive skills—skipping, hopping, moving their eyes without moving their heads, riding a bicycle, or learning to read and write. In one study, significant retardation in bone growth was found among developmentally delayed youngsters. It may be that for some LD children, other aspects of development are slowed.

Unfortunately, there is no guarantee that a child with a delay will catch up. Experts have not found a system for hurrying or speeding up brain maturation. There is little evidence that programs or training designed to bring these children up to age levels in all areas of development are effective (learning to hop or skip may simply waste valuable time, but efforts to improve handwriting may be useful). Nevertheless, developmentally delayed youngsters do respond to the compensatory strategies that benefit other LD students. Offering individualized instruction, including special help in learning to control their behavior, and allowing them to do part of an assignment with neatness and accuracy instead of overwhelming them with the same amount of work other children can accomplish easily, are techniques that do seem to help.

A developmentally delayed child can also benefit from being chronologically more mature than others in his class; however, placing him in first grade at six-and-a-half or seven years of age is not enough to help any learning-disabled child, even if he is merely delayed. A few children with minor disabilities do seem to make sudden academic progress around ten, if they have received individualized or compensatory instruction. It is at ten that myelination of the corpus callosum, connecting both hemispheres of the brain, appears to be completed.

These three clusters of learning-disability syndromes can occur separately or together. It is possible for one boy to be dyslexic, hyperactive, and developmentally delayed. Martha Denckla, whose long practice in clinical neurology has specialized in learning disabilities, found elements of all three kinds of symptoms in more than half the LD patients in one clinic. Also, symptoms tend to change over the years. One boy with reading and handwriting problems in first grade may be working at grade level in these subjects by third grade, but need one-on-one instruction in math. Children who are having trouble with school and show any of these symptoms should be considered for LD testing.

Could Your Son Be Learning Disabled?

It is easy to overlook differences between children, particularly if our experience is limited to our own offspring. It is disappointing to think that one of our children may have trouble in school, and perhaps especially so when there are signs that might indicate a long-term learning problem. Unfortunately, neither denial nor attempts to downplay a boy's problems in school will help an LD child.

Parents who have reason to suspect a little boy is learning disabled should first seek educational and psychological testing. These can be done at no charge through the public school system, although in some localities there may be a backlog for such services and testing can take several months. Private examination by a developmental psychologist or educational testing facility is often quicker but can cost as much as $300 to $600. The Wechsler Intelligence Scale for Children—Revised (WISC-R) is commonly used in such testing. The advantage of this test is that it contains a series of subtests that examine specific abilities. Experts generally agree that a scattering of scores (high in some areas, low in others) is a frequent indicator of learning disabilities. Whenever a significant discrepancy appears between a child's potential for learning and his actual performance, he may be considered at risk for learning disabilities.

Unless a firm diagnosis is made, many school districts suggest that a child have a physical examination as well. A developmental pediatrician or pediatric neurologist may find symptoms of hyperactivity or learning disabilities that a psychologist can only suggest. Other testing occasionally recommended can include an opthalmic examination, psychiatric consultation, and speech and hearing evaluations. The availability of diagnostic facilities depends somewhat upon the community, but parents would do well to seek experts with an interest in and knowledge of learning disabilities. It is also important to be skeptical of those offering simple cures. For almost all children, a learning disability is a lifelong condition. With proper help, a child may learn to adjust to his difficulties or develop ways to compensate for them. A learning disabled child is *learning disabled for twenty-four hours of every day.* "He has trouble learning the do's and don't's of life in *every situation*," one neurologist points out, "in school, at home, on the playing fields, and in social groups."

If a positive diagnosis of learning disability is made, it is natural for parents to feel guilty, angry, concerned about their son's future, or envious of other parents whose children are not different. They may try to blame his teachers ("They don't understand him."), his doctors ("Why didn't someone catch this problem sooner?"), or even each other ("We never had any problems like this in *my* family!"). It's important for parents to deal with their feelings, and if need be, to seek help in doing so. How well you handle your own emotions can help your son deal with his.

How to Get Help at School

A diagnosis of learning disabilities is usually necessary for a boy to receive special help at school. The sooner his problems are recognized, the sooner remediation can begin. If a boy is lucky enough to have his learning prob

lems discovered before he starts school or early in his
academic career, it is possible to prevent his "turning
off" learning or believing that he's stupid.

Professional educators, whether kindly classroom
teachers, supportive principals, or special-education experts, can assist parents in recognizing a child's changing
needs and providing the knowledge about how best to
meet them. In the past, families were forced to seek private instruction for children whose learning problems
could not be adequately addressed by public schools.
With the passage of Public Law 91-142 in 1975, however,
school districts nationwide were required to provide educational opportunities for all children from three to
twenty-one years of age who were learning disabled or
handicapped in some other way. Through special-
education programs in the public schools, a wide range
of facilities is available free of charge to LD students.

The aim of special education is to help an LD child
learn and function competently in a regular classroom.
The best instructor for an LD student is one who can be
flexible, trying a new approach if the standard method
doesn't work, and who functions as a cheerleader root-
ing for the child. One expert suggests three rules for any
adult working with learning-disabled students:

- Don't act angry, or if you do lose control, apologize
  (your lack of perfection gives you something in common with the LD child).
- Don't expect speed.
- Be explicit and precise in your directions, using a step-
  by-step approach to teaching.

What Parents Can Do to Help

While schools have made great strides in understanding
and helping LD youngsters learn, they are often a daily
source of frustration for these children. A bright boy
with learning disabilities may resent that his classmates,

who don't work nearly as hard as he does, get better grades. For LD youngsters of average intelligence, school may represent a constant struggle just to get by and pass.

For a learning-disabled boy, there is literally no place like home—especially if his parents are accepting and loving. The more you can learn about the way his mind works, the better equipped you will be to help him. A number of organizations provide information, sponsor research, and offer support for families of the learning disabled:

Association for Children with Learning Disabilities (ACLD)
4156 Library Road
Pittsburgh, Pennsylvania 15234
Telephone: (412) 341-1515

Council for Exceptional Children
1920 Association Drive
Reston, Virginia 22091
Telephone: (703) 620-3660

The Orton Dyslexia Society
724 York Road
Baltimore, Maryland 21204
Telephone: (301) 296-0232

It is now believed that any diagnostic evaluation of learning disabilities should routinely include checking for childhood depression. Family therapy may be useful, as a learning-disabled youngster, like any handicapped child, can strain the patience of even those who love him the most. An LD boy's brothers and sisters may not be as tolerant of his problems as parents can be. Occasionally, LD youngsters—often messy, sometimes unable to complete chores adequately—can become the family's scapegoat. In some homes, siblings may feel guilty about their own accomplishments or neglected by parents who seem to be always taking an LD child to some specialist or helping him with his homework.

Experts usually advise parents against trying to tutor an LD child (or any child, for that matter). Most of us are simply too involved with child rearing or providing the emotional support youngsters need to be very objective teachers. However, parents can do a great deal to create an environment in which an often disorganized, rarely inspired LD student can work. For many learning-disabled children the normal day-to-day busyness of a classroom, even a self-contained one, may be distracting; homework can offer these youngers another chance to learn.

In establishing standards for studying at home, parents may need to be less rigid and more creative with an LD child than with other children. Short periods of concentrated effort are often more efffective than one long homework session. You can set a kitchen timer for three-, then five-, and eventually ten-minute spurts of focused, uninterrupted work. As simple a technique as offering two choices, with the more attractive one second, may encourage an impulsive, inattentive child to listen more carefully to directions rather than jumping automatically at the first alternative. Asking a hyperactive boy, "Would you like to clean off your desk now or have a snack?" helps him to listen for the second option.

Many children, especially those who have trouble learning at school, need to unwind and relax when they come home. Setting a regular snack time and encouraging your son to go outside to play before he starts his homework may actually help him settle down when he does start to work. With some LD youngsters, having to finish their work before play means they will race through their assignments, working carelessly. For children apt to daydream their homework session away, or those who seem anxious about being able to do their work, a parent's presence in the same room often helps —your example of reading or working on a project can give your son a mode of how competent adults spend their time. Parents may be wise to look over an LD boy's papers from time to time ("I like the way you write your answers on the line. They are easy to read that way.") and may answer an occasional question without teaching or assuming responsibility for the child's homework.

It is often difficult to know just what a learning-disabled youngster can accomplish. An LD child may need extra time learning outside of school, but he should not spend more than an hour a day on homework in first or second grade; one and a half to two hours is the maximum a third to sixth grader should spend studying at home. (See page 141 for further guidelines about homework.)

Flexibility is important for any adult working with learning-disabled children, but a number of youngsters may try to use it to their own advantage, avoiding work they are able to do but would rather not have to undertake. If your son claims his homework is too hard, offer to help him get started, but don't allow yourself to fall into the trap of doing it for him. Another common problem occurs when LD children "forget" to bring home what they need. One family asked their learning-disabled son what he thought might help him remember his homework; at his suggestion, they set up a system by which bringing his assignments and the necessary books home guaranteed television privileges one hour that day. However, parents need to balance the attractiveness of TV with its risks for boys (see Chapter 6).

To encourage real learning at home, parents should keep in close touch with a child's teachers at school. Weekly communication between home and school may be necessary at times when your son is having trouble mastering a new subject or getting along with others. If they understand what's happening at school, parents can help an LD youngster adjust. Change often seems threatening to these children; a new teacher or a new subject can make their trouble learning all too evident to the rest of the class. Your son may resist going to a special classroom, teacher, or school, even though he was clearly miserable before. You can help him deal with change by showing him your interest in what he does. Get to know his new classmates and their parents; help out at his school if you can.

While you want to be honest with your son about his learning difficulties, it is important to be optimistic as well. In one family, a learning-disabled boy was told— many times and in many ways—that he had his own special mode of learning, which made some of his schoolwork hard. At the same time, his parents reassured him that he *could* learn what he needed to and that other people like him not only survived school but sometimes grew up to be famous and important.

With appropriate teaching, learning-disabled youngsters can achieve the same levels of education and adult occupational status as children without disabilities. Dyslexics often have superior spatial skills that reveal themselves in model building, sculpture, or painting. Your son may draw wonderfully but have illegible handwriting— these tasks utilize neighboring, but different parts of the brain. Hyperactive children possess boundless reserves of energy that, with training and encouragement, may be channeled into athletics or hobbies. Provide opportunities for LD youngsters to find interests outside of school. *Emphasize what your son does right.* In the early years of school, a weekly chart of tasks that a learning-disabled boy can accomplish and/or needs to work on will allow him to check off his own successes. As your son matures, a contract to fulfill certain responsibilities may be a useful tool.

Success Chart

One mother of an LD boy found this chart helped her son accomplish tasks and feel good about himself.

WHAT I DID:	WHEN I DID IT:
	M T W Th F S Sun
Fed the dog	
Did the dishes	
Finished homework	
Put my bike away	
Hugged somebody	
Went to scouts	
Used "happy" words*	
Practiced writing	
Helped somebody	
Listened quietly	
Read	
Put my clothes away	
Gave a compliment	
Cleared the table	
Made my bed	

A structured home life is important to all boys, but especially learning-disabled ones. Consistency in your own behavior is one way to see that your son's life runs smoothly and helps him achieve more consistent behavior himself. Don't deprive him of reasonable discipline. Setting sensitive but firm guidelines, with predictable rewards and consequences, is far more effective than flying off the handle and administering punishments on the spot that may be too harsh. Many parents of LD children find parenting courses useful in helping them establish sensible boundaries for behavior and a sound basis for communication with all their children.

*Happy words are those that make you or someone else feel good—words like nice, kind, friendly, help, *and so on.*

Learning-disabled youngsters often feel out of control. In addition to firm discipline, they need training in many areas. Teach your son to tell time, and provide him with a watch so that he can be punctual in getting himself where he needs to be. Encourage him socially, allowing visits and outings with friends. A boy with learning disabilities may enjoy playing one-on-one within the structured environment of his own home and make better friends that way than at school. Tell him what to expect before you expose him to a new social situation. A learning-disabled boy can benefit from practicing his handshake or passing food at an open house. Making him aware of other people's feelings and the consequences of his own actions helps any boy develop his own social sense.

A learning-disabled boy's self-esteem may always seem fragile, but his parents and family can do much to bolster it. Your patience can help him accept his disabilities; laughing at your own mistakes sets an example that can be invaluable to your son. Like any child, an LD youngster deserves the opportunity to try things on his own, and he is far more likely to learn from his mistakes if the people around him don't take their own too seriously. A boy with learning disabilities is very much like any other boy—only more so!

THE GIFTED

Gifted children demonstrate exceptional abilities in intellectual, creative, academic, and leadership areas, or in the performing and visual arts. The number of boys and girls who are gifted appears to be roughly equal. However, by late adolescence, boys generally score higher than girls in tests of mathematics and science.

In preschool youngsters, giftedness sometimes manifests itself by the ability to speak early and in complex sentences. Some wait until they are older to speak, but then show greater facility with language than other children do. Motor skills in many gifted preschoolers are well-developed. They may learn to walk, run, climb, use pencils and scissors, draw and write before most children do. Facts and events are remembered easily, and even at this young age they seem to draw associations between ideas. Boys have great imagination and often wish to initiate immense projects, demonstrating a remarkable ability to keep on task and carry their plans to completion. Gifted preschoolers are more likely than their peers to feel empathy for others and to demonstrate leadership ability. Many have an exceptional sense of humor.

In the elementary-school years, gifted children express ideas verbally in great detail, and reason in a complex way. They see relationships among concepts and ideas, and understand historical and cultural differences easily. Learning and comprehension are often accelerated. These youngsters may have an unusually wide range of interests and a larger than average fund of general information. They may well display a high level of leadership and have a finely developed sense of justice and idealism. Gifted children are more likely than others to direct activities toward a specific goal.

If you have a son who is gifted, you are probably aware of the intriguing, sometimes unanswerable questions that he may ask, or the oddball way he has of juxtaposing ideas that make their own kind of sense. He and a brother or sister may share an offbeat brand of humor, or engage in complex word-play together. Contrary to the popularized image of the myopic bookworm, your gifted son may very likely be athletic, enjoy the out-of-doors, and be well-coordinated.

A popular misconception about the intellectually gifted is that they are narrow, overly specialized, and do not become well-rounded adults. The opposite is true. By and large, gifted children become adults who are more emotionally stable and better able to handle personal problems than others. Louis Terman's Stanford Longitudinal Study of gifted children, which has followed more than six hundred individuals into late adulthood, reveals just how exceptional they are. Not only did these gifted adults achieve educational levels three to five times higher than comparable groups, their professional achievements by age forty were also prodigious and included books, professional and scientific articles, short stories, and plays. Especially significant in this study is the number of men who put great emphasis on a satisfying family life and felt that they had succeeded in this regard. Your gifted son may be able to look forward to high academic and professional achievement during his lifetime, and to a similar level of emotional fulfillment, as well.

Characteristics of Gifted Children

Identifying gifted children is one of the thornier problems faced by educators. It is, at this time, a less than exact science. There is no universally accepted definition of intelligence. Furthermore, educators do not always agree on the kinds of gifts they should be looking for, or how to tell if children have them.

Programs for the gifted may vary from specialized instructions given from one to several hours per week to entire school programs devoted to the needs of these youngsters. Teachers encourage students in more advanced thinking skills than those used by children in regular classes. One teacher of gifted children offered an example. In studying the human body in third grade, identifying parts of the skeleton and understanding how certain organs work is required of all students. In addition, gifted third graders might well be shown skeletons of other animals and asked to compare them with a human one, drawing appropriate conclusions. What might this animal do that a human could not? How could the animal be changed to make it more adaptable? Work that is challenging for these children requires more analysis, synthesis, and evaluation than many of their peers are ready for.

A number of school systems select children to be tested for gifted programs in the early elementary grades. Scores on achievement tests and a child's grades are frequently the signals indicating that his performance is above average. One survey of the departments of education in all fifty states found that achievement tests are used in over 90 percent of the responding states as a measure by which children are evaluated. Seventy-three percent also use IQ tests. Typically, a school system will devise a number of criteria for selection. In addition to attaining a certain score on IQ or achievement tests, for example, students might also be required to demonstrate qualities such as leadership.

Not all gifted children are identified by currently used selection procedures. IQ scores are not static, and can fluctuate from test to test, varying by a number of points; a single test is a dubious measure of anyone's intellectual potential. As children mature, they sometimes show increases in their IQ scores. In one longitudinal study in which IQ increases were found in children between three and twelve years of age, twice as many boys as girls showed large increases. Even if a boy is exceptionally gifted in mathematics, his ability may not always be detected. Precocious students can sometimes be bored with simple arithmetic and not perform very well in the classroom.

A small percentage of students reason so well mathematically that they can make a higher grade on an algebra test before taking the course than other children who have taken the course for a full year. A majority are male. As early as seventh grade, gifted boys substantially outperform gifted girls on college-level tests of mathematical ability. Among the seventh graders selected to participate in the John Hopkins Study of Mathematically Precocious Youths (SMPY), an annual talent search, there are five boys for every girl who scores 600 on the Scholastic Aptitude Test for Mathematics. At 700, there are thirteen boys for every girl. Among students who scored above 700 in one recent year, no girls at all were represented.

Regardless of their sex, children who show this mathematical precocity may or may not have high overall test scores. Few of the children in the Hopkins SMPY program, who rank above 97 percent of their peers nationwide in mathematical reasoning ability, are in gifted programs in their home schools.

A broadened definition of giftedness now includes a number of children who may not score extremely high on an IQ test but who, nevertheless, display outstanding abilities. Talent is usually regarded as exceptional skill in the areas of music, art, or drama. Tests designed to measure creativity in children differ from IQ tests. In one, a child is asked to list all the things he can think to do with a common object such as a tin can. The boy who offers novel uses for the can that depart substantially from the replies of most children is considered to be creative in his thinking. Defining creativity is very difficult, but most experts agree it is a quality that brings into being something new and of value. Creative children wonder why things happen; they make guesses about causation, and are willing to take risks to find out if they are right. They often see patterns and relationships others miss, enjoy problem solving, and welcome new challenges.

For a long time people assumed that a person had to possess high intelligence to be creative. However, an intriguing study supported in part by the U.S. Office of Education shows that they may be independent qualities. The researchers concluded that, for schoolchildren, "Creativity is a different type of cognitive excellence than general intelligence."

Creative boys can be a challenge for parents and for teachers. They interject offbeat questions that steer a class discussion away from the planned lesson, or find their own way of performing a science experiment instead of following directions in the lab manual. A creative boy may drive his teacher wild with his zany sense of humor, or his mother crazy with his roomful of "collections." Naturalist-author Gerald Durrell, at ten, filled one room in his family's home with dissecting instruments, nets and collecting bags, and cardboard boxes of birds' eggs, beetles, butterflies, and dragonflies. There were, as well, shelves on which he kept preserved specimens in bottles. These included a four-legged chicken, lizards, snakes, frogs' eggs in various stages of maturity, and a baby octopus.

Creativity does not appear to be more prevalent in either sex, although in males, the firstborn tend to be more creative than the later born. Reasons for this are less than clear. Researchers who study creativity in adults find that many creative people blend both masculine and feminine interests. This quality, called androgyny, has also been found by some studies in adults of both sexes who achieve unusual success in their chosen fields. Comfortable with their ability regardless of its designation as "masculine" or "feminine," these individuals express their talents and interests fully.

It is sometimes difficult to distinguish among children who are gifted, gifted and talented, or talented and creative. Some, of course, are all three. Talent, though, is especially easy to recognize once a child has reached a certain level of skill. In areas such as music, art, and athletics, it is often a child's parents who first notice his abilities. Chicago educational expert Benjamin Bloom indicates that the intersts of the parents determine the qualities they note as special in their child. In his investigation of the distinctive characteristics of Olympic swimmers, noted mathematicians, and pianists, Bloom concluded that these differentially gifted individuals displayed three outstanding qualities with consistency:

- unusual willingness to do great amounts of work (practice, expend time and effort) to achieve at a high level
- great competitiveness with peers in their field of talent and a determination to do their best at all cost

- ability to learn rapidly new techniques, ideas, or processes in their field of talent

Individuals of high achievement share these qualities of persistence and tenacity of purpose.

Parents Can Encourage a Boy's Natural Gifts

There is no question that parents make a difference in the accomplishments of their children. In the Hopkins SMPY program, the students whose parents become involved make the most progress. Bloom found this to be true of talented athletes, musicians, and mathematicians. It is parents who encourage these youngsters, take them to recitals and meets, pay for lessons and coaches, and provide the means by which their abilities are developed. Helping a talented youngster to do his best is not only rewarding, it is frequently a lot of fun as well.

Parents of gifted boys, though, sometimes face special challenges. If your son is gifted, here are some ways you can meet these challenges:

- Help your son to understand that being intelligent does not mean being better than others. Schoolwork will be easier, grades will be higher, and comprehension of certain subjects or concepts will be faster, or greater, for him than for others. Particularly if he attends special classes or schools, a gifted child may begin believing that he matters more than other children. This can have obvious repercussions in families, where brothers and sisters may resent this superior attitude. Friends don't like it, either. Gifted youngsters can be sensitive to others if encouraged by their families to help or be understanding of those who may not find school as easy as they do.
- Help your son find ways to extend his knowledge when he shows an interest in a particular area. Be will-

ing to drive him to the library for books, transport him to meetings, or expend reasonable amounts of money on his behalf. The old saw, "Well, he can do it provided he earns the money," may be one of the greatest interest killers of all time. If your son is serious about pursuing a hobby or interest, give him reasonable help and financial support.

- Boys who display artistic or musical talent sometimes face an image problem that their athletically inclined brothers do not. The family can inadvertently contribute. The young musician whose father insists on sports participation that cuts into practice hours may well be a boy who fails to develop his ability to the fullest. If you are a country music fan and your son shows real talent for classical violin, it may take special devotion on your part to help develop his ability—but remember, it's worth it!

- Help him to understand why some children tease him. "Brain!" can be a hated epithet to a bright boy. Even though the explanation that some children say such things to make themselves feel more important will be comprehensible to a gifted child, it still doesn't make being called a name any easier to take. Active listening techniques described on page 58 can defuse an overloaded temper.

- Do not pressure you son to bring home straight A's on his report card. Like everybody else, gifted children may be better in some subjects than in others. It is even more important to avoid challenging the teacher and principal every time a child's grade is not as high as you think it ought to be. Behavior like this does two things: it tells your son that grades are more important than other aspects of life (do you get just as upset if your child fails to be kind, well-mannered, or helpful?); and it puts up a red flag at your child's school. Parents who spend all their time worrying about a bright child's grades and achievement, and comparing him with others are letting their son down. "Poor kid, he wouldn't dare come home with less than straight A's," one assistant principal said of a seventh-grader.

"He doesn't want his mom up here again making a scene." Don't be the kind of parent kids feel they can never satisfy and principals wish would move to Timbuktu.

- Be especially careful of becoming a zealous, arrogant caretaker. Some parents go overboard in their efforts to protect gifted children, like the mother who refused to accept telephone calls or admit friends when her eight-year-old son was at work on his stamp collection. Taking messages for a teenage musician who asks for this service during his practice hours, however, can be of real assistance. It is equally important not to brag about your son in his presence. Like all children, he needs to hear himself praised for his accomplishments, but it should not be overdone. *The most helpful kind of parents for gifted children (or any others) are those who can show interest without smothering, facilitate without pushing, and applaud without being overweening.*

Keep in mind, too, that you may well have a truly gifted son even if the schools don't know it. In 1984, the editors of *Science Digest* asked a distinguished panel of researchers and directors of national laboratories to select the one hundred most distinguished young scientists in the United States. The one hundred, 90 percent of whom are male, were interviewed and asked to respond to a questionnaire about themselves. From the 78 percent who responded, some interesting facts emerged. Nearly one third did not excel in elementary school at all. "Almost twenty-five percent hadn't distinguished themselves by high school," *Science Digest* reported, "and even in college fourteen percent considered themselves to be less than outstanding." Many had, however, become interested in science by the age of eight-and-a-half. So, rather than despairing of your frog-catching, swamp-tromping offspring, whose teachers would like him to read more books and practice his handwriting, you might buy him some netting and a good flashlight.

Of Risk to Boys

DIVORCE, INADEQUATE SUPERVISION, TELEVISION AND ROCK MUSIC, SUBSTANCE ABUSE

As parents of boys, most of us are aware of the everyday risks our sons encounter in the course of growing up. We know that boys fall off bicycles and out of trees, and cut their fingers on penknives or fish hooks. Boys are more accident prone than girls; for this reason alone, some parents are all too familiar with hospital emergency rooms. Fortunately, in most cases, the bones mend, the wounds heal, and life gets back to normal.

Some hazards in the environment seem to have a stronger effect on boys than on girls; many show delayed or cumulative effects. What we may consider no more than an ordinary risk can be more serious than a broken arm or a scraped knee if our child is a son. Violence is a staple of television programming that concerns many parents; what we may not know is that boys, more than girls, can act aggressively if it becomes part of their regular viewing. Furthermore, the type of shows our sons watch when they are seven or eight years old may influence how violently they act as adults.

While many American parents worry about the dangers of illegal drug use by teenagers, few of us realize

170

that because of certain genetic propensities, some young males are nine times more likely than other boys and girls to become alcoholic. We may also be unaware that a boy's early school experiences and level of self-esteem may influence drug use later in life.

Stresses on the growing child may be expressed differently in boys and girls. All children experience stress when parents divorce, but family discord seems to encourage antisocial, often destructive behavior in our sons. In rates of referral to child guidance clinics and psychiatrists, boys outnumber girls two to one; delinquency is five to ten times more common among boys than girls.

As children mature, parents play more of a managerial role than that of a caregiver, but throughout childhood and adolescence, they remain an important source of support, facilitating their son's social growth while offering enough supervision to help him stay out of trouble. Although a school-age child still spends half his waking hours at home, middle-class working parents are becoming increasingly complacent about leaving him all alone.

Most sensible parents take precautions to minimize the risks their children inevitably encounter. We use infant safety seats in cars, warn our preschoolers never to go off with a stranger, and instruct schoolchildren in first aid and CPR. The risks to boys associated with divorce, self-care at too young an age, and television and rock music, are less well known, however; because of the frantic pace of many parents' lives, these risks may not be routinely addressed. Fortunately, these are risks over which parents do have some control. Their effects can be minimized and even eliminated, if we are aware of them.

DIVORCE

Few families today are immune from divorce. If we are not ourselves divorced, we have sisters, brothers, parents, or friends who have been through this experience. For a variety of reasons, adults in growing numbers are no longer willing to remain in marriages that they find unsuitable.

"Divorce occurs to solve the problems of parents—not the problems of children," one leading psychologist says. While it may bring escape from an undesirable situation, divorce carries with it the unwelcome baggage of emotional distress, lowered self-esteem, and uncertainty about the future for everyone concerned. If you are a child—especially a boy child—the baggage is loaded even more heavily.

During the upheavals that accompany divorce, and for long periods after the event, little boys are more likely than girls to have behavioral and school problems. Some boys, perhaps distracted by worry about what will happen to them, become accident prone. Others undergo prolonged depression as they yearn for their absent fathers and have unrealistic fantasies about their dad's return. For adults, divorce is second only to the death of a spouse as a major life stress; for children, the impact is similar. Because boys are often more fragile in their psychological functioning, the effect can be even greater than it is on girls.

Adults often look upon divorce as a single act, with temporary consequences. Those who have been divorced testify to the unreality of this notion; divorce is a process that takes place over an extended period of time. The legal aspects are but a beginning. Adjusting to a new way of life—single status, loneliness, possible new employment, and increased child-care responsibilities—can last for years. For children, the effect of divorce can extend throughout childhood and beyond. Even ten years after their parents' divorce, many young adults still regard themselves as "children of divorce."

A Boy's Age Is a Crucial Factor

A child's age at the time the divorce occurs determines his response. Children from eight to eighteen months of age are in the attachment period of late infancy when the presence of a continual caregiver is most needed. A divorce that interrupts this process by removing one parent entirely and causing the other to work full time can make the child anxious and overdependent. Slightly older boys of two can react by regressing to earlier infantile behavior and may have trouble sleeping.

Regression is also typical of children from three to five. A little boy of four may fear his mother will not return for him at the babysitter's (after all, daddy left, didn't he?). He may wet his pants, or fondle his genitals more often. As Judith Wallerstein and Joan Kelly, directors of the California Children of Divorce Project, state, "The child who regresses tells us by his behavior that it is all too much, that he must hold back in development, mark time or move backward, in order to gain strength for the next step forward."

Children of preschool age may blame themselves for causing the divorce. A five-year-old boy may believe that his father left because he didn't put away his toys, or because he makes too much noise. The loss of a father just when a little boy is beginning to identify with him can make the child both angry and insecure; typically, this anger is directed at his mother and other adult females.

Overwhelming sadness characterizes the little boy from six to eight whose parents divorce. As Linda Francke says in *Growing Up Divorced*, "It is as if children this age, who have just begun to recognize the unique benefits of their parents, have lost the promise of a relationship to come, a collaboration they will never know, and the loss they feel is close to the grief of death."

Even talking about the divorce may cause these boys

to cry. Unrealistic worries about being abandoned, left in a foster home, or starving may be one reason for the disorganized and sometimes bizarre behavior of children this age whose parents divorce. Compounding these fears is a real inability to divide their loyalty. Demands that they "choose" one or the other parent bring unremitting anxiety. One boy showed through his artwork the intensity of this conflict by depicting himself with a "hatchet cleaving his head."

The greater maturity, ego strength, and understanding of the older elementary-age child mask his deep anger at the disruption to his life caused by divorce. Children of seven to around eleven can have a black-and-white, right-or-wrong view of the world. Often they have feelings of betrayal, embarrassment, outrage, and unrelenting anger at one or both parents. Alignment of a boy this age with one parent is frequent. These older children often make deliberate attempts to bring their parents back together.

At every age, the first year of separation and divorce is the most disruptive, when anxiety is at its highest. If the child is male, behavior problems at home and at school are typical. Boys with older brothers to help them through the experience have fewer school-related problems, however, and are more likely than others to have interests and enjoy activities considered "masculine." Some younger boys of preschool and early elementary-school age may overreact to the absence of their fathers by displays of exaggerated masculinity. Each child's response is colored by his own personality, the quality of the family's predivorce relationships, and, most important, by how well his divorcing parents handle the event.

In approximately 90 percent of divorces involving children, custody is awarded to the mother. It is upon her that the lion's share of effort rests, and often the odds against success are overwhelming. She must suddenly assume almost all responsibility for her children—homemaker, role model, disciplinarian, and often breadwinner as well.

The Divorced Mother and Her Children

Syndicated columnist Ellen Goodman once noted that "the quickest way for a mother and children to get poor is to get divorced." The financial shock many women experience when they divorce is the stuff of nightmares: the necessity to work full time, to move to a less expensive neighborhood, and, for fully half of the families in one survey, the realization that their income is so reduced their children qualify for free lunch. Goodman reported that in one western state the income of the average wife a year after divorce dropped by 73 percent.

However numbing her economic plight, it is minor compared to the anxiety and panic a mother can feel when she realizes the full magnitude of her new responsibilities. The emotional overload of fear, guilt, lowered self-esteem, and the adjustment to single status can so preoccupy her that the problems her children are experiencing get lost in the shuffle. It is easy to make light of a son's very real concerns, or offer "quick fix" solutions to complex problems that resurface at a later time. Distracted by her own concerns, a mother may be inconsistent in discipline, erratic in maintaining schedules; little parent-child interaction may take place beyond that needed to accomplish the necessities of daily living. This "minimal parenting" contributes to the problems many divorced mothers have with their sons.

A feeling of lingering dissatisfaction can sometimes exacerbate a woman's burdens. Wallerstein and Kelly found that eighteen months after the divorce, 40 percent of the men and close to 50 percent of the women had negative feelings about the event. "Nearly one-quarter were unhappily resigned to their divorced status, 13 percent had considerable misgivings, and 9 percent remained bitterly opposed to divorce."

Boys Are Severely Stressed by Divorce

As is so often pointed out, expectations for boys are higher than those for girls. In a divorce situation, parents call upon a son to "be a big boy," whereas a daughter may be comforted. Researchers have found parents often engage in conflicts in front of a son while they restrain their anger around a daughter. In a study conducted by University of Virginia psychologist E. Mavis Hetherington, family interactions were observed when children were picked up by the noncustodial parent. Says Hetherington, "Fights were much more likely to occur in front of boys, and when they occurred they were more prolonged." Unable to live up to expectations, and under great stress himself, a little boy may retaliate by increasing his demands on his mother. She reacts with harsher discipline—screams and shouts take the place of reason. Tension escalates. The boy becomes aggressive, sullen, or openly defiant. A "cycle of coercion" begins between mother and son which can have destructive results. As Hetherington points out, "Under stress, boys develop a lot of characteristics we don't like."

Effects can widen to include a boy's classroom and friends, especially if the divorce has precipitated a move. Finding a place in a new peer group is sometimes more difficult for boys than for girls; accompanied by stress, the difficulties multiply. Boys who were observed two months, one year, and two years after their parents divorced were found to play alone more often; when they did play with others, the quality of their interactions seemed diminished in subtle ways. It was difficult for some of them to make adjustments in the roles they took in games of pretend, for example.

To boys in the early grades, the approval of their same-sex peers is very important; children may be shunned if they are anxious, uncertain, aggressive, or withdrawn—all characteristics that a boy may exhibit in the first year following his parents' divorce. Even if he receives acceptance by his peers, there may be hidden dangers. A boy is more likely to adopt the values of a peer group that conflict with those of his family if his home is one in which he is not given the nurturance he needs.

Boys from mother-alone families may have trouble in school. In a fourteen-state survey sponsored in part by the National Association of Elementary School Principals, it was found that 20 percent of the elementary-school children were from single-parent families. Of the high achievers, a low 17 percent were children of divorce. The acting-out behaviors of little boys are seen by teachers as well as parents. One experienced principal noted the frequency with which first-grade boys from divorcing families encounter reading problems that last well into their school years.

Another finding in some studies of divorce is a lowering of mathematics achievement scores in boys whose fathers are absent from the home. Fathers often use problem-solving dialogue with their sons and participate with them in activities that involve spatial or mechanical skills—building the toolshed, laying out the new sidewalk, fixing the bicycle, or tossing a ball around. These kinds of activities may tap some of the same skills researchers find associated with mathematics achievement; there appears to be a relationship between spatial ability and mathematics. If a boy's father is unavailable, he will lack this exposure.

On balance, a boy may gain verbal skills from a single mother. As in two-parent homes, mothers are less likely than fathers to treat sons and daughters differently and enforce appropriate sex-role behavior. In one interesting study of young men whose fathers had been absent since their preschool years, SAT results showed the same scoring pattern as that of females.

Boys Need Their Fathers— Divorced or Not

How a father treats his son during and after the divorce can have profound effects on a little boy's sexual identity, his self-esteem, and his school performance over time. Boys need an authoritative figure who is reasonable, consistent, and firm to set out specific rules of behavior and stick to them, and to explain why particular methods of discipline have been chosen—a role traditionally assigned to a boy's father. In some cases, this role can be adequately filled by a mother.

If a boy's father continues his interest in his son, however, a great deal of potential harm can be avoided. Boys whose fathers are available to them perform better in school. One study showed improvement in the reading and math scores of boys whose fathers attended their school conferences. There appears to be a real association between a father's persistent interest in a son and a boy's level of performance. The psychological impact of perceived rejection by a divorced father can exacerbate a little boy's already stressful state. His basis for trust in all adult males can be called into question. Fathers are important to their young sons as nurturers and models, as well as economic providers.

Researchers have found that some single-parent families operate more smoothly if the child is the same sex as the custodial parent. Boys whose fathers have custody (roughly 10 percent of single-parent households) have the advantage of a male role model. The aggression and disobedience single mothers often encounter in sons may not occur as often if a boy lives with his father. There appear to be more sons than daughters in father-custody families. A percentage of fathers view their son's sex as a compelling reason to seek custody in the first place, and some parents and courts assume that fathers are better at rearing boys. Also noted is the frequency with which older children, given a choice in custody hearings, elect to live with the parent of the same sex.

It has been found that fathers who seek custody were usually more deeply involved with their children prior to the divorce than most fathers are. While they experience the same emotional turmoil women do, most single fathers with custody have at least two advantages: a higher level of income, and a fierce determination to prove their competence in the nurturing role.

Parents Can Make Divorce Easier for Boys

While divorce is traumatic to everyone concerned, several factors can offset its impact. The emotional climate of the family and the child's psychological well-being prior to the divorce have obvious carry-over effects. How much a father remains involved in his son's life is a further variable, as is the economic status of the postdivorce family. Most important of all to a child's development is the relationship of the divorced spouses after the break. Experts generally agree that the following steps can help a little boy adjust to the stresses of divorce:

- Remember that you divorced your spouse—not your son. If you are a noncustodial parent, maintain frequent and consistent contact with the boy. It is difficult to foster a close relationship if you are not living with him. Work hard at it.
- If you are the custodial parent, don't place obstacles in the way of visitation with the noncustodial parent. ("He's not ready." "He's sick." "You can't take him there!" "He has to be back by one o'clock instead of five because I'm going out.") Your son needs this relationship, even if you resent having to deal with your ex-spouse.
- Don't fight with your ex-spouse in front of your little boy. No matter how intense your feelings, your son

doesn't share them. He continues to care deeply for both parents, even if you can't understand why he loves the other one. *Don't force him to choose between you.*

- Particularly devastating can be criticism that links a little boy with his absent father. "You are acting just like your father!" Find more reasonable (and caring) ways to change his behavior.
- Exert firm, but loving, discipline, and foster high expectations that can be met without stress. Encourage your son to take on suitable household responsibilities, and praise him for his efforts.
- If you are a mother with custody, help your little boy to see that tenderness and caring are not just "female" attributes. Encourage relationships with adult men who exhibit these qualities (an uncle, his grandfather, a kindly neighbor). Point out specific situations where these qualities are exhibited by men.
- If your son needs it, see that counseling is provided for him. Parents seek such help for themselves, but seldom think of it for a child.
- Avoid moving frequently. It is important for a little boy to have the security of a familiar home and a stable group of peers.

Boys in Stepfamilies

Approximately 11 percent of all American households contain "blended" families; one child in six lives in a stepfamily. For preschool and elementary-school-age boys, the entrance of a caring stepfather into their lives can be an exciting, positive experience; attachment can take place readily. For a somewhat older boy, acceptance is not as easy.

Two problems may be encountered in blended families right from the start. The first has to do with the role of the stepparent. Since there is no institutionalized set of expectations, the role must, in a very real sense, be created. Personality, a liking for children in general, and the quality of a couple's relationship all influence the role a stepparent will take in a child's life. A second problem may occur if the natural parent expects a boy and his new stepparent to love each other right away. It takes time for adults to learn to know and love someone; children need time, too. Demanding that a little boy "love" his stepfather can be perceived as a threat. It can sometimes take two to four years for children to really accept their stepparents.

Step-siblings can precipitate further problems, especially with regard to each child's place in the new family. As one divorced mother points out, "There is no shared family history, no continuity of memory, and often the differences rather than the similarities between stepfamily members are emphasized." Discipline of stepsiblings is a frequent sore spot in blended families, especially if one parent is reluctant to deal with a spouse's offspring.

A very big problem for children in blended families is coping with divided loyalties. Even if a little boy likes his father's new wife, he may be reluctant to admit it to his mother for fear that he will seem disloyal. Problems can also occur in the relationships between natural parents and stepparents, often caused by mothers. Hetherington emphasizes that women who are severely stressed by divorce and faced with major life upheavals and new responsibilities can maintain a "keenly honed sense of outrage" for a considerable period of time. Unresolved anger can spill over into relationships with a former husband and his new wife.

Stepfamilies can get off to a far better start with counseling prior to the marriage. Of five hundred families counseled at a New York foundation, only four went on to divorce later. Of equal importance is the determination of all adults—natural parents and stepparents—to make relationships work.

INADEQUATE SUPERVISION

One expectation that is increasingly placed upon school-age children, whether or not their parents are divorced, is greater responsibility for themselves. Record numbers of children are home alone while their parents work. Even first graders may be expected to get themselves ready for school or let themselves into empty homes with their own latchkeys.

Parents who work are faced with the problems of long-distance care-taking and discipline. You may train your son to call when he gets home from school, but if he fails to call, how do you know where he is? Despite your immediate panic when your call home is not answered, your boy may simply be playing outside and have forgotten to phone you. Conscientious parents set firm rules; parents of latchkey boys know that maturity plays a part in how well they are carried out.

Latchkey Children

No one really knows for sure how many children take care of themselves before or after school. Experts estimate that two to five million American children under thirteen are unsupervised for a good part of every workday; in Canada the figure may be half a million. There are historical precedents for self-care by youngsters. On the western frontier in the United States, an older child was frequently placed in charge of younger siblings while their mother worked in the fields and their father went off hunting. During the Second World War, experts expressed their concern over the plight of "door key" children—youngsters whose mothers worked outside the home while their fathers fought overseas. But these earlier examples of self-care differ substantially from the phenomenon occurring today; a parent or another adult (a neighbor, relative, or family friend) was usually nearby, available to children if needed. One latchkey boy sums up the difference quite succinctly: "There are no grownups at home in my neighborhood, only other kids."

A number of factors in recent years have changed the way we live. Age-segregated housing has limited the number of retired citizens residing near families with school children. Not only are fewer older people available to babysit, there are also fewer teenagers because of the tendency toward smaller families. Increased social isolation, in the suburbs and urban high-rises, has made us wary of entrusting our children to people we don't know very well, and less aware of our neighbors' childcare needs. One survey of a New York City private school showed that approximately 15 percent of first and second graders stayed at home alone. In sixth and seventh grades, all the students took care of themselves until working parents came home.

Fear and Latchkey Children

"I don't like being home alone," says one eleven-year-old boy who takes care of himself after school. Another boy locks himself in the bathroom whenever he feels afraid, but doesn't tell his parents of his fears. "I asked to stay alone and I have to show I can do it," he says. While our society may still attempt to socialize males to be tough, latchkey boys appear as susceptible to fears when left alone as girls are. Sleep disturbances—nightmares and insomnia—can be a signal to parents that a child is not ready to care for himself, despite his protestations against going to a sitter's or a childcare center.

Many boys, especially those concerned about what their peer group thinks of them, don't want to continue day care in elementary school. A first-grade boy hates being teased because a day-care van picks him up after school. Older boys think it's a sign of "being cool" to sport a latchkey around their necks. In reality, some of these boys, as well as latchkey girls, lock themselves in closets or wield baseball bats when they hear a strange noise. Many a latchkey child conducts periodic security checks when he's home by himself or turns up the TV or radio to make himself feel less lonely (and to convince any would-be prowler that he's not alone in the house).

Parents may actually compound a child's fears if they, themselves, feel ambivalent about leaving him unsupervised. Some parents worry a good deal about a youngster at home alone while they're at work. And there seems to be cause for concern. Fire, someone's breaking in or molesting a latchkey child on his way to or from school, a child's having a serious accident with no one to help, youngsters' experimenting with sex, alcohol, and drugs, or simply hanging out with the "wrong crowd" and getting into trouble—each of these unfortunate events has taken place in the lives of some latchkey children.

One out of every five children who takes care of himself before or after school appears unable to cope without supervision and may experience long-term negative consequences. Many feel rejected; others are bitter about missing out on their childhood. Twenty years later, some latchkey casualties still blame their parents for leaving them alone too often when they were children.

Thomas and Lynette Long, educators in the Washington, D.C., metropolitan area, who have interviewed over three hundred latchkey youngsters and their parents, found that mothers and fathers who have to work, "not to buy designer jeans, but to put a roof over their families' heads," are also angry—at society and government agencies that seem unresponsive to children's needs. Even though there are thought to be three million young school children who require monitoring, only 1.6 million are enrolled in before- or after-school programs that provide adult supervision, largely because of a dearth of adequate facilities for latchkey children. There is evidence that such child-care programs reduce abuse and neglect, boost academic progress, and decrease vandalism. Some experts suggest that 50 to 80 percent of working parents would use after-school programs for their children if they were available.

Other Concerns for Latchkey Boys

Children who are unsupervised before or after school appear pretty equally divided by gender; however, the rules parents set and the experiences of these youngsters differ, depending upon their sex. Latchkey boys are frequently given responsibility for getting themselves to and from after-school activities like scouts or sports practice. Most parents who live in neighborhoods they consider safe acknowledge boys' higher activity level by sending them out to play; almost all the school-age sons of working parents are allowed to play outside unsupervised.

The need for friends is strongest during the school years, but in choosing their friends, boys are less sensitive to adult opinion than girls are. Your son is as likely to pick a buddy who is great at "poppin' wheelies" as he is a boy who has nice manners or does what is expected of him. In middle childhood, leadership and popularity among boys seems based on their independence from adult authority—boys high in qualities of which parents approve may be the least popular in a neighborhood or classroom group. Unsupervised boys are apt to get into mischief, especially if there are other boys to urge them on.

Oregon researcher Gerald Patterson has studied delinquency extensively and finds parents' inability to monitor their son's behavior is an important factor. Wandering off, lying, and stealing are three behaviors that require supervision to discourage. Without an adult to know where a child is, when he is fibbing or taking what does not belong to him, and to help him see the consequences of these behaviors, a boy is liable to continue to misbehave. Authorities today report growing rates of vandalism, arson, shoplifting, and vagrancy by unsupervised youth.

Parents of latchkey children often worry that their son's grades suffer. Says one working mother: "When I was home (my son) used to be a good student with awards for grades, behavior, and attendance. Now his teacher says he's not doing his best." One study of unsupervised and supervised school children suggests that boys who have a parent at home score higher on measures of adjustment and academic achievement than those who are merely supervised, presumably by a caregiver who has less personal involvement in the child than a parent would. Boys with no at-home supervision appear to do most poorly.

The possibility that a boy who takes care of himself for part of the day will hurt himself is also of concern to parents. Boys have more accidents than girls, and a small number of accident-prone children have been found somewhat maladjusted and less able to cope with everyday decisions. An accident-prone boy may not be as capable as another youngster the same age, especially if he has to cope with wounds and minor traumas that accompany accidents.

Children who are left unsupervised before or after school appear more vulnerable to sexual molestation. In their interviews with latchkey youngsters, the Longs refrained from asking questions about sexual behavior. Nevertheless, a number of children volunteered incidents of sexual abuse (both homosexual and heterosexual), often of younger children by older latchkey siblings supposedly taking care of them. Some experts believe that 70 to 80 percent of all molesters are related to their victims.

The Threat of Sexual Victimization

The National Center on Child Abuse and Neglect predicts that 20 percent of all children—both boys and girls

—will be victimized sexually before their eighteenth birthdays. Parents are likely to be more protective of daughters than of sons; nonetheless, several experts believe boys are as much at risk for sexual victimization as girls are. Whether or not parents work, their little boys may be in danger:

- Boys are traditionally allowed more freedom to roam, which expands their contacts. This, by itself, makes them more vulnerable in some ways to abduction or abuse than girls are.
- Boys are less likely than girls to report abuse and more resistant to discussing it when referred to professionals for help. Some of this hesitancy is due to an unwillingness to seem helpless or passive. Many boys, and some parents, are reticent to report sexual molesting because of its homosexual nature, even though the child was forced into sexual activity.
- Boys are often the preferred victims of sex offenders whom they do not already know. Pedophiles, or sexual molesters who tend to prey solely on boys, find youngsters who are emotionally troubled or need attention and affection their easiest targets.
- According to one report, boys in single-parent families are more frequently abused than girls are.

Researchers define sexual abuse as exposure to sexual stimulation inappropriate for a child's age, level of psychosexual development, and role in the family. To a child, this means being touched, looked at, or spoken to in ways he feels invade his privacy. Most sexually abused children suffer some degree of emotional disturbance as a result.

Often children who have been molested blame themselves for an incident that happened to them. If your child should try to confide in you what appears to have been sexual abuse (he may tell you a hypothetical scenario), it is important that you listen calmly and sympathetically. Youngsters rarely lie about this subject. You can help your son by emphasizing that he is not at fault, and by recognizing some of the conflicts he may be feeling. Your support can be vital.

Unfortunately, a study of child abuse in the Boston area suggests that two-thirds of children victimized do not tell their parents or anyone else about it. Parents or teachers may suspect sexual abuse if a child exhibits the following types of behavior:

- Suddenly withdraws from group activities, or behaves aggressively when he didn't before.
- Acts in a self-destructive manner. For older children this can include alcohol or drug abuse, self-mutilation, promiscuity, running away from home, and suicide threats or attempts.
- Imposes sex play on other children with an emphasis on coercion rather than the kind of "you show me yours and I'll show you mine" exploration experts consider normal sex play for children.
- Displays guilt, depression, low self-esteem, and sleep disturbances for no apparent reason.
- Seems preoccupied with his own genitalia. Young children may draw sex organs in their artwork; older youngsters might refuse suddenly to undress in front of schoolmates in the locker room.

Recently the media has focused enormous attention on child abuse and abduction, which had previously been touchy subjects. Some of this attention has been helpful. Talk shows suggest ways parents can prevent sexual victimization or abduction of their children, hotline numbers are publicized, actors like Henry (the Fonz) Winkler appear on video cassettes educating parents and their children about the issue and helping them to discuss sex more openly. At the same time, it is alarming for both adults and children to watch coverage of child-pornography rings in day-care centers or read reports of court testimony of preschool teachers accused of victimizing their students. As one mother says, "It's amazing how easy it is to mistrust neighbors, friends, even relatives. Perhaps because it suddenly seemed that every woman I knew had been abused, I began to wonder if my own child had ever been a victim. Underlying my anxiety was the nagging thought that if something happened to my child...God forbid, it would be my fault."

What Parents Can Do about Child Abuse or Abduction

Open communication between parents and their children is always important, but boys, especially, need to know that it's all right to express their fears and to feel helpless and vulnerable sometimes. A parent who can listen without criticizing may be an important asset to a child who has a shameful secret to share.

Obedient children are easy targets for molesters. Let a child know it's all right not to obey every adult who tells him what to do. Any child should be told he needn't hug or kiss unless he feels like it. But preschool and elementary-school children, especially those who respect adult authority greatly, benefit from periodic reminders that they must not talk to strangers.

Parents can work with their son's day-care center, preschool, or school to provide education regularly about abuse and abduction. Local professionals (police, social workers, abuse-clinic personnel) are available to talk with schoolchildren, explaining the dangers youngsters face and how best to avoid them. Experts cannot replace parents, however, and our own efforts, repeatedly and over time, to encourage independent and logical thinking, to set reasonable rules and guidelines, and to help our children become competent and wise are important.

• When you take a young boy shopping with you, teach him where you will meet if you should be separated (a cashier or check-out counter). For active toddlers, a well-designed safety harness can keep a child from wandering off before he's old enough to learn to "mind." A few nasty looks from other shoppers or criticism about your child-care methods are a lot easier to endure than a lost (and possibly abused) little boy.

- Young children need to be instructed never to take food or toys from strangers. They also should be taught never to get into a car with someone they don't know, even if it's to help find a lost kitten or go to the ice-cream store.

- Train your children always to tell you where they will be and expect them to stay within the boundaries you agree upon.

- Teach all children, young or maturing, to run away, scream, and make a fuss if they are ever followed or grabbed by a stranger.

- A three-year-old is capable of learning his own phone number. Older children should memorize their home address (including zip code and how to tell the police to get there). In addition to learning phone numbers, young children need to know their area code, how to dial long distance, and how to use both push-button and dial telephones; they also should memorize the numbers for fire, rescue, and mother and dad at work.

- It's wise to have a special "code word" (such as your middle name or a favorite nonsense word) known to all your children that means "It's okay, you can trust this person, even if I'm not with you." Molesters and abductors have used a powerful lure for a number of children—telling them their mother is hurt and they will take them to her. Your son may be wary of this technique if the person presenting himself as a helper does not know the special code.

- As your son becomes more independent, getting himself to and from school, he needs specific training. Teach him to choose well-lighted, frequently traveled routes when walking, or to bike only with a friend. No child should be allowed to play in a parking lot alone.

Warn him against getting too near a car if a stranger stops to ask directions.

- For children at home alone, it is important that they do not answer the door and that they tell callers, "My mom can't come to the phone right now. May I have her call you back?" Latchkey youngsters need to be trained not to show off their keys (never to wear them outside their clothes) and should always call a parent immediately when they come home from school.

- Encourage your son to run to the nearest public place —store or police station—if he feels unsafe in any way, and to call you.

- Neighbors who are well known to you might be given telephone numbers of your place of business. If they notice anything suspicious (signs of someone breaking into your house or your child going off with a stranger) they may be more comfortable calling you than the police.

When Can a Boy Take Care of Himself?

Responsibility grows, much as children do, in small increments and occasional spurts. Even the most effective training requires reinforcement and a different approach as children mature. The preschooler who refused to speak to anyone he didn't know may, in later years, casually hitchhike home from school if his buddies do. Parents need to match a child's responsibility with his individual personality, level of maturity, and other factors. A boy who is having trouble in school may not be ready to be alone when he gets home. A child who has poor relationships with peers or parents may be more likely than some to reach out to others for love and affection.

The neighborhood in which we live and where our son attends school are also factors in his independence. Approximately 15 percent of all American youngsters live in areas where undesirable characters can be found on the streets (drunks, drug addicts, or tough older kids). Obviously, parents need to question their child's safety walking home from school. Some neighborhoods have "block homes" with special signs in the windows where children can go if they feel frightened; working parents in a tough area can train their children to stay together in groups while walking or taking public transportation.

Before deciding to leave a boy at home alone, you may want to ask yourself these questions:

- Is he mature enough to take care of himself? Most parents consider an eight-year-old (a third grader) old enough to handle a latchkey arrangement. Interestingly, this is also the average age when juvenile delinquency begins. Michelle Seligson, director of the Wellesley School Age Child Care Project, feels most children are not ready to be without some supervision until they are eleven or twelve.
- Is your boy left unsupervised for more than three hours a day? One former latchkey youth recommended that parents never leave a child longer than three hours, and then only if there are neighbors who can be depended upon for help. Latchkey youngsters are often afraid if a parent doesn't come home when expected. These fears can be heightened for children after the trauma of divorce. Parents may be wise to arrive home before their son expects them, and always call if they are going to be late.
- Is your son functioning well in all areas of his life? A boy having trouble at school or making and keeping friends does not need the added stress of self-care. If your son is accident prone, you will undoubtedly want to think long and hard before leaving him alone at home. Siblings who do not get along well when a parent is with them have no business being left alone together.
- Does your son follow directions, abide by your rules, and show an ability to solve problems by himself? If so, you will want to set up a routine together that he

can follow: to call you when he gets home, and to do homework or chores until a certain time. Clear guidelines that you can enforce are most useful: no visitors without your permission and regulations about snacking, TV, telephone calls, and so on. Many parents do not allow latchkey youngsters to use the stove or kitchen appliances. In situations where there are siblings who are close in age, parents may want to divide responsibilities, putting one child in charge of the daily call and settling any issues that arise, while giving a second the same duties the following day.

- Does your son understand why you are leaving him alone part of each day? It seems crucial that latchkey youngsters feel they are contributing to the family by taking care of themselves, much the way working parents contribute their paychecks to the whole family's welfare. A boy's sense of worth can benefit from a successful latchkey experience, if he is ready for responsibility and knows he is helping, rather than feeling rejected or stressed.

- Will you be able to make time for your child when you are home? Working parents often come home exhausted, frustrated by problems at work or rush-hour traffic. It's easy to snap at children who have neglected their chores or who assail you at the door with their own problems and disputes. It seems essential to make a routine of relaxing with a youngster for a little while every day—reading together, playing a game, or simply chatting over dinner.

- Does your son have some time each week to be with other children outside school? Even mature, well-adjusted children who appear to thrive on the responsibilities of self-care need an opportunity to play with friends and to learn new skills. Any child, latchkey or not, can benefit from scouts, lessons, or sports, but the logistics of getting youngsters to and from extra-curricular activities when you are working can be overwhelming.

Some innovative programs are beginning to provide enrichment as well as adult supervision for latchkey children. "Checking In" is one such program recently pilot-tested in Fairfax County, Virginia. It provides flexible care and supervision for elementary and junior-high-school students. Each youngster is assigned to a trained neighborhood-based daycare provider who can transplant him to after-school functions, supervise his play with friends, provide a snack, and be available to help with homework or problems that might arise. A family works out its own system, deciding how much freedom and responsibility each child is to have. Some children simply check in by phone; others prefer to spend all afternoon with a caregiver. Day care can cost as little as a dollar an hour under this system; a kit with step-by-step procedures for setting up a "Checking In" program in your community is available. For further information, get in touch with Judy McKnight; Family Day Care Check-In Project, Fairfax County Office for Children; 11212 Waples Mill Road; Fairfax, Virginia, 22030; Telephone: (703) 691-3175.

Increasingly, school districts are making their facilities available in before- or after-school programs for children of working parents. Schools throughout the country offer extended day programs from dawn until late afternoon; in many such programs, parents pay two-thirds of the extra costs to the school with local jurisdictions picking up the rest of the bill. A study of one program in North Carolina showed significant improvement in reading and math scores among children in after-school care. The Wellesley School Age Child Care Project, Center for Research on Women, Wellesley College, Wellesley, Massachusetts, telephone: (617) 431-1453, provides technical assistance in setting up or upgrading extended day programs in schools. Their book, *The School Age Child Care Action Manual*, may be helpful to parents and school administrators interested in extended care.

In addition, a number of organizations, from local recreation departments to YMCAs, provide de facto child care on a part-time basis through classes in arts and crafts, sports, music, and photography, as well as field trips to museums or cultural events. Groups like the American Red Cross, Campfire, and Cooperative Extension Services teach survival skills for latchkey children.

It is important to give any child, boy or girl, a "trial run" for a few weeks or even months. Let your son know that this is simply an experiment and encourage him to talk honestly about his response to being home alone. Even if a child has asked to be allowed to stay alone and does not complain to you, it may be wise to recognize signs that suggest he's having trouble coping —lack of interest in age-appropriate activities, low frustration tolerance, intense or angry outbursts, restless irritability, provocative or attention-getting behavior, overeating, nightmares, or insomnia—all may be clues that your son is not ready to stay alone on a regular basis.

TELEVISION AND ROCK MUSIC

The electronic media is taken for granted. Like Big Brother, it is everywhere. In a bizarre, Orwellian twist, however, it is not Big Brother who intrudes upon us; rather, it is we who turn to its slickly packaged stimuli of sight and sound, all too willing partakers of whatever is offered. We breakfast with the latest "Today" host. Muzak lulls us as we shop. Jivers and joggers plug into headsets, and radio and television stations operate twenty-four hours a day. More Americans own television sets than own refrigerators, or have indoor plumbing. Months and years of continuing media exposure can give legitimacy to practices and values we do not share.

Earlier generations of adolescents turned to jazz, swing, or rock 'n' roll as a means of self-expression and harmless rebellion. Today's children may begin listening to rock music before they start school. It is not uncom-

mon for five-and six-year-olds to have favorite rock stars
or to wear clothing styled after media idols. Many of our
children watch twenty-six hours of television every
week—more than one full day. Stereo sets and portable
radios are standard equipment. Words we didn't learn
until late adolescence sprinkle the speech of our six- and
seven-year-olds; some of us even take pride in their precocity. Third graders discuss the escapades of rock stars,
mouthing the "put down" language of the disk jockey.
We acknowledge their worldliness with a mixture of joc-
ularity and uneasiness. Times change, we reason. Kids
just grow up faster these days. Besides, everybody
watches TV and listens to rock. You can't make your
child different—can you?

If your child is a little boy, you might want to think
about it. Responsible studies, one lasting over twenty
years, suggest that the media—especially television—
contributes to higher levels of aggression in boys, influences children's perception of the world in negative
ways, and may affect, as well, their behavior as parents.

Some TV Programs Are Bad
for Little Boys

Television influences children in both form (the "sensory
package" of sight and sound) and content (the type of
programming watched). The technical forms of television—camera cuts, zooms in and out, pans across a
scene, and never-ending sound—are not found in ordinary perception. Some experts question what this might
do to a child's developing mental processes.

Of particular appeal to children are programs that
have characters displaying a lot of physical movement.
A rapid tempo, loud music, sound effects, and a number
of differing scenes are also favored. Young children, who
begin paying more attention to television around two-
and-a-half, understand little of program content. Children of eight and nine remember only about 65 percent

of the content in shows that have a story format, and boys and girls of all ages recall more content if someone describes what is happening. A comparison of children who watched a televised version of a picture book with others who read the same material showed that the readers remembered more of the story. Not only did the readers draw upon their own experience, they also asked more questions, made more comments, and were able to remember more of the vocabulary used in the story.

The content of television programming in this country ranges from "Mister Rogers' Neighborhood" to cable-erotica. Critics have rightfully focused on subjects considered unsuitable for children, citing research that shows that violent programs raise the general level of violence throughout society. In 1984, researchers found a rise in violence in five countries where violent television programs had been imported—many of them from the United States.

Children do learn from what they see on television. The physical movements, tone of voice, and idiosyncrasies of an admired television or rock video star who condones or uses violence on the screen may be copied faithfully.

A little boy of about five, observed in a doctor's office, provides a case in point. While a second boy listened wide-eyed, and his mother shifted uncomfortably in her chair, this youngster delivered a nonstop reenactment of programs he had seen on television. Fingers curved about an imaginary steering wheel, the boy "crashed" his four-wheeler, falling on the carpeted floor. "You got to pretend I got blood all over my shirt," he advised his audience. Then, with staccato chops of his hand, he dispatched two victims who, he said, "bugged" him. Asked to join the second boy as his mother began reading a story, the TV-watching youngster declined. "I don't like looking at books," he said. "Me and my sister, we just watch our shows."

The American Academy of Pediatrics issued a call to reform in 1985. Said spokesman George Gerbner, dean of the University of Pennsylvania's Annenberg School of Communications, "Whoever tells most of the stories to the children of a culture influences, in a very fundamental way, the way people grow up. For the first time in human history, it's no longer parents, the school, or the church, but television that tells most of the stories."

TV Violence Can Cause Aggressiveness

In the early 1960s, psychologist Leonard D. Eron of the University of Illinois began a series of studies to discover which child-rearing practices contributed to the development of aggression. One of the questions he asked the children in his survey had to do with the television programs they watched. Almost accidentally, Eron uncovered a relationship between the violence of the television programs some boys watched and their level of aggression. This finding was not nearly as strong for girls (although it is now increasing as more aggressive female role models appear on TV).

Children around eight seemed to be unusually susceptible to TV's effects. Boys who had problems in school and spent more time than average in front of the set had an inclination to be aggressive, especially if their parents punished them physically. Sifting through the factors that appeared significant, researchers found three especially important. First of all, the level of aggression among children in general increases from first to fifth grade and then declines. Second, among children in the third grade, viewing of TV violence was at a peak; children responding to Eron's survey watched more violent programs during this period than they did before or after. A third factor was that eight-year-old boys (third graders) believed the violent behavior they observed on TV was more realistic than did girls the same age.

The convergence of these factors at eight—a rising level of aggression among children, maximum exposure to TV violence, and the interpretation of the portrayed events as real—seemed to be important forces in the level of aggression of a number of boys. Continued watching seemed to reinforce their aggressive behavior.

This finding alone would be enough to deter many parents from allowing their boys to watch violent shows. Even more frightening are Eron's follow-up studies of the children at the ages of nineteen and thirty. Aggressive eight-year-olds became aggressive teenagers and aggressive men. Not only that, they punished their own children harshly, were prone to even more combative behavior when drinking, and had more encounters with the law than boys who had watched less TV violence.

Of course, not every eight-year-old who watches a few violent TV episodes is going to turn into an angry, aggressive adult. Intelligence, socioeconomic factors, and the level of parental involvement in a child's life are significant variables. However, Eron and his colleagues point out that there are physiological and psychological components to aggression in males that seem absent in females. In one experiment the heart rate and blood pressure of males was "routinely" reduced when they had an opportunity to respond to aggression previously directed against them. Females did not respond in this way. In addition, expectations and socialization practices of parents and society reinforce aggressive behavior as being more appropriate for males than for females. More than girls, boys imitate aggressive models. Thus, there are elements of risk for boys that do not exist for girls, and parents need to be aware of them.

Eron's team also developed intervention methods for some groups of children who were "high violence viewers." Youngsters were shown excerpts from violent shows and informed about how film makers used sound and visual effects to create an appearance of reality. The researchers asked them to write paragraphs telling why TV violence was unrealistic and watching too much of it was bad. The children were videotaped reading their responses and had an opportunity to see themselves perform. The level of aggression of the children who had

written the paragraphs was reduced. As Eron emphasizes, adults can counteract television's negative effects.

TV Affects Imagination and School Performance

Too much television appears to diminish a child's creative and imaginative capacity. Fantasy, make-believe,
or imaginary play is very important to development. It is
a means by which children acquire vocabulary, learn
how it feels to be somebody else, pretend to act out adult
skills (use of a block as a hammer by a three-year-old),
and practice cognitive skills like counting. Yale psychologists, Jerome and Dorothy Singer found that the most
imaginative children were those whose parents played
fantasy games with them or made a practice of reading
fairy tales.

Child psychologist Bruno Bettelheim says one great
value of fairy tales is their ability to help the child deal
with his inner problems; the unreality of the stories is
very important. Through the actions of the characters
and the dilemmas they face and overcome, the child's
questions about life often may be answered. Bettelheim
finds it sad that many of today's children do not know
fairy tales as their parents did, and regrets that films and
TV shows all too often turn beloved stories into "empty-
minded entertainment."

According to the surgeon general's 1982 report on television and behavior, separate studies found that older
boys who scored highest in an interview that measured
how imaginative they were, watched more situation
comedies than action/adventure shows. Preschoolers
who watched cartoons with large amounts of violence
were the children in their classes most likely to be aggressive in school. Young boys with imaginary friends
watched few action/adventure shows and were not especially aggressive in nursery schools. Clearly, what a boy
watches on television affects his everyday behavior.

It can also affect his school performance. While moderate amounts of television watching (up to ten hours per week) seem to have no ill effects on elementary-age children, by high-school age, reading scores are inversely related to the amount of television watched—the higher the score, the less TV a teenager watches.

Television's Other Effects

One physician compared the "trancelike" behavior of TV-watching children to the shut-down mechanism of newborns—the way in which infants tune out excess stimuli such as bright lights. However, some children, who may appear passive while they are watching, can become difficult to manage as a result of too much television. One young mother allows her son a bare minimum of weekly television fare. "If he watches any more," she says, "he's off the wall."

Arousal refers to the level of excitability or provocation we feel as the result of our experiences. Someone who has had a bad day at the office and sat for an hour in a traffic jam is usually in a high state of arousal when he gets home. Physical effects of arousal are measurable changes in blood pressure, heart rate, and skin temperature. Television can have an effect on our level of arousal. Watching a show with pleasant content may reduce the tension resulting from the traffic jam and the bad day at the office. One's state of arousal is not as likely to be reduced by watching erotica, news broadcasts, or intense athletic competitions. The arousal left over from one stimulus may affect subsequent behavior. The boy who becomes anxious while watching a program about crime or a news broadcast about an airplane disaster may be unable to sleep, or may overreact to the taunting of a sibling.

Very young children may be frightened by what they see on television, especially if it involves human transformation. The changing of a benign character into what

appears to be an evil one is particularly terrifying. The
TV series "The Incredible Hulk" and the film of *The
Wizard of Oz* were found in one study to be more upset-
ting to preschoolers than other kinds of shows. Older
children find TV presentations of events that could really
happen more frightening than fantasy. *Jaws* and *Hal-
loween* are examples of frightening fare for many
elementary-school-age children, as is the evening news.
Heavy viewers are more likely than light viewers to regard the world as "mean and scary."

In terms of TV viewing, habituation refers to the increased tolerance for violence that results from watching
it repeatedly. One research showed a violent movie to
boys between five and fourteen years of age. Those accustomed to watching a lot of television were not as
aroused by the scenes as those who watched less. As
with many other kinds of stimuli, repetition accustoms
us to its presence. At first violent episodes arouse us—
make us anxious, frightened, or repelled. With continued
exposure, however, each episode seems less traumatic,
and we become more tolerant of violence in general.

Children who watch a great deal of television sometimes have a distorted sense of reality. Boys who race
and crash their bikes in emulation of TV heroes rarely
see the real effects of automobile accidents on the
screen. The handsome hero doesn't go to the shock-
trauma unit in a helicopter, he rarely even has a broken
bone, and he almost never dies. In real life, automobile
accidents are one of the leading causes of death among
young men. Alcohol use is also distorted by television.
One conservative estimate is that a child can see ten episodes of drinking during an average day's viewing,
hardly typical of most American adults. Even if your
own drinking habits are moderate, or nonexistent, your
son can be influenced by his adult TV heroes whom he
sees drinking every day—and most of them are males.

Many parents are ambivalent about the effects of the
evening news on their children. "They ought to know
what the world is really like," some believe. "But they

don't have to see such a steady diet of mayhem," others counter. Each family has to decide whether or not the news is appropriate viewing for their children. Some choose not to have the television on during these hours; others, if they watch the news at all, do so in a room to which young children do not have access. However, it is important to realize that many school-children can be terribly frightened by events portrayed on the news. They know these "stories" are real. These things really happen and, they think, "They could happen to me." In his helpful book, *Mister Rogers Talks to Parents*, Fred Rogers relates that his mother would counteract the effect of newsreel or newspaper presentations of disasters and tragedies by saying to her son, "Always look for the helpers. There's always someone who is trying to help."

Saturday-morning cartoons are also a cause for concern to many parents. One reviewer characterizes this programming as "nonstop combat between good and bad guys," with no suggested alternatives other than violence for resolving conflict. On the other hand, some experts believe that much of the violence portrayed by cartoons is "sanitized." Cartoons are a part of the culture of most American children, these experts say, and a reasonable amount of exposure to Saturday-morning television will not permanently harm our children.

Parents should be aware that some Saturday programs are created for the purpose of promoting specific toys. Manufacturers now invent a product and develop a television show to convince children they would like to have one. Mickey Mouse products were among the first to be marketed as an offshoot of a filmed character; now, one writer comments, today's toy manufacturers "put the watch before the mouse."

Some parents counteract the appeal of these morning cartoons by loading up the VCR with more suitable fare. However, even films one can rent for children have elements parents often object to, such as violence, sex, and gratuitious swearing. One psychiatrist suggests letting children help select the programs within the guidelines parents set for viewing. Boys, especially, would respond to the added sense of control derived from this approach.

Rock Video and Cable TV

The relatively new phenomenon of rock video, available on many cable networks twenty-four hours a day, adds an unfortunate dimension to televised violence. One commentator characterizes these three-minute presentations as "studies in rage, retribution, and outer-space sexuality." The tapes used by rock video stations are supplied by record companies for purposes of promotion. Up to two hundred thousand dollars may be spent on a single video.

Of concern to parents of all children is that these films offer a mixture of sexuality and violence. Women are presented in ways that most mothers—if they watched —would scarcely condone. A significant percentage of these videos feature violence of a sexual nature.

One rock video director was recently quoted by *The Washington Post* as saying that he did not allow his own little boy to watch what MTV has to offer, "because of the incredible sadism" of the presentations. A second MTV director characterized young people who watch his videos as those "raised on television, drugs, and rock 'n' roll."

Some of these films can be especially troubling for the very young. Early in 1984, the Boston-based Action for Children's Television (ACT) was beseiged by calls from pediatricians and psychiatrists treating children between three and five years of age who had been frightened by the rock video "Thriller." Unable to deal with the theme of human transformation in this film, many could not sleep, had nightmares if they did, and clung mournfully to their mothers for long periods of time.

Cable TV also offers sexually explicit movies and programs dubbed suitable for children that may well not be up to your own standards of acceptability. R-rated movies are available on cable TV stations not just during adult viewing hours, but throughout the day. "There's no way we're going to have cable in this house," one mother said. "It's hard enough to say no as it is. With cable, kids can find something to watch that isn't really 'bad' just about any time they want."

You can affect what comes into your home via cable television. In the summer of 1985 Ann Landers, responding to a query from parents concerned about the suitability of presentations on the cable network to which they subscribed, pointed out that some types of programming are prohibited by the Cable Communications Policy Act passed by Congress in 1984. She suggested writing to Attorney General Edwin Meese III, Department of Justice, Constitution Avenue and 10th Street, N.W., Washington, D.C., 20530, and that PTAs and other interest groups inundate cable companies with complaints. "The cable companies are motivated by profit," this popular columnist stated. "If complaints and cancellations begin to pour in, they will clean up their act."

Rock Music

Popular music is a multibillion-dollar-a-year industry, much of which is targeted at the 10–16 age group. As a genre, rock music glorifies youth, freedom from adult constraints, and a we-them approach to adolescence. While many rock songs are harmless and entertaining to their listeners, others legitimize drug use. "Drugs and rock music are closely related," one sociologist says. "They support each other."

Rock music may be particularly harmful to boys, who are more likely than females to use drugs in the first place and are more concerned about what their peers think. The approval of older boys is also important. Boys who are becoming aware of the adolescent world for the first time may be extremely attracted to a milieu that seems to offer freedom, good times, and popularity. They will often imitate the mannerisms and clothing of adolescent boys and even adopt their values. Eighty-two percent of the university students in one survey felt that the lyrics to rock songs could help shape an individual's values at the subconscious level.

The ubiquitous "box" carried about by boys of all ages to enable them to plug in to their favorite rock station or disc jockey may well be a merchandising marvel; however, it could be a mistake to give one to your son. The boy who is especialy vulnerable—struggling in school, at odds with his peer group, generally immature, or at risk because of family problems like divorce—can readily turn to a world that promises the companionship and self-esteem he lacks at home or school. Asked about the influence of rock music on her fourth-grade son's group of friends, one mother said, "They all have a box —except my son. And it's getting harder and harder to keep him away from it." Fortunately, parent organizations are becoming aware of the effects of the media on their children. By taking collective action, and being willing to say no, parents can help redirect patterns of behavior.

Two groups are urging the record industry to adopt a rating system similar to that used for films. The National PTA proposed in 1984 that rating labels be placed on records, tapes, and cassettes featuring lyrics some consumers might find offensive. Association president Ann Kahn stresses that parents should have a way to assess what kind of music is being brought into their homes.

In the spring of 1985, Susan Baker, wife of the Secretary of the Treasury, and Tipper Gore, whose husband is a Tennessee senator, helped to found the Parents' Music Resource Center. Citing the blatant obscenity and violence in some rock songs, this organization also endorses labeling and wants record companies to print lyrics on album covers so buyers will know what they're getting. If you support the positive steps these groups are taking, let them know and ask how you can help:

The National PTA
700 North Rush Street
Chicago, Illinois 60611-2571
Telephone: (312) 787-0977

Parents' Music Resource Center
300 Metropolitan Square
655 Fifteenth Street, N.W.
Washington, D.C. 20005
Telephone: (202) 639-4085

Parents Can Influence a Boy's Taste

To help your little boy derive the greatest benefit from his exposure to the media, and to minimize the dangers, there are a number of steps parents can take:

- Watching television with your children ensures that they see programs of which you approve. Television has much to its credit, and can be used to help children gain information, be entertained, and observe socially desirable behavior. At least one college student first became interested in his major field of biology through watching Marlin Perkins's "Wild Kingdom." In his quiet, reassuring way, Mister Rogers helps millions of youngsters to feel that they are special. Discuss programs with your little boy, and emphasize the positive behavior of television characters.
- If your son watches aggressive cartoons or violent police or action shows, talk them over with him. Tell him your concerns about violence, and let him know that violence on a dramatic show is an exaggeration, not reality.
- Encourage an interest in live music and theater from an early age to counter the "canned" versions so readily available. An occasional night out to see a high-school or professional production, and family

participation in community theater or choral groups can give your son an appreciation for a wide variety of performing arts, if not an active outlet for his own talents.

- Previewing cable and rental films for young children can ensure the suitability of presentations. Not all films with "good" ratings may be right for your child.

- Analyzing your own watching habits may cause you to reexamine the place of the media in the life of your family. Is television so important that you have multiple sets? Are you, or your children, at loose ends if the television needs repair or the power goes out? Do you play games, talk, listen to music, visit friends or relatives, or engage in other pleasurable activities as often as you watch television? A boy's parents are his primary role models. What you do matters far more than what you say.

- Bedroom TV sets, radios, and stereos prevent family interaction and allow unsupervised access to the media. As one medical expert says, "To me, a second television spells the disintegration of family. With one set, at least you're all sitting together—there's some interaction. But with a second set, you've lost that one positive aspect." Personal sets also make it less likely that a child will engage in other more active mental pursuits, and this can affect school work. Yale Pediatrics Professor Victor Strasburger has a solution. Asked what to do about a child who is failing in school, "My first response," he says, "is to get the TV out of his room."

- Personal stereo sets and hand-held radios provide further access to the world of rock. If you allow such access, be prepared for your little boy to imitate disk jockeys, express an interest in clothing and hair styles modeled by rock stars (even if your boy is younger than ten), and, eventually, to show a desire to attend rock concerts. Exposing children to traditional music from an early age, providing music lessons to introduce them to classic musical forms, and taking the whole family to musical events can counteract the appeal of the rock subculture.

- Be careful that your child does not become accustomed to eating while watching TV. A number of experts see a connection between increasing rates of obesity in children and excessive television watching —with junk food as an ever-present accompaniment.

- Encourage independent thinking in your son by fostering self-sufficiency—family and church activities, sports, reading, or perfecting a musical or artistic skill. It also makes him less susceptible to the "groupthink" of the young. Many of today's teenagers are able to resist the appeal of forces that pull them away from the positive influence of family, church, and school. Help your little boy to develop this kind of independent thinking.

SUBSTANCE ABUSE

More than girls, boys experiment with and become dependent upon alcohol and drugs. Over half of today's adolescents have tried illegal drugs; in a major metropolitan area, it is not surprising to find third graders who have smoked pot. A recent study reported that one out of every three high-school seniors who admitted to smoking pot began his drug use when he was between twelve and fourteen. No national survey of substance use has looked at children below twelve, but the *Weekly Reader*, a newspaper for elementary-school students, conducted a national survey and found one in four fourth graders felt some pressure to try alcohol or marijuana. Almost 20 percent of these children saw no risk in smoking a joint of pot a day.

School officials report that sometimes older students in nice, middle-class suburbs aggressively foist drugs on younger ones. Also, older siblings may introduce a younger brother or sister to drinking or drugs. If a younger sibling is involved in drug use, he is far less likely to tell mom and dad about an older child's habit.

Genetic Factors Can Make Drinking Hazardous

Males show a greater genetic tendency to become alcoholic than females. Patterns of alcohol abuse run in families and are influenced by environmental factors. Adopted children of problem drinkers, who were reared away from their alcoholic parents, developed more serious drinking problems as adults than children with no family history of alcohol abuse. Some boys whose fathers are alcoholic appear nine times as likely as the general public to become problem drinkers. Boys of European and Oriental descent are more at risk than those of African heritage.

Researchers have recently identified personality traits—impulsivity, attention-seeking behavior, rebelliousness, manipulation of others, and self-centeredness—that can also be found in one-quarter of all alcoholics. Such antisocial personality traits are almost as strongly linked to alcohol abuse as is direct inheritance of genetic traits from father to son. Because boys, more than girls, exhibit these kinds of antisocial behaviors, they may be vulnerable in yet another way to alcoholism. One expert believes that both alcoholism and antisocial personality characteristics are associated with a brain anomaly that weakens an individual's ability to control his emotions and his behavior.

Pennsylvania State University researchers examined alcohol and drug use among individuals whose temperament had been followed over a period of years. They found that people who had been considered "difficult" at five years of age (slow to adapt, negative in mood, and intense in their reactions) tended to be the heaviest substance abusers as they approached adulthood. Since temperament, itself, seems to have a genetic basis, it is possible that an underlying vulnerability, both toward personality problems and substance abuse, may be inherited.

Environmental Factors Also Put Boys at Risk

In addition to genetic factors, there are social forces inherent in American culture that put boys at risk for abusing alcohol and other drugs. Low self-esteem is a key factor in substance abuse among young people today. The Chicago study conducted by Sheppard Kellam and his colleagues linked antisocial behavior, particularly aggressiveness in first-grade boys, with alcohol and drug abuse ten years later. First graders who were both shy and aggressive (those "angry loners" who often have classroom difficulties) became the heaviest drinkers and pot smokers in adolescence. The immaturities and poor social adjustment of younger boys, who rarely adjust as well to school as older children do, may contribute to a lack of self-esteem and vulnerability to substance abuse in the adolescent years.

Peer pressure contributes to the initial experimentation with drugs, and having friends who drink and "do drugs" is likely to influence a boy's continued use. Boys most susceptible to peer influences are insecure and have a strong need for acceptance. A study of over eight thousand children from a hundred New York schools showed that close family relationships are a powerful influence against a youngster's turning to alcohol and other substances. *Positive family relationships, deliberately and systematically reinforced from a child's earliest years, can be a bulwark against negative peer influences in adolescence.*

Conformity to one's peers is pronounced in the early teenage years, and boys are more likely than girls to follow the group in behaviors of which society disapproves. Boys are also more willing than girls to take risks. As they grow more independent in middle childhood, and especially during adolescence, boys seem to need to prove something to themselves and their peers. Parents' acknowledgement of a son's increasing independence may be reflected in a lessening of some kinds of controls, which can inadvertently contribute to a problem of drug use. Many boys, for example, supervise themselves when parents go out in the evening.

When famous personalities, ads in magazines, and his own parents tell him by their behavior that a drink makes them feel great, it is hardly surprising that a boy tests his limits with beer or bourbon. Drinking is one rite of passage almost all American males experience. "Recreational use" of drugs may be fast becoming another. If a boy experiences pleasurable sensations when he drinks or uses other drugs, then he is apt to keep on doing so unless there are forces in his life stronger than his peers to influence his behavior.

Drug Use May Begin at Home

Recent research suggests that drinking is more family influenced than peer oriented. One study of white middle-class youngsters, aged ten to thirteen, found that most young drinkers, both those imbibing regularly and those just experimenting with alcohol, usually drank with their families. Morris Chafetz, founding director of the National Institute on Alcohol Abuse and Alcoholism, believes parents are important role models. "If a parent demonstrates that alcohol is a special substance that turns him from sad to glad in minutes, at the same time it helps him to win the approval of others, you can be sure that the lesson won't be lost on the kids," he says.

Currently, alcohol is the most abused drug in the United States. Four million youngsters drink twice, or more often, weekly; many of these children are not yet adolescents. One researcher thinks the reasons for early use of alcohol by our children are clear:

First, alcohol is readily accessible to children in liquor cabinets or is put into plain view. Second, for those children who do not have alcohol present in their homes, it is inexpensive and relatively easy to obtain from peers, adult friends, or store sales personnel. Finally, because parents often use it themselves, alcohol use generally does not receive the same degree of adult criticism, scrutiny, or concern as other substances. For many teenagers, alcohol provides the same tranquilizing or numbing effect as marijuana, or sedatives, without the social penalties often accompanying other drugs.

Similarly, dependence on other drugs may begin at home. The casual use of medication and the media's blatant promotion of pills to cure all manner of problems makes even young children aware of the effectiveness of modern drugs. "Uppers," stimulant drugs such as amphetamines, are used by 35 percent of all high-school seniors; similar numbers use over-the-counter legal drugs that are stay-awake or diet pills. Many experts suggest that young people's drug use moves from legal substances, such as over-the-counter drugs, to illegal ones. Parents need to teach their children early on that medicine is only given by a physician. Keeping a little boy home from school when he's sick, rather than sending him off armed with medication for the school nurse or teacher to administer, can help put drug use in perspective, as can our own careful use of medicine for ourselves. Some parents keep medication in the top of the closet or in a locked cabinet, where young children cannot reach it. The lesson of respect for drugs, learned early in life, may help a boy avoid them as he matures.

Drinking and abuse of other drugs affect children from all socioeconomic groups. High tuition provides no insulation from this pervasive problem. In fact, there now seems to be a slightly higher rate of marijuana use among students in parochial and private schools than in public schools. Children who grow up in small towns and rural environments appear less likely to drink or use drugs than youngsters who live in urban and suburban communities, but coming from a "good home" does not mean a boy won't experiment with drugs. In many middle-and upper-income communities, eleven is the average age children begin marijuna use. Recently, health officials have reported cases of PCP intoxication among very young children and infants, who apparently inhaled this drug while their parents or sitters smoked joints laced with it.

Drugs Can Affect the Unborn

Since the time of the ancient Greeks, people have wondered whether drugs or drink might affect the unborn child. Recently, evidence of addiction in babies born to heroin addicts and fetal alcohol syndrome (FAS) identified among the offspring of alcoholic women have brought the horrifying reality of at least some maternal drug use to light. The physical risks are clear for children of problem drinkers. Perinatal mortality is substantially higher among the offspring of alcoholic women than among children of nondrinking mothers, carefully matched for education level, socioeconomic and marital status, race, and age. Almost half those FAS infants who survive birth have been found to be marginally retarded; many show abnormal features of the face, hands, and heart.

As yet, no one has set a safe lower level for alcohol consumption in pregnancy. This substance is known to pass the placental barrier rapidly, and it reaches the fetal bloodstream in at least the same concentration as it is found in the mother. By birth, a large baby is still only a fraction of his mother's size, so *it is difficult even to theorize a level of alcohol that might not harm a developing child*. Nursing mothers can also pass alcohol on to a suckling infant whose brain cells are still forming.

Mounting evidence of the risks of alcohol from both

human and animal studies led the Food and Drug Administration in 1981 to advise total abstinence from alcoholic beverages during pregnancy. However, efforts to place warning labels on liquor bottles have been unsuccessful. As little as one or two ounces of maternal alcohol (the amount found in a mixed cocktail, glass of wine, or can of beer) may produce serious changes in fetal growth and development, particularly of the central nervous system. Research has linked drinking by pregnant women to later hyperactivity, delayed psychomotor development, inability to attend to tasks, and other school behavior problems in their offspring. Chemicals in marijuana have also been found toxic to the developing fetus. Fetal marijuana syndrome is reported to be five times as commmon today as fetal alcohol syndrome. Those children born to pot-smoking mothers weigh less than normal babies and may show developmental anomalies.

Mom, if You Use Drugs...

Many adults of childbearing age use recreational drugs. Because the total number of eggs a woman has is present from birth, drug use creates long-lasting potential for damage to her offspring. No one really knows yet what the results of pot smoking may be in the children of women whose eggs may have been affected. But in animal studies, babies born even two generations after their pot-smoking grandmothers showed disturbed physiological responses.

- If you are a pot smoker, your menstrual cycle may be disrupted for several months. Marijuana is not, however, an effective method of birth control as some believe.
- You may have problems with infertility.
- You may have a long or arrested labor.
- Your baby may show signs of stress at birth, such as an abnormal heart rate or the need for oxygen.

In her 1985 book, *Marijuana Alert*, Peggy Mann reported that *one hundred percent* of the babies born to heavy pot smokers in one study showed abnormal behavioral effects, including exaggerated tremors and startles, and a slower than average response to visual stimuli.

With the increasing popularity of substances like cocaine comes evidence that it, too, is damaging to fetal development. A 1985 study suggests that using coke while pregnant may be even more harmful to a mother's unborn child than taking heroin has proved to be.

The Younger a Boy Is, the More Likely Drugs Will Harm Him

It is obviously impossible to test the effects of alcohol or drugs on growing children, but the evidence that is available from youngsters who have tried them indicates that the effect on the developing organism is extreme. Differences in body chemistry make young drinkers more vulnerable to alcohol than adults are. The National Institute on Drug Abuse reports that 7 percent of the adult population in the U.S. has trouble handling alcohol, but the percentage is almost three times as high among children and adolescents who drink. Experts predict that one out of every five teenagers who drink will become an alcoholic by his twenties. A child's physical addiction to alcohol can occur within twenty to thirty days of daily drinking, or six months of frequent drinking. Alcoholism is a disease from which only one out of thirty-five victims recovers.

Alcohol addiction develops from sensitivity in the hypothalamus region of the brain. This area of the brain, which helps control the automatic functions of the body (heartbeat and the action of several important glands) does not mature until adulthood. The younger a child begins to drink alcohol, the more likely the hypothalamus will be affected, possibly obstructing normal growth. For growing boys, alcohol also reduces the amount of testosterone in the body, and may interfere with normal development of secondary sex characteristics during adolescence.

Children who have not reached their maximum growth have a lower tolerance for alcohol and drugs than adults do. Automobile accidents are the leading cause of death among fifteen- through thirty-four-year-olds; approximately half are alcohol-related. Lowering the drinking age in many states during the early 1970s seems to have contributed to increased drinking among teenagers. When eighteen is the legal age to purchase alcohol, the effective drinking age becomes fifteen or younger. Eighteen-year-olds buy liquor for younger friends, and some fifteen-year-olds look old enough to purchase their own wine or beer if clerks don't ask for identification. During the 1970s and 1980s, the death rate for young people, age fifteen to twenty-four, has risen at the same time life expectancy for every other age group has improved. Increased numbers of automobile fatalities are largely responsible for the difference.

Boys are more likely than girls to drink and drive, or to drive under the influence of drugs. A survey of two thousand teenagers in the Boston area found that fully one-third believed they could safely combine drink with driving. Statistics suggest that higher drinking ages correspond to decreased fatalities for teenagers.

Fortunately, both federal and local governments recognize the problem and are taking action. Any Marylander knowingly serving alcohol to a minor can spend up to two years in jail and/or pay a thousand-dollar fine. "Dram shop laws," which make proprietors of restaurants and bars liable for accidents that result when they serve alcohol to either minors or adults who are obviously intoxicated, have been regarded as a "top legislative priority" by members of MADD (Mothers Against Drunk Drivers). The federal requirement that only states where twenty-one has been set as the legal minimum drinking age can receive full highway funding may prove even more persuasive.

Boys Can Get Hooked on Many Chemical Substances

The pattern of substance abuse tends to run from legal drugs, like beer or cigarettes, and nonprescription stimulants, to illegal ones such as marijuana or PCP. Over one million teenagers in this country are trapped into multiple drug use, compounding the dangers. From his experience helping young drug users at the Haight-Ashbury Free Medical Clinic, one expert knows the full potential of mixing marijuana and alcohol:

> These young people are unaware . . . that marijuana has some sedative hypnotic properties. Therefore, it is partially cross-tolerant when added to alcohol. A kid who uses X amount of alcohol and Y amount of marijuana, one day combines the two. He does not realize they are partially additive and it puts them over the top.

Drinking to excess generally causes nausea and vomiting, the body's protective response against too much alcohol. But chemicals in marijuana turn off the nausea centers in the brain. Complete intoxication, often acute alcohol poisoning, can result.

Marijuana alone is also risky business, especially for boys, who are twice as likely to smoke it as girls. Unlike alcohol, which is water soluble and metabolizes quickly in the body, the chemicals in marijuana are fat soluble. THC and other cannabinoids released in the body when pot is smoked can remain there for up to thirty days. Fatty tissues—the brain, sex organs, liver, spleen, and lungs—are prime sites for these chemicals. The Boston study of seventh and tenth graders found that three out of five youngsters had tried marijuana.

Some of the risks marijuana holds for boys include:

- Reduction of male hormones in the body. Even one month of heavy smoking, generally considered to be five or more joints a week, lowers sperm count and motility; however, these effects can be reversed within several weeks, if a boy stops using pot.
- Increased incidence of abnormal cells. Dr. Gabriel Nahas of Columbia University's College of Physicians and Surgeons discovered in the 1970s that marijuana disrupts cell chemistry, inhibiting the formation of DNA, the genetic material essential to cell functioning and division. "Today's pot smoker may not only be damaging his own mind and body, but may be playing genetic roulette and casting a shadow across children and grandchildren yet unborn," this researcher is quoted as saying.
- Reduced immune response to disease. THC's effects on cell chemistry extend to white blood cells, which divide more slowly in pot smokers than in non-drug-users.
- Altered brain tissue and functions. Marijuana appears to widen the synapse or gap that exists between nerve cells, to increase abnormal deposits of fatty granules (usually associated with old age) that clog the gap between nerves, and to lower the level of neurotransmitters in the brain—in short, to slow down brain functioning. A number of physicians report that short-term memory is significantly impaired in pot smokers; it may improve, but often fails to come back to what it was before heavy drug use. Marijuana also seems to distort perception, behavior, and personality, cause sluggish thinking, and reduce motivation in its users.

When marijuana use first became popular, some experts believed it to be nonaddictive. In reality, it can be very addictive. Flu-like symptoms (irritability, sweating, nausea, diarrhea) result when heavy pot smokers stop using marijuana. Depression and fatigue affect lighter smokers as their "high" wears off. According to a 1979 survey, over 40 percent of American males, aged eighteen to twenty-four, smoke marijuana. Many of these individuals began their habits as adolescents, and have been unable to break them.

American children use other chemical substances in record numbers. Unfortunately, not enough research has been undertaken to demonstrate the whole effect of these drugs on the developing body. What evidence there is, however, is frightening. Chronic high doses of stimulants, like amphetamines, can produce psychotic symptoms in psychologically healthy human beings— disorganized thought processes, paranoia, and unprovoked violence. Even lower stimulant dosages often cause irritability, personality changes, elevated blood pressure, and sleep disturbances.

A stimulant that has recently become fashionable is cocaine. Despite its relatively higher cost, coke, as this drug is usually known, is popular for the feeling of lift, confidence, and control it gives its users. One drug expert sees cocaine as "more dangerous than marijuana in the sense that people tend to become more preoccupied with it than other drugs." Cocaine may rupture blood vessels to the brain while contributing to high blood pressure, brain hemorrhages, and stroke; recent evidence suggests irreversible damage to the vascular system of the brain from large doses. Continued consumption often leads to "free basing," or smoking coke, an extremely hazardous practice. "Large amounts of the drug can be absorbed in a short period of time," a National Institute of Drug Abuse researcher reported. "The danger here is purely physiological—you can die from it."

Hallucinogens, like LSD and PCP, can cause panic and disorganization, indistinguishable from schizophrenia. MDMA, or "ecstasy," is another psychedelic drug that has recently become popular with college students and young professionals in the U.S. and Canada. In May 1985, the Drug Enforcement Agency announced its intention to outlaw this hallucinogen because research suggests it may cause permanent brain damage to users.

Depressants (barbiturates and Quaaludes) may be both physiologically and psychologically addictive. Their effects—slurred speech, disorientation, and drunken behavior—are similar to alcohol's. The overdose potential is great and can lead to death.

What Parents Can Do to Prevent Alcohol and Drug Abuse

The causes of substance abuse are similar no matter what drug a child uses, and may begin early in life. Poor self-image, sometimes manifested in shyness, aggression, or a combination of these behaviors, seems to be a prime cause of substance abuse among young people today. Most drug experts advise parents about the importance of the following factors:

- Close, strong family relationships. Open communication is important, as are firm guidelines. *Make it clear that your child is not allowed to use alcohol or drugs* and, furthermore, that their use by minors is illegal.
- Appropriate supervision and consequences for a child's actions. For older children as much as younger ones, a parent's presence and willingness to enforce rules are essential. Grounding, especially if it means cutting off a child's telephone privileges, is an effective deterrent, as is taking away use of television or stereos.
- Knowing your son's friends and their parents. Are their behavior and standards compatible with your own? Boys need strong peer relationships, but with children who influence them in positive ways. If you know your son's friends and parents well when your little boy is in preschool, first grade, or third grade, chances are you will continue to be involved with the parents of your son's friends as he grows.
- Continued concern for a maturing boy. Independence does not mean your son wants you to abandon him.

Take an interest in his hobbies and activities. Make your home the kind of place where he feels comfortable bringing his friends. Supervise them adaequately. Make sure that when your son visits his friends, parents are there to keep an eye on things. What you don't know about older children *can* hurt them.

- Sound values. Studies show that discussion of moral issues is important in a boy's development. Do members of your family express how they feel about issues in the media? In your local community? In your son's school?

- Adequate male role models for boys. It is useful to include children in adult gatherings, and for boys to have grownup friends who will take an interest in their activities. Teenagers involved with drugs tend to be wary of all adults. Accustom your son to the company of responsible adult men who provide good role models.

- Looking closely at your own behavior. Are you setting the kind of example you want your children to follow? Announcing that you really need a drink may be telling your son that alcohol is okay. Popping pills, even antacid tablets or vitamins, may teach a boy that drugs are harmless or beneficial.

- Instilling the concept of moderation early. "Pigging out" on snacks, or spending an entire day in front of a television set are addictive habits that an older child might carry into alcohol or drug abuse.

- Knowing your son's inheritance. If there is a family history of alcoholism or drinking problems, a boy should be made aware that he may develop similar problems if he uses alcohol. If your son is adopted, obtain enough genetic information to help you understand his risks. The age at which you warn a boy about possible alcoholism, and the way you tell him, need careful thought and will vary from child to child.

- Helping children to realize the dangers of alcohol and drugs to the growing body. Government-funded agencies have information available for families:

National Institute on Drug Abuse
15600 Fishers Lane
Rockville, Maryland 20857
Telephone: (301) 443-4577

National Clearinghouse on Alcohol Abuse
P. O. Box 2345
Rockville, Maryland 20852
Telephone: (301) 468-2600

- Organizing drug programs in the schools. One effective program for sixth through eighth graders combined training in group skills, values clarification, moral development theory, and decision-making strategies; it produced significant differences in attitudes about drinking and drug use. The late elementary-school years seem to be an ideal time to begin antidrug campaigns.
- Recognizing the signals of alcohol or drug abuse. An unexpected drop in school performance, or a drastic change in the kind of friends your son sees may be the first clue that something is wrong. Trouble getting along with other members of the family, a loss of interest in former activities, especially if accompanied by unexplained mood changes, hostility, or irritability, are reasons for adults to look more closely at a boy's behavior. If your son is acting strangely and receiving mysterious telephone calls, or his coordination, reflex activity, or memory are lessening noticeably, he may have an addiction problem. Lying and stealing often indicate a serious habit.
- Getting help immediately for a child discovered to be using drugs or alcohol. Denial that your son has a problem only encourages continued destructive behavior. Parent support groups have been established in many communities. These organizations can provide information and give parents insight into how they can help a boy hooked on drugs. Two national groups that

can put you in touch with local support organizations and provide help in starting your own are

PRIDE (Parent Resource Information for Drug Education)
100 Edgewood Avenue, NE
Suite 1216
Atlanta, Georgia 30303
Telephone: (800) 241-7946

National Federation of Parents for Drug Free Youth
1820 Franwall Avenue
Silver Spring, Maryland 20902
Telephone: (800) 554-5437

As is often pointed out, it is hard to find something that is not risky or hazardous to our health these days. Just listening to the late news can keep us from getting a good night's sleep. All of us daily face risks of one sort or another over which we have little or no control. The risk factors presented here, however, are under our control. More important, the way we handle them directly affects the development of our children.

In the General Mills American Family Survey conducted in 1976, it was revealed that over 40 percent of the parents questioned regarded themselves and their own self-fulfillment as top priorities in their lives. Not only were these parents unprepared to make sacrifices for their children, they also did not believe that they should place a child's interests above their own. In view of the hazards presented in this chapter, such an attitude is disturbing.

Parents face decisions about their children every day. Like the adolescent who considers the choice of whether or not to drink or take drugs, we also must choose. Giving your son free rein to watch TV or listen to his favorite rock station habitually might mean you can enjoy a few hassle-free minutes of newspaper-reading time. The money you save in child-care expenses by letting a son

stay home by himself might underwrite a summer vaca-
tion. Small or large, decisions must be made—every
day—and we make them. We all face continual choices
between our own needs and desires and those of our
children.

By our overindulgence or moderation, our willingness
or unwillingness to be consistent about the guidelines we
set for behavior, our choices of where our money goes
and the way we deal with conflict, we reveal the level of
our commitment to our children. It seems almost ines-
capable that eliminating certain risks requires that we
put forth the time, spend the money, and yes—in some
cases, even sacrifice—in order to show our children we
care what happens to them.

Weathering the Storms

*Sometimes I think I'm a total failure as a
parent, but I'm all they've got. Before Jem
looks at anyone else, he looks at me, and
I've tried to live so I can look squarely back
at him. . . .*

In these words from Harper Lee's Pulitzer Prize–
winning novel, *To Kill a Mockingbird*, Atticus Finch reveals with eloquent clarity the mixture of responsibility
and vulnerability most of us feel as parents. Who of us
has not, at some time, doubted his ability to be a good
parent? How many of us have not known the determination to stand a bit taller because our children were
counting on us? As Jem looked to his father, our own
children look to us as models of what is right.

While Atticus Finch is a fictional southern lawyer, he
embodies the virtues of courage, tolerance, and kindness
many of us try to cultivate in our own lives and those of
our children. Like him, we try to be the best parents we
can. Mother or father, single or happily married, well-to-

do or financially strapped, we share with our sons goals for the future as well as a genetic inheritance. If our boys are adopted, our experiences together make us family. This bond, cemented by love, will last a lifetime.

"I think one of my biggest challenges," one young mother said, "is helping my boy learn to cope. Somehow I have to prepare him to 'weather life's storms,' if you know what I mean." We all know what she means. Each of us has weathered our own particular storms, and we know that our children will face their storms, too. Some of their challenges will be very much like those we encountered; others will be different—perhaps so very distant from our own that we cannot even imagine them. Our grandparents coped with life-threatening diseases that are now treated routinely with antibiotics; the thought that their children would come face to face with the threat of nuclear destruction was incomprehensible. We do not know, nor can we even envision, what the world will be like for our own little boys when they are men.

"Parenting," one father said, "is a kind of balancing act. You have to know when to push forward, when to pull back, and when to just hang on." As in any other venture, the more we know when we start out, the greater the odds will be for success. Some of us have had excellent role models in our own parents; we already possess much useful information. We may raise our children very much the way our parents raised us. "If I can do the job half as well as my father did," one man said in reminiscing about his childhood experiences, "my kids will be really lucky."

In other cases, though, our parents may have imparted more negative lessons than positive ones. One mother admitted to a parenting class that, "Growing up in my house, I learned at least a thousand things *not* to do. What I need now is to learn what I *ought* to do. My parents never taught me that."

The way our own parents treated us, the practices relied on by other adults of our acquaintance, the child-care books we read and courses we take, and our own temperamental characteristics and experiences influence our approach to child rearing. Much like the children we have described in earlier chapters, some of us may be easygoing and others may find life more difficult to cope with; most of us are somewhere in between. Our moods, likes and dislikes, and characteristic ways of reacting to stress influence how we communicate with and discipline our children.

To become the kind of effective parents most of us would like to be, we need to assess our own idiosyncrasies as objectively as possible. If a mother knows, for example, that she is prone to panic attacks around large groups of noisy children, she might decline the invitation to chaperone her son's Boy Scout field trip to an amusement park. Volunteering to work with three or four boys on a cooking badge would be a more appropriate choice for her particular temperament. Recognizing that he has a difficult time controlling his anger, a father might make a practice of waiting at least fifteen minutes before confronting his son when the boy misbehaves.

We also need to keep in mind our own value systems in making judgments and teaching our children right and wrong. "My dad's always spouting off about how important it is to be a good sport," one boy told a friend. "But the first thing he wants to know when I get home from a match is, 'Did you win?' " Another parent may realize that the emphasis he places on honesty and hard work won't mean much if he continues to pay his son money for high grades. Throughout the child-rearing years, our relationships with our children can be colored by how well our personalities and values fit with theirs.

Our Goals for Our Sons Are Influenced by Our Environment

Whoever we are, and wherever we live, there are certain parental standards to which we adhere, and correspond-

ing aspirations that we have for our children. Some are
born of our cultural or religious traditions, while others
are influenced by the norms and practices of our particular community. In metropolitan areas, a matter of great
concern to many parents is their child's acceptance to a
specific private school. A boy's performance once he
gets there is monitored with similar care; his parents
want to ensure that he gains admission to the right prep
school or college.

Standards of a different kind may apply in other parts
of the country. In some rural locations, boys of five or
six accompany their fathers when they hunt. By ten,
many boys own their own guns and can successfully
bring down squirrels, rabbits, or even turkeys. Their parents want their sons to be able to hold their own in the
field. In both kinds of communities, parents' aspirations
for their boys determine, to an extent, the opportunities
they provide and the kinds of pressure they apply. Urban
parents realize that among their son's friends, competence in school is a mark of status. Parents in some rural
settings know that, even if their son is good in school,
his skill at field sports will affect his sense of competence
among his peers.

Parents Have Their Own Storms to Weather

We want our little boys to grow up confident, to be good
people, and to be able to handle what life brings their
way. In helping them to do this, we all have our own
problems to cope with. The fast pace of society yields
stress as well as opportunity. One busy working mother
confessed, "My life is geared for things to run smoothly,
but when they don't—when the babysitter quits or my
school-age child is sick—this family's active schedule
comes to a grinding halt."

Our life-style choices can make child rearing relatively simple or enormously complex. The stay-at-home

mother in a small Indiana town who volunteers at her son's school one afternoon per week and acts as den mother for his scout troop can scarcely comprehend the logistics of office demands and child care faced by the Manhattan executive with preschool children. The businessman who faces a heavy travel schedule and what seem like endless meetings will have a more difficult time playing an active role in the life of his son than will the farmer in Iowa whose boy works beside him every day.

The ordinary turmoil of schedules and family demands can be multiplied when we experience a crisis with our son. Difficulty in school, a serious behavior problem, or a diagnosis of long-term educational or psychological difficulty like dyslexia or childhood depression can severely strain the resources of the most well-put-together parents.

"I thought I was slowly losing my mind," one mother said, speaking of a prolonged bout of misbehavior on the part of her eleven-year-old son. Methods she had found effective with two of her children failed to work when her third child developed a problem the books seldom talked about. The communication skills she learned in an effective parent training course, however, not only helped her deal with her son's problem, but made a positive difference in the behavior of her older children, as well.

In another family, therapy was necessary when a father was unable to come to terms with a diagnosis of his son's learning disability. Hyperactive and difficult to manage, the boy's behavior demanded more than his father could give without assistance. A sympathetic counselor helped this man resolve the conflicts he felt about being responsible for the problem and put him in touch with a parent support group for learning-disabled children. Sometimes we all need help in managing our children. When this happens, recognizing our need and taking positive action are important.

There are steps all parents can take to increase our

own competence and help us address the needs of little boys today.

- *Get to know your son's moods.* Learning to predict a boy's moods, times when his fears are apt to get the best of him, or situations that produce a certain kind of reaction to stress can make our job a lot easier. "There is no way you are going to that movie," one mother declared, putting her foot down. "Whenever you see one of those scary films, the entire family is awake for nights afterward." Another mother could tell when her son was getting into a melancholy mood by the music he played.

- *Know his limits.* Taking the time to reflect on our son's feelings and behavior will give us a better understanding of his energy level and resistance. One especially active ten-year-old participated in a community play that held rehearsals two nights a week, was catcher on a baseball team, sang in the church choir, and made straight A's in school. A less gregarious friend had a difficult time just keeping up with baseball. He enjoyed being at home, puttering about with his bicycle, and playing with his friends. From long experience, the mother of the active little joiner knows that he can take it. "Jerry can't handle too many things at once," the mother of the more retiring boy wisely acknowledges. "When he's ready for something new, he lets us know."

- *Read his signals.* If we are aware of our son's energy level, moods, and feelings, we are better able to read all of his signals, from appetite to body language. We can also help our son to interpret his behavior for himself. One learning-disabled boy developed such an awareness of his own abilities that he could warn his family when he was having a "bad day"—unable to focus on his work or feeling especially sensitive. Knowing how he felt, his parents could make a special effort to encourage or praise him. But a far more important benefit of being able to read our boy's signals is that the sensitivity we show for his unique way of behaving—of just being himself—says, "You're okay. We like you the way you are." The boy whose parents are accepting will have higher self-esteem than the one whose parents find themselves at odds with his moods, his interests, and his behavior.

- *Help your son see the consequences of his actions.* Helping a child realize the results of what he does is a very effective parenting technique, and can be used with even very small boys. Posing questions allows him to figure out for himself what might happen. For example, the boy who is determined to respond to a dare to fight may think twice if his mother asks, "What do you think it will feel like when he hits that loose front tooth?" or "What would happen if you told him you thought fighting was silly?" Asking, "What do you think will happen when the fight is over? How will you and Billy feel?" may cause a boy to reflect on the implications of winning, losing, and what friendship is all about.

  Reasoning or questions that show consequences for others seems to work better for boys than self-oriented logic or simple prohibitions. "How do you think it makes Tim feel if you call him a 'fatty'?" is much more effective than saying, "If you do that, this will happen," or "Don't do that!"

- *Moderate your reactions.* Intensity—whether in punishment or reasoning—seems to be an effective discipline method for girls, but not for boys. Even overemphasizing our own reactions, as in the warning, "I'll be very, very upset if you don't do as I say!" can encourage negative behavior in boys. Moderation in the way we discipline, and sensitivity in how we reason with our sons seems to help them develop their own internal self-controls.

- *Give praise.* Accentuating the positive also appears to encourage good behavior in children of both sexes. Praising school children when they were helpful was found by Canadian researchers to boost their willingness to help. Being told that he is kind and generous will strengthen the conscience of a boy who shares his allowance with needy children, and lead to continued helpful behavior.

- *Encourage sensitivity.* A number of experts believe boys should be raised much the way society tradition- ally trains girls. Psychologist Leonard Eron states: "Rather than insisting that little girls should be treated like little boys... it should be the other way around. Boys should be encouraged to develop socially posi- tive qualities such as tenderness, sensitivity to feel- ings, nurturance, cooperativeness, and aesthetic appreciation. The level of individual aggression in so- ciety will be reduced only when male adolescents and young adults, as a result of socialization, subscribe to the same standards of behavior as have been tradition- ally encouraged for women." Because boys place more emphasis on "the rules" in evaluating the rightness or wrongness of a situation, training in sensitivity may help them approach these issues from a more caring perspective.

- *Give your boy a code of values.* Children learn from what we do and say from infancy on. If we wish to impart a particular set of beliefs in our youngsters, we must share these precepts with them in their early years. Many of today's families belong to churches or synagogues, and membership can give the growing child a sense of being part of a larger group whose values reflect his own and those of his family. A boy who observes his father's attendance at religious ser- vices benefits from a strong model demonstrating a continued commitment to faith. Getting to meet and know men who affirm their values through group wor- ship, or share their beliefs with children in Sunday school or youth groups can be an important force in the lives of sons of single mothers.

- *Have the courage to hold your son back if he's not ready for school.* "It's really difficult to keep your per- spective sometimes," one young mother said. "When my friends comment that Aaron will be ready for first grade next fall and I tell them he's going to kindergarten instead, there's this sudden silence in the conversation. One of my friends even suggested we were taking a whole year out of his life by holding him back." It is often difficult to do what we believe is best for our children in the face of social pressures of various kinds, especially if they come from more experienced parents. We all have at least one friend or acquaintance who seems to do everything right, has the answer to all problems, and knows the path we ought to take. It helps to remember that she doesn't live with our little boy; she doesn't know him as well as we do, and won't have to face the consequences if her advice is wrong. If there are sound and compelling reasons for you to suspect that your little boy should wait until he's older before starting school, take sensible measures to confirm your suspicions rather than accepting the advice of well-meaning friends. See that a developmental test is given. Consult with the principal of your son's school, and with his teacher as well. Read as much as you can about readiness. *Is Your Child in the Wrong Grade*?, an excellent book by Gesell's associate director, Louise Bates Ames, is not only informative, but also comforting to parents trying to make the right decision about school for a little boy.

If you ask experienced educators, they will tell you that they have frequently come across situations in which parents regret sending a boy to school too soon. "In eighteen years as a teacher and principal," one administrator said, "I've met only one parent who was sorry she held her child back—and her child was a little girl."

- *Respect the progress your son makes in every area of his life*. It is important to recognize that a little boy's efforts in aspects of life besides school need your support and approbation. What if he isn't such a great student? What if his standardized test scores fall in the middle range instead of in the high one like the child's next door? Shouldn't you push him to do better? That depends. One male school principal, asked what he would tell parents to remember about boys, said, "They need to keep in mind that no child is only what the school says he is. School is just one aspect of his life." A refreshingly frank teacher told parents, "Your son is curious and will always learn. It's just that he may not do most of his learning in school."

The boy whose school success is fair to middling instead of superior may be achieving the most he can at a particular time in his life. It is unfair of schools— and parents—to insist continually that a boy work harder when he is already doing his best. If teachers persist in telling you, "Johnnie could do better if he would only try harder," a serious look should be taken at his grade placement. Not every boy is going to do well in school, and even if a child does make adequate progress, he may not enjoy going to school; some children hate it throughout their school careers. Nevertheless, these same boys may be considerate of other people, love animals, have a consuming interest in science or computers, show good sportsmanship, and be all-around nice kids. The trouble is, we don't give them grades on these aspects of their lives. Little boys want to be competent. They need to be competent. And, most of all, they must feel their parents believe they are competent, too. Make sure that grades and school performance are not the only yardsticks used in measuring your little boy.

What Is Your Little Boy Really Like?

Everyone seems to be an expert on children today. Neighbors, relatives, and sometimes even perfect strangers are quite willing to give us their opinions, even if we do not ask for them. Each person, though, may see only one side of any little boy, however sound or valid his advice may seem.

To his teacher, Daniel may be a B-minus student from a middle-class family with no history of behavior problems, but with few outstanding qualities. To the neighbor who observed him one day in an uncharacteristic bad mood and saw him throw a rock in anger, Daniel is a nasty little boy. The elderly widow down the street whose lawn he mows and whom he sometimes "forgets" to ask for payment tells his mother that Daniel has a heart of gold. Daniel's three-year-old brother idolizes him and copies his every move; but his teenage sister would be happy to trade him for a used car. What is the boy, Daniel, really like? Do even his parents know the "real" Daniel?

All too often, we become so caught up in the busyness of life that we don't really get to know our children as we should. If we work, we may spend very little time with them until the evening hours. If television or homework claim even a small portion of the remaining time, that is lost to us as well. Even if we spend a good part of every day with our youngsters, we may not be privy to their fantasies, their doubts and fears, or their real feelings. Parents may believe they know their child better than anyone else does; and, to an extent, they do. However, it is sometimes possible to live with someone for years and not be aware of some very important things about him.

Even though you may know what your son's favorite TV show is, do you know who he pretends to be when he is playing? You may know his best friend better than you would like to, but can you say who his adult friends are—grownups he admires and likes to be around? Although he withstood the pain of falling off his bicycle and endured the necessary stitches without flinching, there are things he fears—can you name two of them? What makes your little boy feel good? What did you last say or do that made him smile? What ticks him off? Makes him laugh? Or causes him to cry? What does your little boy do when he doesn't have anything else to do?

Many of us find it hard to answer questions such as

these, not because we are indifferent to our children, but simply because we have never really thought about them. Yet it is precisely the answers to questions of this kind that matter most of all. What good does it do us if we remember every grade on our son's last two report cards, but can't tell someone what makes him laugh? How many of us can list his major illnesses year by year, but are hard put to say who our boy's heroes are?

While it is important to know our son well, it is equally essential to be accepting of him and use our own knowledge to encourage his development in every way we can. The toddler who is determined to climb the stairs despite spills and bumps may become an adventuresome schoolboy who, at seven, breaks his arm falling from a tree. This boy's parents will want to help him realize that he is not invincible, encourage friendships with more cautious boys, and, by their questions, help him see the consequences of the risks he takes. They will not be able to change his personality, but they can encourage such a boy to moderate the level of risk he considers acceptable, and to learn his own limits. They can't prevent him from skateboarding, but may be able to help him learn to wear protective headgear or avoid those steep hills.

Another boy, who is naturally shy, may be less aggressive than many of his friends. Taunting may be a problem, as others try to goad him into a response. One shy boy, who was very interested in snakes, was helped when his parents enrolled him in a herpetological society that met monthly. The interested adults in this group made the boy feel at ease and his shyness was less in evidence when he was involved with the subject he knew most about. Even the more gregarious boys in this club came to respect the youngster because of his expertise. Recognizing their son's need for companionship as well as finding a way to expand his interests, these parents came up with an exceptionally suitable answer to his problem.

A third boy, Sean, was always easygoing, even-tempered, and rolled with the punches, but showed a stubborn streak about some things. As a fourth grader, he refused to accept the dominance of the playground bully who unofficially set the dress code for the "in group" of boys. Teased because he refused to wear camouflage clothing like the rest of his classmates, Sean was fortunate to have a family who supported his independence and saw that he had plenty of opportunities to be with other boys outside of school. By the end of the year, "camo" was out, most fourth graders were fed up with the bully, and Sean had as many friends as ever at school without losing his self-respect or his principles.

A Boy's Family Is His Backup System

In a middle-sized town in southeastern Pennsylvania, there is a sixty-year-old converted frame dwelling that fronts on a narrow sidewalk. On one wall in the kitchen of an upstairs apartment hangs a faded sampler with the words, HOME IS WHERE THE HEART IS. The apartment dweller is an elderly widow who has outlived both of her sons. The children of one of these sons, the woman's grandchildren, return to that small kitchen several times each year to visit with the grandmother who has been there since they were born. Grandma makes up a pot of chicken corn soup, a batch of her best-ever sugar cookies, and they sit around the kitchen table, renewing ties and recalling special times together. For these young adults, the words on the faded sampler do not constitute a time-worn cliché. They are alive with meaning.

The sense of identity and continuity a little boy receives from his family is the most important force in his life. It is within his family that a child first perceives the idea of who he is, and what makes him and his people different from all others. The values his family espouses, the causes they believe in, and the way they conduct their everyday life transmit lessons to a son that are lifelong in their impact. For today's young boy, a rich family life can be the first and most important line of defense against the storms life will inevitably toss his way.

"The family is a child's backup system," one school administrator says. If the school says he's not such a hot student, his family can counter with, "Maybe not, but he's still a great kid." If a neighbor complains about his behavior, his family can deal with the problem and love him anyway. If the bully down the street picks on a little boy, his brothers and sisters will go to his rescue. (They will pick on him later.) Family members stick up for one another. They are still there when everybody else goes away.

Family ties enrich a boy's life as nothing else can. One young mother recounts the memories her small son has of being treated regularly to lunch in a certain restaurant by his grandfather, who died when the boy was three. In a family whose members are scattered across the country, an aunt each year takes a niece or nephew backpacking in the mountains where their fathers grew up. Not only are these children given an experience to share with dad, but cousins, who live far apart and whose lives differ greatly in other ways, have at least one summer's outing in common. In another family, a grandmother makes a special treat of telling each grandchild the story of "The Day You Were Born," tucking them into bed beside her on their overnight visits. Tradition, shared experiences, and the memories they give a child are the very stuff of life which translate into a child's sense of self.

Because it is often females who carry on family traditions—ensuring that the pictures get taken and saved, writing the letters, and making the phone calls—it is important for mothers to share these ties with a boy when he is young. We need to encourage our boys to correspond with that favorite aunt or grandparent, or a cousin who lives in another state. Let him help address Christmas cards, or write a postscript on letters you write yourself.

Even if your own family life was empty of ritual or

tradition, establish new ones in your home to give added meaning to special family events. A recently divorced mother, who lives in a city far from her own family, has "adopted" a grandmother for her little boy through a church friendship. Not only does her son have the traditions she continues from her own past, he is also learning new ones from his very special "grammy."

Sadly, divorce can disrupt family ties, unless adults make special efforts to keep in touch. Often cut off from association with the custodial parent, relatives on the noncustodial side of a family may be deliberately thwarted in their attempts to maintain contact with grandchildren, nieces, and nephews in the shuffle of visitation rights. In later years, children of divorce often regret these sundered relationships. If a divorce has occurred in your family, go the extra mile to provide family continuity for your little boy.

Growth Brings Both Joys and Stresses for Parents

"It's hard to believe he's the same boy," one mother said of a well-dresssed six-footer who was helping a sweet-faced girl into the family car to take her out to dinner. "Three years ago it was a struggle just to get him into the shower."

Each period of our son's life has its own particular delights and special set of stresses. The worries we faced about teething and toilet training seem inconsequential when we encounter failing grades at nine or experimentation with alcohol at fourteen. When our toddler takes his first tentative steps, we think we shall never again be as proud. Yet this milestone seems trivial compared to the look of satisfaction he exhibits when he wins the spelling bee in sixth grade, or his glow of achievement when he graduates from college.

Faced with what seems like an endless round of diapers and sleepless nights, brand-new parents sometimes yearn longingly for deliverance. Coping with the bathroom words of the four-year-old makes us fantasize about a fairy godmother who will come along and turn him into a respectable adult by morning. Then, when he is sixteen and sometimes surly, we wish for a return to the days of the placid five-year-old who told us each night, "I really love you, Mom!"

A speaker at a PTA meeting once told a group of parents to remember that our children do not really belong to us; they are ours "on loan." Ultimately each of our sons will become his own person—in his own time, and in his own way. As we cope with the diapers, the bathroom words, and eventually the surliness, it is important to remember the speaker's message.

Like Atticus Finch in Lee's wonderful story, most of us try hard to be good parents. We accept the responsibilities that go with having children, even when we're not really sure we're up to the job. We willingly read the same story every night for six months, sleep outdoors in all kinds of weather, schedule carpools, teach Sunday school, sponsor book fairs, cheer at games, and volunteer for things nobody else in his right mind would do— except another parent. "Because that's how," one mother said, "they know we love them."

Try to enjoy each and every stage of your little boy's life. Store up memories for the times to come—the feel of his hair against your cheek as you read him a bedtime story, the look of expectation on his face on Christmas morning, the sound his clarinet makes as he practices for the spring recital. Write down the preschool mispronunciations you find so adorable and believe you will never forget—because you will forget them if you don't. Save the doily-laden card with the crooked, "Be My Valentine," and the pencil holder he made for Dad from an empty orange-juice can.

Give your son his own special memories—a surprise trip to a favorite place when he thinks it's going to be just another Sunday, the privilege of making a long-distance call to the pal who moved far away, or a soft answer and understanding when he's expecting the roof to cave in.

Remember that he is yours for a brief time only. Show him—and tell him—that you love him. And help your little boy in every way you can as he follows his own individual path to manhood.

Notes

1. What Little Boys Are Made Of

1 In *Huckleberry Finn*...with satisfaction. Mark Twain, *The Adventures of Huckleberry Finn* (New York: Bantam Books, [1965] 1975), pp. 53–60.

4 Psychologist Sandra Scarr...right kind of environment. Authors' interview with Sandra Scarr, Commonwealth professor of psychology, The University of Virginia, July 12, 1984. Also from Sandra Scarr, *Race, Social Class, and Individual Differences in I.Q.* (Hillsdale, N.J.: Lawrence Erlbaum Associates, 1981), pp. 16–21; and Elizabeth Hall, "What's a Parent to Do?", *Psychology Today*, May 1984, pp. 58–63.

5 Genetic information is transmitted...throughout life. P. B. Medawar, J. S. Medawar, *Aristotle to Zoos, A Philosophical Dictionary of Biology* (Cambridge, Mass.: Harvard University Press, 1983), p. 56.

6 The tendency in humans...secretes testosterone. Charles H. Doering, "The Endocrine System," *Constancy and Change in Human Development* (Cambridge, Mass.: Harvard University Press, 1980), p. 249; and Eleanor E. Maccoby, *Social Development, Psychological Growth and the Parent–Child Relationship* (New York: Harcourt Brace Jovanovich, 1980), p. 206.

7 Even though more males are conceived...respiratory problems. Maccoby, Ibid.

7 A second, and equally important... different amount of information. Christopher Ounsted, David C. Taylor, "The Y Chromosome Message: A Point of View," *Gender Differences: Their Ontogeny and Significance* (London: Churchill Livingstone, 1972), pp. 241–262.

8 The late Norman Geschwind... human brain,... Marilynn Mansfield, "YOU: What a Difference a Brain Makes," *Washington Post*, October 10, 1983, p. D5.

8 Brain weight... brain hemispheres. Sandra F. Witelson, "The Brain Connection: The Corpus Callosum Is Larger in Left-Handers," *Science*, August 16, 1985, pp. 665–68; Christine deLacoste, Ralph L. Holloway, "Sexual Dimorphism in Human Corpus Callosum," *Science*, June 25, 1982, pp. 215–216.

8 During fetal life... within the right." Wray Herbert, "Not of One Mind," The *Washington Post Magazine*, December 12, 1982, pp. 44–45.

9 This increased communication... both sides of the brain. Jo Durden-Smith, Diane de Simone, *Sex and the Brain* (New York: Arbor House, 1983), p. 78.

9 Pioneering work... with sex hormones. Ibid., pp. 146 and 154–55.

9 One neurotransmitter, serotonin, which inhibits aggressive and impulsive behavior... Herbert, op. cit.

9 Some researchers... suicidal and alcoholic individuals. Durden-Smith, diSimone, op. cit. p. 159.

9 More men than women... problem drinkers... D. W. Goodwin, "Genetic Components of Alcoholism," *Annual Review of Medicine*, 1981, vol. 32, pp. 93–99.

9 ... carry it to completion. Herbert, op. cit.

11 Winston Churchill... difficulty learning as a boy. Robert Lewis Taylor, *Winston Churchill, An Informal Study of Greatness* (Garden City, N.Y.: Doubleday & Company 1952), pp. 52–79.

11 Albert Einstein's headmaster... succeed at anything. Ronald W. Clark, *The Survival of Charles Darwin* (New York: Random House, 1984), p. 6.

11 Beatle John Lennon's school... at best. Vic Garbarini, Brian Cullman, with Barbara Graustark, *Strawberry Fields Forever: John Lennon Remembered* (New York: Bantam Books, 1980), pp. 42 and 133–34.

11 ...F. Scott Fitzgerald...was a poor student. Matthew J. Bruccoli, *Some Sort of Epic Grandeur: The Life of F. Scott Fitzgerald* (New York: Harcourt Brace Jovanovich, 1981), p. 28.

11 Darwin's father once told him...yourself and the family." Clark, op. cit.

11 Bertrand Russell once observed...abilities in several fields. Carl Sagan, *The Dragons of Eden* (New York: Random House, 1977), p. 202.

12 Fear of failure is cited...in the 15–24 age group. Bruce Alan Kehr, "Perspective: Teen Suicide," *Washington Post*, September 13, 1983, p. B5.

12 A Virginia physical education specialist...young men are fed up. Roon Frost's interview with Richard Stratton, associate professor of physical education, Virginia Polytechnic Institute and State University, November 1984.

2. Infants and Toddlers

15 Besides the obvious...organism." Josef F. Garai, Amram Scheinfeld, "Sex Differences in Mental and Behavioral Traits," *Genetic Psychology Monographs* (Provincetown, Mass.: Journal Press, 1968), pp. 183–88.

16 A boy's average weight gain...first birthday... Ronald M. Deutsch, *The Family Guide to Better Food and Better Health* (New York: Bantam Books, 1973), pp. 414–15.

16 Newborn...throughout life. K. B. Hoyenga, K. T. Hoyenga, "Theoretical Review, Gender and Energy Balance: Sex Differences in Adaptations for Feast and Famine," *Physiology and Behavior*, vol. 28, 1982, p. 553.

16 A male infant...stomach. Melvin Konner, "She and He," *Science 82*, vol. 3, no. 7, September 1982, p. 58.

16 In many unseen...boy. Garai, Scheinfeld, op. cit.

16 For a number...to calm. Diane McGuinness, "How Schools Discriminate Against Boys," *Human Nature*, February 1979, pp. 82–88.

16 One reason boys may be harder to calm...less acute. McGuinness, op. cit.

16 Your daughter is likely to be quieted...infant son may not be. Diane McGuinness, "Perception and Cognition," *Exploring Sex*

Differences, Barbara Lloyd, John Archer, editors (New York: Academic Press, 1976), p. 125.

16 It appears that the auditory system in girls ... is in boys. Richard H. Restak. *The Brain: The Last Frontier* (New York: Doubleday & Co., 1979), p. 198.

16 Newborn girls, hearing another infant cry ... longer than boys. Diane McGuinness, Karl H. Pribam, "The Origins of Sensory Bias in the Development of Gender Differences in Perception and Cognition," *Cognitive Growth and Development: Essays in Memory of Herbert G. Birch* (New York: Brunner/Mazel, Inc., 1978), p. 18.

16 Not only do girl babies ... more readily than males. McGuinness, *Human Nature*, op. cit.

17 The babies who seem to lose interest ... more often boys. Eleanor Emmons Maccoby, Carol Nagy Jacklin, *The Psychology of Sex Differences* (Stanford, Calif.: Stanford University Press, 1974), p. 27.

17 ... who until seven months of age lag behind girls in visual maturity ... Robert Cooke, "Baby Girls Found to Lead Boys in Brain Development," *Boston Sunday Globe*, August 12, 1984, p. 16.

17 From infancy on, boys tend to notice ... interest in the unusual. Eric Taylor, "Development of Attention," *Scientific Foundations of Developmental Psychiatry*, Michael Rutter, editor (London: Fakenham Press, Ltd., 1980), p. 192.

17 Because we humans are such overwhelmingly visual creatures ... Martha Bridge Denckla, M.D., National Institutes of Health, personal communication, May 1984.

17 Very young babies can follow a moving object ... like checkerboards. Bryant J. Cratty, *Perceptual and Motor Development in Infants and Children*, 2nd edition (Englewood Cliffs, N.J.: Prentice-Hall, 1979), p. 105.

17 Even before birth ... cause some babies to seem stressed. Thomas Verny, M.D., with John Kelly, a condensation of *The Secret Life of the Unborn Child*, in *Families*, February 1982, pp. 55–58.

18 We humans are programmed ... twenty-four months of life. Sandra Scarr, James Vander Zanden, *Introduction to Psychology* (New York: Random House, 1983), pp. 59–61; Scarr, *Race, Social Class*, p. 21 and p. 88.

18 There is very little evidence ... development. Hall, op. cit.

18 There is, in fact, substantial evidence...development not to take place. Robert B. McCall, "Nature-Nurture and the Two Realms cf Development: A Proposed Integration with Respect to Mental Development," *Child Development*, 52, 1981, pp. 1–12.

18 All babies...are blind;... Scarr, *Race, Social Class*, op. cit., p. 88.

18 ...babbling occurs on schedule even if a child is deaf. Paul H. Mussen, John J. Conger, Jerome Kagan, *Child Development and Personality*, 3rd edition (New York: Harper & Row, 1969), p. 186.

18 They have no idea...what he touches. David Elkind, *Child Development and Education* (New York: Oxford University Press, 1976), p. 84.

19 Underlying a baby boy's growing sensory-motor coordination ...brain growth. Sandra Scarr, *Mother Care/Other Care* (New York: Basic Books, 1984), pp. 149–51.

19 An infant's brain...girls do. Herman Epstein, "Growth Spurts During Brain Development: Implications for Educational Policy and Practice," *Education and the Brain*, Jeanne S. Chall, Allan F. Mirsky, editors (Chicago: University of Chicago Press, 1978), pp. 343–68.

19 From about six to fifteen months...which we call memory. Floyd E. Bloom, Arlyne Lazerson, Laura Hofstadter, *Brain, Mind and Behavior* (New York: W. H. Freeman and Co., 1985), p. 160.

19 For example, between sixteen and twenty-four months...they look in a mirror. Jerome Kagan, Ph.D., *Psychological Research on the Human Infant: An Evaluative Summary* (New York: William T. Grant Foundation, 1982), p. 17.

19 "The brain is acutely dependent...emotional performance." Herbert L. Meltzer, *The Chemistry of Human Behavior* (Chicago: Nelson-Hall, 1979), pp. 51–54.

19 Severe malnutrition...brain cells from growing properly. Meltzer, op. cit.

20 Overwhelming evidence...superiority of mother's milk over formula...Nutrition Commission of the Canadian Paediatric Society and the Commission on Nutrition of the American Academy of Pediatrics, "Breast Feeding," *Pediatrics*, vol. 62, no. 4, October 1978, pp. 591–601.

20 ...infant boys are prone to...and allergies. Durden-Smith, DiSimone, op. cit. pp. 172–74.

20 It can also reduce the body's defense...respond to others as positively. David E. Barrett, Marian Radke-Yarrow, Robert E. Klein, "Chronic Malnutrition and Child Behavior: Effects of Early Caloric Supplementation on Social and Emotional Functioning at School Age," *Developmental Psychology*, vol. 18, no. 4, July 1982, p. 540.

20 Certain youngsters . . . detrimental to bone growth. Anna Kanianthra, public health nutritionist for northern Virginia, personal communication, February 27, 1985.

21 Burton White . . . first six months. Authors' interview with Burton White, director, Center for Parent Education, Newton, Massachusetts, June 14, 1984.

21 Information for the paragraphs on temperament in this chapter came from the following sources:

Alexander Thomas, M.D., Stella Chess, M.D., Herbert G. Birch, Ph.D., *Temperament and Behavior Disorders in Children* (New York: New York University Press, 1968).

Alexander Thomas, Stella Chess, Sam J. Korn, "The Reality of Difficult Temperament," *Merrill-Palmer Quarterly*, vol. 28, no. 1, January 1982, pp. 1–24.

H. H. Goldsmith, "Genetic Influences on Personality from Infancy to Adulthood," *Child Development*, 54, 1983, pp. 331–55.

Eleanor E. Maccoby, John A. Martin, "Socialization in the Context of the Family: Parent-Child Interaction," *Handbook of Child Psychology*, Paul H. Mussen, editor (New York: John Wiley & Sons, 1983), vol. 4, pp. 62–63.

Sandy Rovner, "Healthtalk: Assessing Emotional Development," *Washington Post*, July 6, 1984, p. E5.

Cynthia Garcia Coll, Jerome Kagan, J. Steven Regnick, "Behavioral Inhibitions in Young Children," *Child Development*, 55, 1984, pp. 1005–19.

Stella Chess, M.D., Jane Whitbread, *Daughters* (New York: Doubleday and Company, Inc., 1978), pp. 11–26.

Thomas Lickona, *Raising Good Children, Helping Your Child Through the Stages of Moral Development* (New York: Bantam Books, 1983), p. 43.

23 However, as infants . . . move farther than girls. Maccoby, Jacklin, op. cit. pp. 173–75.

23 Besides moving more . . . than girls do. George F. Michel, "Sex Differences in Motor Skill: Looking Glass or Cheshire Cat?", *Sex*

Differences in Dyslexia, Alice Ansara, Norman Geschwind, Albert Galaburda, Marilyn Albert, Nannette Gartrell, editors (Towson, Md.: Orton Dyslexia Society, 1981), p. 33.

23 One such boy...grocery bag. Anne M. Brown, Adam P. Matheny, Jr., Ronald S. Wilson, "Twins: Did You Know...?", vol. 3, Louisville Twin Study, Child Development Unit, Department of Pediatrics, University of Louisville School of Medicine, 1977, p. 5.

26 Chipping and peeling...lead solder. Kenneth W. Holt, environmental health consultant, Centers for Disease Control, personal communication, September 9, 1985.

26 Just as boys are more active, they are also more curious... Jeanne H. Block, "Differential Premises Arising From Differential Socialization of the Sexes: Some Conjectures," *Child Development*, 54, December 1983, 1334–54.

26 From the beginning, boys seem as interested...wide variety of cultures. Jerre Levy, professor of behavioral sciences, Committee on Biopsychology, University of Chicago, presentation to the National Association of Independent Schools, Washington, D.C., March 1, 1985.

26 Strings and sticks...especially as tools. Mary Ann Spencer Pulaski, *Your Baby's Mind and How It Grows* (New York: Harper & Row, 1978), p. 89.

26 Even as babies, boys use their toys in "creative" ways. Dr. Corinne Hutt, in Ounsted and Taylor, op. cit. pp. 99–102.

27 Boys' curiosity shows up...to talk. Madorah E. Smith, "The Influence of Age, Sex, and Situation on the Frequency, Form, and Function of Questions Asked by Preschool Children," *Readings in Language Development* (New York: John Wiley & Sons, 1978), p. 291.

27 From infancy, boys are more interested...unusual or novel. Maccoby, Jacklin, op. cit. p. 144.

27 Information for the section on attachment in this chapter came from the following sources:

Jerome Kagan, Richard B. Kearsley, Phillip P. Zelazo, *Infancy: Its Place in Human Development* (Cambridge, Mass.: Harvard University Press, 1978), pp. 64–90, 113–17.

Joseph J. Campos, Karen Caplowitz Barrett, Michael E. Lamb, H. Hill Goldsmith, Craig Sternberg, "Socio-emotional Development," *Handbook of Child Psychology*, op. cit., vol. 2., p. 879.

Kagan, op. cit. pp. 130–33.

Megan R. Gunnar-vonGnechten, "Changing a Frightening Toy Into a Pleasant Toy by Allowing the Infant to Control Its Actions," *Contemporary Readings in Child Psychology*, op. cit. pp. 95–100.

Candice Feiring, Michael Lewis, "Sex and Age Differences in Young Children's Reactions to Frustration: A Further Look at the Goldberg and Lewis Subjects," *Child Development*, 50, 1979, pp. 848–53.

Cornelis F. M. Van Lieshout, "Young Children's Reactions to Barriers Placed by Their Mothers," *Child Development*, 46, 1975, pp. 879–86.

29 By two, girls placed behind a barrier...than girls. Feiring, Lewis, op. cit.

29 From infancy on...more words in phrases than little boys do. Frances Fuchs Schachter, Ellen Shore, Robert Hodapp, Susan Chalfin, Carole Bundy, "Do Girls Talk Earlier? Mean Length of Utterance in Toddlers," *Developmental Psychology*, vol. 14, no. 4, July 1978, pp. 388–92.

29 Infant girls rely on speech...seek information. McGuinness, op. cit.

29 It is clear that speech problems...boys than girls. James W. Hillis, professor of speech and hearing, George Washington University, personal communication, March 5, 1985.

29 From his first...three hundred words. Arnold Gesell, M.D., Frances Ilg, M.D., and Louise Bates Ames, Ph.D., in collaboration with Janet Learned Rodell, Ph.D., *Infant and Child in the Culture of Today, the Guidance of Development in Home and Nursery School*, revised edition (New York: Harper and Row, 1974), p. 193.

29 A vocabulary of at least fifty words...two-year-olds. Scarr, Vander Zanden, op. cit., p. 366.

30 This higher level of thought...beginning of conflict. Pulaski, op. cit., p. 109.

30 From a very early age...less compliant than a girl. Eleanor Maccoby, *Social Development*, op. cit. p. 221.

30 All children have bouts of anger...than girls do. Ibid., p. 120.

30 At two, boys and girls seem equal...more likely to use anger. VanLieshout, op. cit.

30 Girls learn to control their frustration...than boys do. Maccoby, *Social Development*, op. cit. p. 117.

31 Material used in the section on toddlers and discipline came from the following sources:

Diana Baumrind, "Authoritarian vs. Authoritative Parental Control," *Adolescence*, vol. 3, 1968, pp. 255–272.

Scarr, *Mother Care/Other Care*, op. cit., pp. 150–180.

Authors' interview with Burton White, op. cit.

Authors' interview with Thomas Lickona, author of *Raising Good Children* and professor of Education at the State University of New York, Cortland Campus, September 27, 1984.

Maccoby, Martin, op. cit.

Maccoby, *Social Development*, op. cit.

34 Mothers who use a policy... "Don't do that!" Maccoby and Martin, op. cit., pp. 51–52.

34 As simple a technique as introducing positive words... negative behavior. Maccoby, *Social Development*, op. cit. p. 152.

34 Thomas Lickona... inappropriate. Lickona, *Raising Good Children*, op. cit., pp. 60–61.

34 Orderly household environments... midst of order. Robert H. Bradley, Bettye M. Caldwell, "The Relation of Home Environment, Cognitive Competence and IQ among Males and Females," *Child Development*, 51, 1980, pp. 1140–48.

35 Many child-rearing experts... more easily than boys. T. Berry Brazelton, *To Listen to a Child, Understanding the Normal Problems of Growing Up* (Reading, Mass.: Addison-Wesley Publishing Company, 1984), p. 158–162.

35 By school age, those children... mostly male. Authors' interview with Benjamin Spock, M.D., author of *Baby and Child Care*, October 30, 1984.

35 There are many reasons... twice as many children are bedwetters. Brazleton, op. cit., pp. 160–62.

37 A little boy plays more vigorously... play of boys in pairs or small groups. Maccoby, *Social Development*, op. cit., pp. 24–25.

37 By his second birthday... show a measure of self-control. Clair B. Kopp, "Antecedents of Self-Regulation: A Developmental Perspective," *Developmental Psychology*, vol. 18, no. 2, 1982, pp. 199–213.

3. Learning to Be a Boy

38 Young children...their own sex...Althea C. Huston, "Sex Typing," *Handbook of Child Psychology*, op. cit., vol. 4, pp. 397–98.

38 Beginning around three...barriers. Willard W. Hartup, "Peer Relations," *Handbook of Child Psychology*, op. cit. vol. 4, p. 109.

38 The years between two...for humans... Maccoby, *Social Development*, op. cit. p. 167.

38 ...boys' metabolism...of girls. Anna S. Espenschade, Helen M. Eckert, *Motor Development* (Columbus, Ohio: Charles E. Merrill Books, 1967), pp. 203–204.

39 Boys may be less advanced...preschool. Michel, op. cit.

39 Gender *identity*...seven years old. Huston, op. cit. p. 397.

39 As a child learns...way they behave. Michael Rutter, "Psychosexual Development," *Scientific Foundations*, op. cit. p. 322.

40 ...if he has an imaginary playmate...boy. Martin Manosevitz, Norman M. Prentice, Frances Wilson, "Individual and Family Correlates of Imaginary Companions in Preschool Children," *Developmental Psychology* vol. 8, no. 1, 1973, p. 76.

40 Even if he has "liberated"...his gender is permanent. Lawrence Kohlberg, Dorothy Zelnicker Ullian, "Stages in the Development of Psychosexual Concepts and Attitudes," *Sex Differences in Behavior*, Richard C. Friedman, M.D., Ralph M. Richart, M.D., Raymond vande Wiele, M.D., editors (Huntington, N.Y.: Robert E. Krieger Publishing Company, 1978) pp. 212–13.

40 They hear their mothers...strength means power. Authors' interview with Jerome Kagan, May 22, 1984.

40 As they mature...masculine traits. Leonard D. Eron, "Prescription for the Reduction of Aggression," *American Psychologist*, vol. 35, 1980, p. 249.

41 While a father tends...with a daughter. Block, op. cit.

41 Dad plays rougher...more severely... Maccoby, Jacklin, "Psychological Sex Differences," *Scientific Foundations*, op. cit. p. 98.

41 They would rather...achievement. Block, op. cit.

42 When preschoolers play house...proper behavior. Evelyn Goodenough Pitcher, Lynn Hickey Schultz, *Boys and Girls at Play: The Development of Sex Roles* (New York: Praeger Publishers, 1983), pp. 71–72.

43 ... *little boys define* ... *males are not* ... Miriam M. Johnson, "Fathers, Mothers, and Sex Typing." *Contemporary Readings in Child Psychology*, op. cit. pp. 391–403.

43 In one of the few ... especially their sons. Michael E. Lamb, "Father and Child Development: An Integrative Overview," *The Role of the Father in Child Development*, second edition (New York: John H. Wiley, 1981), p. 4 and pp. 16–17.

43 Even if most fathers ... generosity in their sons. Ibid., pp. 20–25.

43 A mother who enlists ... active participation in child care. Frank A. Pedersen, "Father Influences Viewed in a Family Context," *The Role of the Father in Child Development*, op. cit. p. 309.

44 When a father is available ... she is on her own. Hugh Lytton, "Disciplinary Encounters Between Young Boys and Their Mothers and Fathers: Is There a Contingency System?" *Developmental Psychology*, vol. 15, no. 3, 1979, p. 262.

44 However, studies ... active fathering. Graeme Russell, "Highly Participant Australian Fathers: Some Preliminary Findings," *Merrill-Palmer Quarterly*, vol. 28, no. 1, January 1982, pp. 137–56; Norma Radin, Abraham Sagi, "Childrearing Fathers in Intact Families, II: Israel and the USA," *Merrill-Palmer Quarterly*, vol. 28, no. 1, January 1982, pp. 111–36.

44 Boys in these families ... traditional families ... Ibid., and Norma Radin, "Childrearing Fathers in Intact Families, I: Some Antecedents and Consequences," *Merrill-Palmer Quarterly*, vol. 27, no. 4, October 1981, pp. 489–514.

44 ... no problems ... opposite sex ... Roon Frost's interview with Kyle Pruett, M.D., October 16, 1984.

44 One such father ... turn out just fine." Kyle D. Pruett, M.D., "Two-Year Follow-up of Infants of Primary Nurturing Fathers in Intact Families," paper presented to the Second World Conference of Infant Psychiatry, April 1983, p. 12.

44 Yale University researcher ... offspring's curiosity. Anita Shreve, "The Working Mother as Role Model," *New York Times Magazine*, September 9, 1984, pp. 50–52.

44 ... these mothers ... to be nurturant ... Lois W. Hoffman, address to American Psychiatric Association, August 1983.

45 In 1980 ... headed by women. Claire Etaugh, "Infant Day Care: Effects and Issues," testimony before U.S. House Select Committee on Children, Youth, and Families, September 1984, p. 1.

45 Fortunately, most boys...house. Rutter, "Psychosexual Development," op. cit. p. 332.

45 But single mothers...assertiveness in their sons. Huston, op. cit. p. 434.

45 In one long-term study...both parents. Sheppard G. Kellam, Rebecca G. Adams, C. Hendricks Brown, Margaret E. Ensminger, "The Long-Term Evolution of the Family Structure of Teenage and Other Mothers," *Journal of Marriage and the Family*, August 1982, p. 548.

46 One of the clearest differences...combativeness. Janet Anne DiPetro, "Rough and Tumble Play: A Function of Gender," *Developmental Psychology*, vol. 17, no. 1, January 1981, pp. 50–58.

46 Cross-cultural and animal studies...emotional upset. Maccoby, Jacklin, op. cit. pp. 242–43.

46 Although the findings are clearer...adult males. Ross D. Parke, Ronald G. Slaby, "The Development of Aggression," *Handbook of Child Psychology*, op. cit. vol. 4, p. 561.

46 In experiments with monkeys...McGuire says. Roon Frost's interview with Michael T. McGuire, M.D., Neuropsychiatric Institute, UCLA, March 1, 1985; Michael T. McGuire, M.D., "Summary UCLA Fraternity Data Relating Whole Blood Serotonin and Social Status: A Preliminary Study," January 20, 1984.

47 It may serve...other children. Maccoby, Jacklin, op. cit. p. 257.

47 Knowing which boy...rankings in boys' groups... Maccoby, op. cit. p. 137.

47 ...usually at the end of the preschool period. Donald R. Omark, Monica Omark, Murray Edelman, "Formation of Dominance Hierarchies in Young Children," *Psychological Anthropology*, Thomas R. Williams, editor, (The Hague: Mouton Publishers, 1975), p. 303.

47 As young children...hierarchial. Zick Rubin, *Children's Friendships* (Cambridge, Mass.: Harvard University Press, 1980), pp. 106–109.

47 As early as two...boys who are friends. Pitcher, Schultz, op. cit. pp. 64–69.

47 Although boys...many young boys. Ibid., pp. 40–52.

48 Strict banning...aggressive play. C. W. Turner, D. Goldsmith, "Effects of Toys, Guns and Airplanes on Children's Antisocial Free

Play Behavior," *Journal of Experimental Child Psychology*, vol. 21, 1976, pp. 303–11.

48 After the age of two...as frequently as girls do. Rutter, "Emotional Development," *Scientific Foundations*, op. cit. p. 312.

49 Boys, more than girls...aggressive behavior. Leonard D. Eron, L. Rowell Huesmann, "The Control of Aggressive Behavior by Changes in Attitudes, Values, and the Conditions of Learning," *Advances in the Study of Aggression*, vol. 1 (New York: Academic Press, in press), pp. 138–67.

49 Boys are more sexually active...early in life. Michael Rutter, "Normal Psychosexual Behavior," paper presented to the British Psychological Society meeting, November 6, 1970.

49 An Israeli study...in reproduction. Ibid.

50 Half of all young children...sex play... Ibid.

50 Preschoolers still associate...until adolescence. Ibid.

50 However, a few incidences...homosexual. Rutter, "Psychosexual Development," op. cit. p. 326.

51 Another mother...privacy. Marguerite Kelly, "Children and Curiosity," *Washington Post*, October 18, 1984, p. D5.

52 Regardless of sex...effective and expressive. Janet T. Spence, Robert L. Helmreich, *Masculinity & Femininity: Their Psychological Dimensions, Correlates, and Antecedents* (Austin, Tex.: University of Texas Press, 1978), pp. 4–7 and p. 23.

52 Gender deviance...girls. Houston, op. cit., p. 445.

52 Little boys...rejected by others. Ibid., p. 442.

52 Many feminine boys...mature. Ibid., p. 447; Bernard Zuger, M.D., "Effeminate Behavior Present in Boys from Early Childhood," *Journal of Pediatrics*, vol. 69, no. 6, December 1966, pp. 1098–1107.

52 Some males...homosexual. Rutter, "Emotional Development," *Scientific Foundations*, p. 331.

52 Berlin endocrinologist...pattern of development. Ibid.; Günter Dörner, M.D., Wolfgang Rohde, M.D., Fritz Stahl, Ph.D., Lothar Krell, M.D., Wolf-Günther Masius, M.D., "A Neuroendocrine Predisposition for Homosexuality in Men," *Archives of Sexual Behavior*, vol. 4, no. 1, 1975, pp. 1–9; Durden-Smith, diSimone, *Sex and the Brain*, op. cit. pp. 100–101.

53 Homosexuals...their fathers. Huston, op. cit. p. 446.

53 Male homosexuals...heterosexual males. Ibid., p. 447; Spence, Helmreich, op. cit. pp. 66–67.

53 For some men...run in the family. Marilyn Mansfield, "FOCUS: Gays, Parents and Their Search for Answers, Research Highlights," *Washington Post*, March 26, 1984, p. C5.

53 ...many parents respond...aggressively than other children. Maccoby, Martin, op. cit. pp. 42–44.

54 Other boys...rough... Ibid., p. 40.

54 Regardless of their sex...compliant and passive. Maccoby, op. cit. p. 243.

54 Shy boys...young children. Ibid., p. 198.

54 Regardless of the high...academic achievement. Maccoby, Martin, op. cit. p. 41.

54 While *permissive parents*...act impulsively. Ibid., p. 44.

54 For preschool boys...very important. Maccoby, op cit. pp. 377–78.

54 Consistently ignoring...physical punishment. Dan Olweus, "Familial and Temperamental Determinants of Aggressive Behavior in Adolescent Boys: A Causal Analysis," *Developmental Psychology*, vol. 16, no. 6, November 1980, pp. 644–59.

54 *Firm parents*...and independence. Maccoby, op cit.; Diana Baumrind, op. cit. pp. 255–72.

54 For boys especially...motivation to achieve. Spence, Helmreich, p. 142.

55 Children reared firmly...long haul. Baumrind, op. cit.

55 Unselfish, nonaggressive schoolboys...young children. Marian Radke-Yarrow, Carolyn Zahn-Waxler, Michael Chapman, "Children's Prosocial Dispositions and Behavior," *Handbook of Child Psychology*, op. cit. vol. 4, p. 608.

56 Respecting your son's...self-worth. Maccoby, op. cit. pp. 407–409.

56 Encouraging problem-solving...control his impulses. Myrna B. Shure, George Spivack, *Problem-Solving Techniques in Child-Rearing* (San Francisco: Jossey-Bass, Inc., 1978), pp. 7–35.

56 Giving a boy...his cooperation. Maccoby, op. cit.

56 Parents who make suggestions...important. Maccoby, Martin, op. cit. p. 51.

57 One psychologist...adult males. Dorothy Z. Ullian, "Why Boys Will Be Boys: A Structural Perspective," *American Journal of Orthopsychiatry*, vol. 51, no. 3, July 1981, pp. 493–501.

57 "Active listening" techniques...clung to his anger. Thomas Gordon, *P.E.T., Parent Effectiveness Training: The Tested New Way to Raise Responsible Children* (New York: Peter H. Wyden, 1972), p. 31.

59 Teaching a child to think...appropriate to his age. Shure and Spivack, op. cit.

60 Little boys...other children. Pitcher, Schultz, op. cit. p. 64.

60 In boys, competition...competitive ones. Mark A. Barnett, Laura M. King, Jeffrey A. Howard, "Relationship Between Competitiveness and Empathy in Six and Seven Year Olds," *Developmental Psychology*, vol. 15, no. 2, 1979, pp. 221–22.

60 In one interesting experiment...attributes. Roger E. Jensen, Shirley G. Moore, "The Effects of Attribute Statements on Cooperation and Competitiveness in School-Age Boys, *Child Development*, 48, 1977, pp. 305–307.

61 One nutritionist...often enough. Anna Kanianthra, op. cit.

69 Young brothers and sisters...their parents. Judy Dunn, "Sibling Relationships in Early Childhood," *Child Development*, 54, 1983, pp. 787–811.

69 Overall, boys seem...brothers or sisters. Ann M. Minnett, Deborah Lowe Vandell, John W. Santrock, "The Effects of Sibling Status on Sibling Interaction: Influence of Birth Order, Age Spacing, Sex of Child, and Sex of Sibling," *Child Development*, 54, 1983, pp. 1064–72.

69 Boy siblings...hit one another. Parke, Slaby, op. cit. pp. 578–79.

69 Younger siblings...tendency is strong. Dunn, op. cit.

70 One researcher..."motherese"... Ibid.

70 In most families, the arrival...time for them. Judy Dunn, Carol Kendrick, "The Arrival of a Sibling: Changes in Patterns of Interaction Between Mother and First-Born Child," *Journal of Child Psychology and Psychiatry*, vol. 21, 1980, pp. 119–132.

71 ...this speech dysfunction...genetic components in some cases. Bruce F. Pennington, Shelley D. Smith, "Genetic Influences on Learning Disabilities and Speech and Language Disorders," *Child Development*, 54, 1983, pp. 369–387.

71 One expert states...tension cannot yet be altogether discounted as a factor. Hillis, op. cit.

71 An excellent suggestion...*talking* things." Dr. Benjamin Spock, *Baby and Child Care* (New York: Pocket Books, Simon & Schuster, 1977), p. 395.

71 Two developmental experts caution...speech production. Gesell et al., op. cit.

71 In the preschool years...sound social relationships. Louise Bates Ames, Ph.D., Joan Ames Chase, Ph.D., *Don't Push Your Preschooler* (New York: Harper & Row, 1980), pp. 7–10.

72 There is even...each tongue represented. Lewis Thomas, *Late Night Thoughts on Listening to Mahler's Ninth Symphony* (New York: Viking Press, 1983), pp. 49–53.

72 A little boy may be popular...less important. Willard W. Hartup, "Peer Interaction and Social Organization," *Carmichael's Manual of Child Psychology*, 3d edition (New York: John Wiley, 1970), vol. 2, p. 394; Hartup, op. cit. pp. 128–29; Pitcher, Schultz, op. cit. pp. 74–80.

72 Obesity...any child. Steven R. Asher, Sherri L. Oden, John M. Gottman, "Children's Friendships in School Settings," *Contemporary Readings in Child Psychology*, op. cit. pp. 277–94.

72 Young boys...early exposure to other children. Rubin, op. cit. pp. 20–22.

72 ...introducing any young child...cooperative play. Ibid., pp. 22–27.

73 Playing on a one-to-one basis...group play. Wyndol Furman, Donald F. Rahe, Willard W. Hartup, "Rehabilitation of Socially Withdrawn Preschool Children through Mixed-Aged and Same-Age Socialization," *Child Development*, 50, 1979, pp. 915–22.

73 Similarly, an aggressive boy...nurture a young friend. Rubin, op. cit. p. 58.

74 A child's responsiveness...is voluntary. Maccoby, Martin, op. cit. p. 85.

74 ...preschool boys spend...building play. Frank A. Pedersen, Richard Q. Bell, "Sex Differences in Preschool Children Without Complications of Pregnancy and Delivery," *Developmental Psychology*, vol. 3, no. 1, 1970, pp. 13–14.

74 Not only are boys...novel ways...Hut, op. cit. p. 99.

74 For boys, the characteristics...creativity. David L. Singer,

Judith Rummo, "Ideational Creativity and Behavioral Style in Kindergarten-Age Children," *Developmental Psychology*, vol. 8, no. 2, 1973, pp. 154–61.

74 . . . play serves serious functions. Catherine Garvey, *Play, The Developing Child Series*, Jerome Bruner, Michael Cole, Barbara Lloyd, editors (Cambridge, Mass.: Harvard University Press, 1977), pp. 4–5.

74 Good relationships . . . encourage play . . . D. B. Rosenblatt, "Play," *Scientific Foundations*, op. cit. p. 296.

74 A young child's attention span . . . what they are doing. Willard W. Hartup, "Peer Relations and Family Relations; Two Social Worlds," *Scientific Foundations*, op. cit. p. 302.

75 In general, boys are more likely . . . nursey school . . . Rutter, "Emotional Development," *Scientific Foundations*, p. 312.

75 . . . and they tend to cry . . . if they are injured or hurt. Maccoby, Jacklin, op. cit. p. 179.

75 Florida researcher . . . hyperactive. Diane McGuinness, "Sex Related Syndromes," *Proceedings of the National Conference of the Montessori Society*, Anaheim, California, June 1981, p. 5.

75 As a rule, boys . . . building together, right? Pitcher, Schultz, op. cit. pp. 64–69.

76 Observers . . . three times as often. McGuinness, op. cit. p. 6.

76 Humor . . . jokes. Pitcher, Schultz, op. cit. p. 69.

76 Boys also differ . . . pictures drawn by girls. McGuinness, "Sensory-Motor Biases in Cognitive Development," op. cit. pp. 15–16 in manuscript.

76 A few girls . . . symbolic. Pitcher, Schultz, op. cit. p. 39.

76 Observations of children . . . threaten them. Ibid., pp. 39–42.

77 One long-term assessment . . . evaluated. Louise B. Miller, Rondeall P. Bizzell, "Long-term Effects of Four Preschool Programs: Ninth- and Tenth-Grade Results," *Child Development*, 55, 1984, pp. 1570–87.

77 . . . intellectual gains . . . diminish over time. K. Alison Clarke-Stewart, Greta G. Fein, "Early Childhood Programs," *Handbook of Child Psychology*, op. cit. vol. 2, p. 967.

77 The opportunity for fantasy play . . . in quantity. Greta G. Fein, "Pretend Play: New Perspectives," *Contemporary Readings in Child Psychology*, op. cit. pp. 308–12.

77 ...less likely than their peers...delinquent behavior in adolescence. Clarke-Stewart, Fein, op cit. p. 968.

79 Reading...intellectual competence rewarding... Authors' interview with Jerome Kagan.

80 Approximately half...employed... Sandra Scarr, *Mother Care/Other Care*, op. cit. pp. 35–36; Bradley Hitchings, "Today's Choice in Child Care," *Business Week*, April 1, 1985, pp. 104–108.

80 ...two million preschoolers...each day. Etaugh, op. cit. p. 1.

80 Sons of mothers...mothers' working... Lois Wladis Hoffman, "Maternal Employment: 1979," *American Psychologist*, vol. 34, no. 1, October 1979, pp. 859–65.

80 ...boys from intact middle-class homes...did not work. Dolores Gold, David Andres, "Developmental Comparisons Between Ten-Year-Old Children with Employed and Nonemployed Mothers," *Child Development*, 49, 1978, pp. 75–84.

80 A separate study...inhibited as adolescents. Hoffman, op. cit.

81 Daughters...educational backgrounds. Authors' interview with Sandra Scarr; Lois Wladis Hoffman, "Effects of Maternal Employment on the Child: A Review of the Research," *Developmental Psychology*, vol. 10, no. 2, 1974, pp. 204–28.

81 From the standpoint of physical health...childhood. Mary Battiata, "Centers Increase Risk of Childhood Disease." *Washington Post*, July 6, 1983.

81 Males have lower...childhood infections. Durden-Smith, di-Simone, op. cit. p. 139.

81 "Glue ear"...inattentive. Ralph Naughton, M.D., National Institutes of Health, personal communication, 1984.

81 Among the most unhappy women...working... Scarr, *Mother Care/Other Care*, op. cit. p. 139.

81 Family discord...problems in boys...Maccoby, *Social Development*, op. cit. p. 222.

82 More recent...most young children. Clarke-Stewart, Fein, op. cit. p. 980.

82 One psychologist...along with other children. Authors' interview with Sandra Scarr.

82 Difficult children...are young. Clarke-Stewart, Fein, op. cit. p. 969.

83 Older preschoolers...part of each day. Ibid., p. 980.

83 Even difficult boys... they enter. Ibid., p. 969.

83 Boys who play... complex ways... Ibid., p. 972.

83 ...their greater social interaction... day-care centers. Ibid., pp. 956–58.

83 If children in centers... trained teachers. Ibid., p. 974.

84 High-quality centers... best care possible. Scarr, *Mother Care/Other Care*, op. cit. p. 237.

4. When Is a Boy Ready to Start School?

86 Generally, children who are older... classes. Three such studies are those by Inez B. King, "Effect of Age of Entrance Into Grade 1 Upon Achievement in Elementary School," *Elementary School Journal*, February 1955; Rosalyn Rubin, "Sex Differences in Effects of Kindergarten Attendance on Development of School Readiness and Language Skills," *Elementary School Journal*, February 1972; Philip Langer, John Michael Kalk, Donald T. Searls, "Age of Admission and Trends in Achievement: A comparison of Blacks and Caucasians," *American Educational Research Journal*, vol. 21, no. 1, Spring 1984, pp. 61–78.

86 Even children regarded as gifted... school. Ann Obrzut, R. Brett Nelson, John E. Obrzut, "Early School Entrance for Intellectually Superior Children: An Analysis," *Psychology in the Schools*, vol. 21, January 1984, pp. 71–77.

87 A long-term study... mature enough for the demands of first-grade tasks. Sheppard Kellam, M.D., C. Hendricks Brown, *Social Adaptational and Psychological Antecedents in First Grade of Adolescent Psychopathology Ten Years Later*, paper presented at the Research Workshop on Preventive Aspects of Suicide and Affective Disorders Among Adolescents and Young Adults, Harvard School of Public Health and Harvard School of Medicine, December 3–4, 1982. Quotations are from p. 18.

87 A second finding... abusers of all. Margaret E. Ensminger, C. Hendricks Brown, Sheppard G. Kellam, "Sex Differences in Antecedents of Substance Use Among Adolescents," *Journal of Social Issues*, vol. 38, no. 2, 1982, pp. 25–42.

87 Kellam also points out... closely is essential. Carol Krucoff, "Education: Grading the System," *Washington Post*, November 17, 1982, p. B5.

88 The Gesell Institute... many school systems. Louise Bates Ames, Ph.D., *Is Your Child in the Wrong Grade?* (Lumberville, Pa.: Modern Learning Press, 1978), pp. 3–14.

88 . . . a 1983 survey . . . likely to fail a grade. Sammie M. Campbell, *Kindergarten Entry Age as a Factor in Academic Failure*, unpublished dissertation, School of Education, The University of Virginia, Charlottesville, Virginia, May 1984. Dr. Campbell's thesis was the basis for an invited paper that she presented to the American Association of School Administrators in March 1985. The Association presented her with its Outstanding Research Project Award.

90 A little boy's performance in school . . . pattern of timing. Scarr, *Race, Social Class*, op. cit. pp. 377–91; Jeannette Jansky, Katrina de Hirsch, *Preventing Reading Failure: Prediction, Diagnosis, Intervention* (New York: Harper & Row, 1972), pp. 1–2.

90 Even before your little boy was born . . . mathematical ability. Wray Herbert, op. cit. pp. 44–45, 51.

90 Even at very young ages . . . objects mentally. Diane McGuiness, *When Children Don't Learn* (New York: Basic Books, Inc., 1985), pp. 148–151.

90 Most girls speak . . . sentences than boys do. . . . Schacter et al., op. cit.

90 . . . performing much better in beginning reading. Mussen, Conger, Kagen, op. cit. p. 619; Verna Dieckman Anderson, *Reading and Young Children* (New York: Macmillan, 1968), p. 303; Emerald V. Dechant, Henry P. Smith, *Psychology in Teaching Reading*, 2nd edition (Englewood Cliffs, N.J.: Prentice Hall, 1977), pp. 97–100.

90 Neurologist Richard Restak . . . implied ideas. Restak, op. cit. p. 199.

91 "For school-related functions . . . life beyond school." Martha Denckla, M.D., "Minimal Brain Dysfunction," *Education and the Brain*, op. cit. pp. 251–52.

91 Even moderate distractions . . . no problem for seven-year olds. Sheldon H. White, Ph.D., "Some General Outlines of the Matrix of Developmental Changes Between Five and Seven Years," *Bulletin of the Orton Society*, vol. 20, 1970, p. 49.

91 Experimenters who were testing memory ability . . . as fourteen-year-olds. Harold W. Stevenson, "Learning," *Scientific Foundations*, p. 114.

92 It is characteristic of children . . . not unusual in five-year olds. Ann L. Brown, John D. Bransford, Roberta A. Ferrara, Joseph C. Campione, "Learning, Remembering and Understanding," *Handbook of Child Psychology*, op. cit. vol. 3, p. 92.

92 Psychologists have discovered that the speed...same perceptual conclusion. Mussen, Conger, Kagan, op. cit. p. 294.

93 Material on kindergarten readiness is drawn from personal experience in the classroom and the following sources:

Jeannette Jansky, *The Marginally Ready Child*, Orton Society Reprint, vol. 25, 1975.

Frances L. Ilg, M.D., Louise Bates Ames, Ph.D., et al., *School Readiness* (New York: Harper & Row, 1978), pp. 6–19, 29–74.

Jeanette Jansky, de Hirsch, op. cit. pp. 1–38.

Louise Bates Ames, Frances L. Ilg, *Your Five-Year-Old* (New York: Delacorte Press, 1979), pp. 57–67.

Your Child Starts to School, Department of Education, Commonwealth of Virginia, 1981.

94 Developmental tests...correspond to his chronological age. Ames, *Is Your Child in the Wrong Grade?*, op. cit. pp. 70–71.

96 NIH neurologist Martha Denckla...at risk in elementary school." Denckla, "Minimal Brain Dysfunction," op. cit. p. 252.

96 Many kindergarten teachers...child will do well in school. Katrina de Hirsch, Jeannette Jefferson Jansky, William S. Langford, *Predicting Reading Failure* (New York: Harper & Row, 1966), p. 3.

96 Full-time monthly charges...amount to $240. Kindercare, Leesburg, Virginia, April 1985.

97 A child who is ready for first grade...its proper conclusion. In part from George D. Spache, Evelyn B. Spache, *Reading in the Elementary School* (Boston: Allyn & Bacon, 1973), pp. 48–89; Emerald V. Dechant, *Improving the Teaching of Reading* (Englewood Cliffs, N.J.: Prentice-Hall, 1970), pp. 137–201; and from personal experience.

98 First graders display a number of tensional outlets...tasks at hand. White, op cit.; Louise Bates Ames, France L. Ilg, *Your Six-Year-Old* (New York: Delacorte Press, 1979), pp. 29–31.

98 The mature first-grade boy...should have repeated. Ames, *Is Your Child in the Wrong Grade?*, op. cit. p. 55.

102 A small percentage of children...begin on the first day of school. Dan Olweus, *Aggression in the Schools* (Washington, D.C.: Hemisphere Publishing Co., 1978), pp. 15–144.

103 A Scottish study found...reject peers in these terms." Paquita McMichael, "Reading Difficulties, Behavior, and Social Status," *Journal of Educational Psychology*, vol. 74, no. 1, 1980, pp. 76–86.

104 In a study at Canada's McGill University... self-defeating outlook." Eigil Pedersen, Therese Annette Faucher, William W. Eaton, "A New Perspective on the Effects of First-Grade Teachers on Children's Subsequent Adult Status," *Harvard Educational Review*, vol. 48, no. 1, February 1978, pp. 1–31.

104 Unfortunately, the opposite... teachers regarded as more competent. Jansky, de Hirsch, op. cit. p. 83.

105 Harvard psychologist Robert Rosenthal... think your child can learn." Authors' interview with Robert Rosenthal, professor, Department of Psychology and Behavioral Sciences, Harvard University, May 22, 1984.

105 Teachers who rely on benign methods of discipline... fewer behavior problems. William W. Wayson, Thomas J. Lasley, "Climates for Excellence: Schools That Foster Self-Discipline," *Phi Delta Kappan*, February 1984, pp. 419–21.

110 "A little boy who is larger than average... one principal says. Elizabeth Decker, principal, Guilford School, Sterling, Virginia, personal communication, March 1985.

111 "Just that half year would make... beyond kindergarten level." Ames, *Is Your Child in the Wrong Grade?* op. cit. p. 143.

111 "You have to realize... difference in age." Authors' interview with Sheppard Kellam, M.D., February 22, 1984.

112 One Virginia principal... transmitted to the children. Sheila Moore, "Education: Making the Grade," *Washington Post*, April 17, 1984, p. D5.

112 "The sense of relief... one specialist says. Ibid.

112 Researchers find... early grades." John Lindelow, "Synthesis of Research on Grade Retention and Social Promotion," *Educational Leadership*, vol. 39, no. 6, March, 1982, pp. 471–73.

112 Gesell's Louise Bates Ames believes... year after year. Authors' interview with Louise Bates Ames, associate director, Gesell Institute, August 5, 1983.

113 One educator proposes... learning-disability resource teachers if necessary. Harry N. Chandler, M. Ed., "Retention: Edspeak for Flunk," *Journal of Learning Disabilities*, vol. 17, no. 1, January 1984.

113 Some researchers emphasize... in school where his needs can be adequately addressed. Authors' interviews with Nathlie A.

Badian, consulting teacher, Holbrook Public Schools, Holbrook, Massachusetts, November 29, 1984, and Jeannette Jansky, op. cit.

5. The Primary School Years

116 Boys are apt to receive almost . . . hear more about the work itself. Carol S. Dweck, Ellen S. Bush, "Sex Differences in Learned Helplessness: 1. Differential Debilitation with Peer and Adult Evaluators," *Developmental Psychology*, vol. 12, no. 2, pp. 147–56.

117 "The male brain . . . rapid muscular responses." Restak, op. cit. p. 205.

117 What a child learns in school . . . education specialist Benjamin Bloom. Benjamin S. Bloom, *Human Characteristics and School Learning* (New York: McGraw-Hill Book Company, 1982), pp. 142–43.

117 The relative size . . . will be very different depending on his environment. Authors' interview with Jerome Kagan.

119 Boys are more active than girls. Block, op. cit.

119 Boys are more exploratory than girls. McGuinness, "How Schools Discriminate Against Boys," op. cit.

119 Boys are more competitive than girls. Block, op. cit.

119 They are also more peer-oriented . . . to gain the approval of their friends. Dweck, Bush, op. cit.

119 Young elementary-school pupils of both sexes believe in stereotypes. Mussen, Conger, Kagan, op. cit. pp. 503–505; Maccoby, *Social Development*, op. cit. pp. 233–40.

119 Boys need to feel in control of what happens to them. Block, op. cit., Sheila Moore's interview with Jeannette Jansky, op. cit.

120 In general, boys have a positive outlook . . . those of their teachers. Carol S. Dweck, Elaine S. Elliott, "Achievement Motivation," *Handbook of Child Psychology*, vol. 4, op. cit. pp. 674–77.

120 A child's image of himself in school becomes less positive. William W. Purkey, *Self Concept and School Achievement* (Englewood Cliffs, N.J.: Prentice-Hall, 1970), p. 42.

121 Boys are reprimanded . . . more than girls, too. Patricia P. Minuchin, Edna K. Shapiro, "The School as a Context for Social Development," *Handbook of Child Psychology*, op. cit. vol. 4, pp. 228–29.

121 Harvard's Carol Dweck found . . . try harder. Dweck, Bush, op. cit., Minuchin, Shapiro, op. cit. p. 229.

122 Teachers have different expectations...white and middle class. Minuchin, Shapiro, op. cit. pp. 228–30.

122 An exceptional teacher...we look at the history of man. Alan Moorehead, *Darwin and the Beagle* (New York: Harper & Row, 1969), pp. 26–30.

123 Columbia University reading expert...the time he gets to school. Sheila Moore's interview with Jeannette Jansky.

124 Approximately one child in a hundred...early ability. Elkind, op. cit. p. 82.

124 Parents of early readers...over-correct them. Bernard Spodek, editor, *Handbook of Research in Early Childhood Education* (New York: Free Press, 1982), pp. 249–250.

126 A child needs to learn...learning process. Arthur W. Heilman, *Principles and Practices of Teaching Reading*, third edition (Columbus, Ohio: Charles E. Merrill Publishing Company, 1972), pp. 222–23.

127 One of the more perplexing problems...referred for special help. Jeane W. Anastas, Helen Reinherz, "Gender Differences in Learning and Adjustment Problems in School," *American Journal of Orthopsychiatry*, vol. 1, no. 54, January 1984, pp. 110–21.

127 A possible reason...less relevant to their progress in reading. Scarr's work cited in McGuinness, *Sensory Motor Biases*, op. cit. p. 34 of draft.

127 A factor as seemingly inconsequential...two to four children. Victor G. Cicirelli, "Sibling Constellation, Creativity, I.Q., and Academic Achievement," *Child Development*, 38, June 1967, pp. 481–90.

127 Emotional problems...frequently have more trouble in school. Elizabeth Decker, personal communication, op. cit.; Minuchin, Shapiro, op. cit. pp. 248–49.

127 How appealing a boy finds...little relevance to their lives. McGuinness, *Sensory Motor Biases*, op. cit. p. 31 of draft.

128 Immaturity, which makes learning...reading performance for boys. Dechant, Smith, op. cit. p. 98.

128 One expert notes that the differences in reading progress... measured by grades. Heilman, op. cit. p. 81.

128 For children of either sex...aspects of school performance. In part from Jansky, de Hirsch, op. cit. pp. 1–38.

129 Educator Thomas Lickona...appealing story. Lickona, op. cit. pp. 344–46.

129 Sex differences in mathematical ability are not found until the end of the elementary-school years. Lynn H. Fox, "Sex Differences: Implications for Program Planning for the Academically Gifted," *The Gifted and the Creative: A Fifty Year Perspective*, Julian C. Stanley, William C. George, Cecelia H. Solano, editors (Baltimore: Johns Hopkins University Press, 1977), p. 116.

129 One interesting difference... in pursuit of mathematical interests. Lynn H. Fox, Sanford J. Cohn, "Sex Difference in the Development of Precocious Mathematical Talent," *Women and the Mathematical Mystique* (Baltimore: Johns Hopkins University Press, 1980), p. 100.

130 Some children may have problems... precisely how he got it. McGuinness, *Sensory Motor Biases*, op. cit. p. 17 of draft.

130 Five teaching practices... learning processes. Leonard M. Kennedy, *Guiding Children's Learning of Mathematics* (Belmont, Calif. Wadsworth Publishing Company, 1984), p. 66.

131 In *Overcoming*... geometric shapes methods. Sheila Tobias, *Overcoming Math Anxiety* (New York: W. W. Norton and Co., 1978), p. 257–65.

131 In one experiment... both hemispheres were more apt to be activated. Sally Banks Zakariya, "His Brain, Her Brain: A Conversation with Richard M. Restak," *Principal*, vol. 60, no. 5, May 1981, pp. 46–51.

132 And he will be close to ten... female classmate. Ilg, Ames, et al., *School Readiness*, op. cit. p. 59.

132 One intriguing hypothesis... repaired electrical equipment. Nora Newcombe, Mary M. Bandura, "Effect of Age of Puberty on Spatial Ability in Girls: A Question of Mechanism," *Developmental Psychology*, vol. 19, no. 2, 1983, pp. 215–24.

132 There was evidence... average men who were compared with them. Tobias, op. cit. p. 116.

133 At almost every age... available for home computers is considered masculine. Jo Shuchat Sanders, "The Computer: Male, Female, or Androgynous?" *The Computing Teacher*, April 1984, pp. 31–34; Leigh Chiarelott, "Cognition and the Media-ted Curriculum: Effects of Growing Up in an Electronic Environment," *Educational Technology*, May 1984, pp. 19–22.

133 Students, in general... minimal use of computers in elementary schools... Henry Jack Becker, "Report #1 from a National Survey," *Journal of Computers in Mathematics and Science Teaching*, vol. 3., no. 1, Fall 1983, pp. 29–33; Henry Jack Becker, "Report #2 from a National Survey," Ibid., vol. 3, no. 2, Winter 1983–84, pp. 16–21.

133 The material for the section on single-sex classes came from the following sources:

Garai, Scheinfeld, op. cit. pp. 185–86.

Carlotta G. Miles, M.D., "Do Boys and Girls Need Different Schooling?" *Independent School*, February 1981, pp. 23–26.

John F. Hurley, "Instructional Grouping by Sex in the Fifth Grade," Pilot Study Research Report, State Department of Education, Richmond, Virginia, 1965.

Sheila Moore's interview with John Hurley, former Director of Research for Fairfax County Public Schools, Fairfax, Virginia, April 1985.

Verna Dieckman Anderson, *Reading and Young Children* (New York: MacMillan, 1968), pp. 303–304.

Dechant, Smith, op. cit. pp. 97–100.

134 However, as Jerre Levy ... psychiatrists." Levy, op. cit.

135 Information for What Makes A Boy a Successful Learner came from Brown, et al., op. cit., pp. 77–166; M. C. Wittrock, et al., editors "The Generative Processes of Memory," *The Human Brain*, (Englewood Cliffs, N.J.: Prentice-Hall, 1977), pp. 153–84.

137 "It is the efficiency ... defines intelligence." Brown, et al., ibid., p. 100.

137 A simple procedure ... can help in getting started. In part from Gerald Wallace, James M. Kauffman, "Remedial Teaching Competencies," *Teaching Children with Learning Problems* (Columbus, Ohio: Charles E. Merrill Publishing Co., 1973), pp. 93–119.

137 Jack Canfield and Harold Wells ... chips to stay in the game." Jack Canfield, Harold C. Wells, *100 Ways to Enhance Self-Concept in the Classroom* (Englewood Cliffs, N.J.: Prentice-Hall, 1976), p. 7.

138 Information for Boys Like Good Schools came from the following sources: Rutter, "School Effects on Pupil Progress: Research Findings and Policy Implications," *Child Development*, 1983, 54, pp. 1–29; Wayson, op. cit.

140 Their achievement is higher. Rutter, op. cit.

141 Homework Is for Kids—Not Their Parents. "Homework," in the *Harvard Education Letter*, vol. 1, no. 1, February 1985.

6. Boys with Special Learning Needs

144 If he were a schoolboy today...taught him at home. Dorothea M. Ross, Sheila A. Ross, *Hyperactivity: Research, Theory and Action* (New York: John Wiley & Sons, 1976), p. 20.

144 Albert Einstein, despite a measured IQ...language disability ... K. Joyce Steeves, "Memory as a Factor in the Computational Efficiency of Dyslexic Children with High Abstract Reasoning Ability," *Annals of Dyslexia*, vol. 33, 1983, p. 143.

145 Of the two million children...at least three to one. Jean Petersen, executive director, Association for Children with Learning Disabilities, personal communication, March 15, 1984.

145 Norman Geschwind...left-handedness in males...Norman Geschwind, Peter Behan, "Left-handedness: Association with immune disease, migraine, and developmental learning disorder," *Proceedings of the National Academy of Science, USA*, vol. 79, August 1982, pp. 5097–100.

145 ...twice as likely...as females. Mansfield, op. cit.

145 ...left-handed individuals appear ten times more likely... right-handed. Durden-Smith, diSimone, op. cit. p. 171.

145 Researchers at Johns Hopkins...as the general population. Camilla Persson Benbow, Robert M. Benbow, "Biological Correlates of High Mathematical Reasoning Ability," in press, p. 22, in draft.

145 Several other studies...make use of spatial skills. Amy Ward, "The Hand Connection," *Northwest Orient*, February 1984, pp. 8–11.

146 According to guidelines...do mathematics." Katherine Geren, *Complete Special Education Handbook* (West Nyack, N.Y.: Parker Publishing Company, 1979), p. 19.

146 Heredity factors...normal reading abilities. Pennington, Smith, op. cit. pp. 369–387.

147 Several studies link alcohol...learning process. Sandra Gold, Lee Sherry, "Hyperactivity, Learning Disabilities, and Alcohol," *Journal of Learning Disabilities*, vol. 17, no. 1, January 1984, pp. 3–6.

147 There also appears to be a higher rate...smoked while pregnant. William Hines, "Smoke Signals," *Families*, March 1982, p. 61.

147 Emotional stress...higher rate of learning handicaps among adopted children. Authors' interview with Martha Denckla, M.D., chief, Section on Autism and Related Disorders, National Institutes of Health, January 12, 1983.

147 Long or difficult delivery...nutritional deficiencies. Hilda Freid, editor, "Plain Talk about Children with Learning Disabilities," (Bethesda, Md.: National Institute of Mental Health, 1979), pp. 3–5.

148 Dyslexics are predominantly male...they conclude. Joan M. Finucci, Barton Childs, "Are There Really More Dyslexic Boys than Girls?" *Sex Differences in Dyslexia*, op. cit. p. 9.

149 Children with specific language disability...two-dimensional tasks...Martha B. Denckla, "Clinical Syndromes in Learning Disabilities: The Case for Splitting vs. Lumping," *Journal of Learning Disabilities*, vol. 5, no. 7, August 1972, p. 405.

149 ...they seem to read as well upside down as right side up). Jeannette Jansky, Katrina de Hirsch, "Patterning and Organizational Deficits in Children with Language and Learning Disabilities," *Bulletin of the Orton Society*, vol. 30, 1980, p. 231.

149 Dyslexic youngsters...memorization and arithmetic computation. Steeves, op. cit. p. 147.

149 These are the children...just my words." *Dyslexia, The Language Disability that Can be Overcome* (Westwood, Mass.: Orton Dyslexia Society, 1982), pp. 7–8.

149 Often dyslexics can succeed...secretarial help"...Denckla, "Clinical Syndromes," op. cit. p. 405.

149 *Attention deficit disorder*...child psychiatrists. Ross, Ross, op. cit. p. ix.

149 One study of suburban schools...one girl. Mark A. Stewart, Sally Wendkos Olds, *Raising a Hyperactive Child* (New York: Harper & Row, 1973), pp. 3, 26.

150 Longitudinal research...academic ability and intelligence. Ross, Ross, op. cit. p. 48.

150 They have trouble separating relevant from irrelevant information...Ibid., p. 48.

150 ...however, they can often work well if an adult helps to get them started. Barbara K. Keogh, Judith Margolis, "Learn to Labor and to Wait: Attentional Problems of Children with Learning Disabilities," *Journal of Learning Disabilities*, vol. 9, no. 5, May 1976, pp. 18–29.

150 At school...IQ scores and classroom grades. Ross, Ross, op. cit. pp. 41–42.

150 A typical report card . . . motivated." Denckla, "Clinical Syndromes," op. cit. p. 406.

150 Stimulant medication . . . will not cure attention deficits. Sources include: Martha Denckla, M.D., personal communication; Judith L. Rapoport, personal communication, March 3, 1984, and with Monte S. Buchsbaum, Theodore P. Zahn, Herbert Weingartner, Christy Ludlow, Edwin J. Mikkelsen, "Dextroamphetamine: Cognitive and Behavioral Effects in Normal Prepubertal Boys," *Science*, vol. 199, no. 3, February 1978; John J. Ross, "On Psychopharmalogical Drugs in Children with Learning Problems," *American Family Physician*, vol. 29, no. 2, February 1984, p. 250; L. Alan Sroufe, "Drug Treatment of Children with Behavioral Problems," *Review of Child Development Research*, Frances Degen Horowitz, editor (Chicago: University of Chicago Press, 1975), pp. 347–407; Stewart, Olds, op. cit. pp. 247–49.

151 As one researcher puts it . . . find him normal. Marcel Kinsbourne, "Minimal Brain Dysfunction as a Neurodevelopmental Lag," *Annals of the New York Academy of Science*, vol. 205, 1973, pp. 268–73.

151 . . . these children are slow . . . motor, perceptual, and cognitive skills . . . Ibid.

152 In one study significant . . . developmentally delayed youngsters. Leon Oettinger, Jr., Lawrence F. Majovski, George A. Limbeck, Ronald Gauch, "Bone Age in Children with Minimal Brain Dysfunction," *Perceptual Motor Skills*, vol. 39, 1974, pp. 1127–31.

152 Unfortunately, there is no guarantee . . . benefit other LD students. Denckla, "Minimal Brain Dysfunction," op. cit.

152 Experts have not found a system . . . brain maturation. Kinsbourne, op. cit. p. 243.

152 There is little evidence . . . benefit other LD students. Denckla, op. cit.

152 A few children with minor disabilities . . . compensatory instruction. Authors' interview with Nathlie Badian; Denckla, ibid.

152 It is at ten that myelination . . . appears to be completed. Roon Frost's interview with Patricia Davidson, Boston Children's Hospital, May 1983.

152 These three clusters . . . half the LD patients in one clinic. Denckla, "Minimal Brain Dysfunction," op. cit.

154 If a positive diagnosis of learning disability . . . ability to overcome his learning problems. Freid, op. cit.

155 The best instructor for an LD student...step-by-step approach to teaching. Denckla, "Minimal Brain Dysfunction," op. cit. pp. 258–66.

156 It is now believed...childhood depression. Roger A. Brumback, R. Dennis Staton, "Learning Disability and Childhood Depression," *American Journal of Orthopsychiatry*, vol. 53, no. 2, April 1983, pp. 269–78.

157 Short periods of concentrated effort...focused, uninterrupted work. Betty B. Osman, *Learning Disabilities: A Family Affair* (New York: Random House, 1979), p. 106.

157 As simple a technique as offering two alternatives...listen more carefully to directions...Maccoby, *Social Development*, op. cit. p. 195.

158 An LD child...studying at home. Suzanne H. Stevens, *The Learning Disabled Child: Ways That Parents Can Help* (Winston-Salem, N.C.: John F. Blair, 1980), p. 97.

159 With appropriate teaching...children without learning disabilities. *Dyslexia*, op. cit. pp. 20–21.

159 Your son may draw wonderfully...different parts of the brain. Denckla, personal communication. January 1983.

159 *Emphasize what your son does right*. Osman, op. cit. p. 35.

161 In preschool youngsters...activities toward a specific goal. Frederick B. Tuttle, Jr., Laurence A. Becker, *Characteristics and Identification of Gifted and Talented Students* (Washington, D.C.: National Education Association, 1980), pp. 13–14; Barbara Clark, *Growing Up Gifted* (Columbus, Ohio: Charles E. Merrill Publishing Co., 1979), pp. 23–27; Wayne Dennis, Margaret Dennis, *The Intellectually Gifted* (New York: Grune & Stratton, 1976), pp. 156–57.

162 A popular misconception...had succeeded in this regard. Frank Laycock, *Gifted Children* (Glenview, Ill.: Scott, Foresman & Company, 1979), pp. 39–45.

163 One teacher of gifted children...their peers are ready for. Marilyn Bos, Search Program Resource Coordinator, Loudoun County Public Schools, Leesburg, Virginia, personal communication.

164 One survey of the departments of education...such as leadership. Betty H. Yarborough, Roger A. Johnson, "Identifying the Gifted: A Theory-Practice Gap," *Gifted Children Quarterly*, vol. 27, no. 3, Summer 1983, pp. 135–38.

164 IQ scores are not static...twice as many boys as girls showed large increases. Mussen, Conger, Kagan, op. cit. pp. 308–309, 470–71, 476.

164 Even if a boy is exceptionally gifted...very well in the classroom. "A Conversation with Julian Stanley," *Educational Leadership*, November 1981, pp. 101–106.

164 A small percentage of students reason so well...for a full year. Julian C. Stanley, Camilla Persson Benbow, "Educating Mathematically Precocious Youths: Twelve Policy Recommendations," *Educational Researcher*, vol. 11, no. 5, May 1982, pp. 4–9.

164 A majority are male. "A Conversation with Julian Stanley," *Educational Leadership*, November 1981, pp. 101–106.

164 As early as seventh grade...no girls at all were represented. Ibid.

165 Regardless of their sex, children...gifted programs in their home schools. Authors' interview with Camilla Benbow, associate director, Study of Mathematically Precocious Youth, Johns Hopkins University, January 12, 1984.

165 Tests designed to measure creativity...creative in his thinking. Albert Rothenberg, Carl R. Hausman, editors, *The Creativity Question* (Durham, N.C.: Duke University Press, 1976), pp. 210–211.

165 Defining creativity is very difficult...of value. Ibid., p. 6.

165 For a long time people assumed...excellence than general intelligence." Michael A. Wallach, Nathan Kogan, "Creativity and Intelligence in Children," *The Creativity Question*, op. cit. p. 211.

166 Naturalist-author Gerald Durrell...baby octopus. Gerald Durrell, *My Family and Other Animals* (New York: Viking Press, 1957), p. 126.

166 Creativity does not appear to be more prevalent...later born. Clark, op. cit. p. 249.

166 Researchers who study creativity in adults...interests fully. Fox, "Sex Differences: Implications for Program Planning for the Academically Gifted," op. cit. pp. 113–37.

166 Chicago educational expert Benjamin Bloom...tenacity of purpose. Benjamin S. Bloom, "The Role of Gifts and Markers in the Development of Talent," *Exceptional Children*, vol. 48, no. 6, April 1982, pp. 516–21.

167 In the Hopkins SMPY program...make the most progress. Authors' interview with Camilla Benbow.

169 In 1984, the editors of *Science Digest*...science by the age of eight-and-a-half. Tom Yulsman, "The 100: Who They Are and What They Think," *Science Digest*, December 1984, pp. 78–79, 102.

7. Of Risk to Boys

170 ... what we may not know ... becomes part of their regular viewing. Leonard D. Eron, "Parent-Child Interaction, Television Violence, and Aggression of Children," *American Psychologist*, vol. 37, no. 2, February 1982, pp. 197–211.

171 ... because of certain genetic propensities ... become alcoholic. Constance Holden, "Genes, Personality, and Alcoholism," *Psychology Today*, vol. 19, no. 1, January 1985, pp. 38–44.

171 ... but family discord ... destructive behavior in our sons. Rutter, Garmezy, "Developmental Psychopathology," op. cit. p. 824.

171 In rates of referral to child guidance clinics ... boys than girls. N. Richman, J. Stevenson, P. J. Graham, *Preschool to School: A Behavioral Study* (London: Academic Press, 1982), p. 132.

171 Although, a school-age child ... leaving him all alone. Linda Barrett Osborne, "Unlocking the Latchkey Child's Interests," *Washington Post*, March 22, 1985, p. C5.

172 "Divorce occurs to solve ... have behavioral and school problems. Authors' interview with E. Mavis Hetherington, March 27, 1984.

172 Some boys, perhaps distracted ... become accident prone. Linda Bird Francke, *Growing Up Divorced* (New York: Linden Press/Simon & Schuster, 1983), p. 133.

172 Others undergo prolonged depression ... dads' return. Judith S. Wallerstein, Joan B. Kelly, *Surviving the Breakup* (New York: Basic Books, 1980), pp. 165, 170.

172 For adults, divorce is second only ... impact is similar. Francke, op. cit. p. 35.

172 Because boys are often more fragile ... greater than it is on girls. Wallerstein, Kelly, op. cit. p. 166.

172 Even ten years after their parents' divorce ... "children of divorce." Rita Rooney, "Helping Children Through Divorce," *McCall's*, April 1984, p. 42.

173 A divorce that interrupts this process ... may have trouble sleeping. Francke, op. cit. pp. 66, 69.

173 "The child who regresses ... too much noise. Wallerstein, Kelly, op. cit. pp. 57–62.

173 Overwhelming sadness ... grief of death." Francke, op. cit. pp. 84–91.

173 Even talking about the divorce . . . parents divorce. Wallerstein, Kelly, op. cit. pp. 66–68.

174 One boy showed through his artwork . . . cleaving hi^ head." Francke, op. cit. p. 94.

174 Alignment of a boy this age . . . parents back together. Ibid., p. 74; Francke, op. cit. p. 115.

174 If the child is male, behavior problems at home and at school are typical. Teresa E. Levitin, "Children of Divorce: An Introduction," *Journal of Social Issues*, vol. 35, no. 4, 1979, p. 10.

174 Boys with older brothers . . . activities considered "masculine." James D. Vess, Jr., Andrew I. Schwebel, John Moreland, "The Effects of Early Parental Divorce on the Sex Role Development of College Students," *Journal of Divorce*, vol. 17, no. 1., Fall 1983, pp. 83–94.

174 In approximately 90 percent . . . mother. Betty Spillers Beeson, "Yours, Mine, or Ours?", *Childhood Education*, September–October 1984, pp. 4–8.

175 Syndicated columnist Ellen Goodman . . . is to get divorced." Ellen Goodman, "Man Supports Child," *Washington Post*, November 8, 1983.

175 The financial shock many women . . . children qualify for free lunch. "One-Parent Families and Their Children," A National Association of Elementary School Principals Staff Report, *Principal*, September 1980, p. 33.

175 Goodman reported that in one western state . . . 73 percent. Goodman, op. cit.

175 This "minimal parenting" contributes . . . mothers have with their sons. Carol E. MacKinnon, Gene H. Brody, Zolinda Stoneman, "The Effects of Divorce and Maternal Employment on the Home Environments of Preschool Children," *Child Development*, 53, October 1982, pp. 1392–99.

175 A feeling of lingering dissatisfaction . . . opposed to divorce." Wallerstein, Kelly, op. cit. p. 153.

176 In a study conducted by University of Virginia psychologist . . . they were more prolonged." Authors' interview with E. Mavis Hetherington.

176 As Hetherington points out . . . characteristics we don't like." Ibid.

176 Finding a place in a new peer group . . . than for girls . . . Mussen, Conger, Kagan, op. cit. p. 575.

176 Boys who were observed two months . . . games of pretend, for example. Kenneth H. Rubin, Greta G. Fein, Brian Vandenberg, "Play," *Handbook of Child Psychology*, op. cit. vol. 4, p. 730.

176 To boys in the early grades . . . given the nurturance he needs. Mussen, Conger, Kagan, op. cit. pp. 576–86.

177 In a fourteen-state survey . . . low 17 percent were children of divorce. Staff report, *Principal*, op. cit. p. 33.

177 One experienced principal . . . well into their school years. Elizabeth Decker, personal communication, March 12, 1984.

177 Another finding . . . fathers are absent from the home. Marybeth Shinn, "Father Absence and Children's Cognitive Development," *Psychological Bulletin*, vol. 85, no. 2, 1976, p. 316.

178 Boys need an authoritative figure . . . assigned to a boy's father. "Small Boys Worst Victims of Divorce," *USA Today*, vol. 107, no. 2409, June 1979, p. 30.

178 One study . . . boy's level of performance. Shinn, op. cit. p. 320.

178 Researchers have found . . . same sex as the custodial parent. Karen W. Bartz, Wayne C. Witcher, "When Father Gets Custody," *Children Today*, vol. 7, no. 5, September–October 1978, pp. 2–6.

178 The aggression and disobedience . . . if a boy lives with his father. John W. Santrock, Richard Warshak, Cheryl Lindbergh, Larry Meadows, "Children's and Parents' Observed Social Behavior in Stepfather Families," *Child Development*, 53, 1982, pp. 472–80.

178 There appear to be more sons . . . elect to live with the parent of the same sex. Bartz, Witcher, op. cit.

179 While they experience the same emotional turmoil . . . competence in the nurturing role. John P. Pichitino, "Profile of the Single Father: A Thematic Integration of the Literature," *The Personnel and Guidance Journal*, February 1983, p. 296.

180 Particularly devastating can be criticism . . . absent father. Authors' interview with E. Mavis Hetherington.

180 If your son needs it . . . seldom think of it for a child. Sara E. Bonkowski, Shelly Q. Bequette, Sara Bromhower, "A Group Design to Help Children Adjust to Parental Divorce," *Social Casework*, vol. 65, no. 3, March 1984, p. 131.

180 Approximately 11 percent of all American households . . . lives in a stepfamily. Santrock, Warshak, Lindbergh, Meadows, op. cit.

180 Since there is no institutionalized set of expectations...be created. Authors' interview with Sheppard Kellam M.D.

181 As one divorced mother points out...are emphᴧsized." Francke, op. cit. p. 186.

181 Hetherington emphasizes that women who are severely stressed...period of time. Authors' interview with E. Mavis Hetherington.

181 Of five hundred families...on to divorce later. Rooney, op. cit. p. 42.

182 Experts estimate that two to five million...unsupervised... Suzanne Higgs Stroman, R. Eleanor Duff, "The Latchkey Child: Whose Responsibility?", *Childhood Education*, vol. 59, no. 2, November 1982, p. 77; Lynette and Thomas Long, *The Handbook for Latchkey Children and Their Parents: A Complete Guide for Latchkey Kids and Their Working Parents* (New York: Arbor House, 1983), p. 22.

182 ...in Canada the figure may be half a million. Nancy L. Galambos, and James Garbarino "Identifying the Missing Links in the Study of Latchkey Children," *Children Today*, vol. 12, no. 4, July 1983, p. 3.

182 One latchkey boy sums up...only other kids." Long, Long, op. cit. p. 63.

183 A number of factors...child-care needs. Galambos, Garbarino, op. cit.

183 One survey of a New York City private school...parents came home. Grace Hechinger, *How to Raise a Street Smart Child: The Complete Parent's Guide to Safety on the Street and at Home* (New York: Facts on File Publications, 1984), p. 134.

183 "I don't like being home alone"...going to a sitter's or a child-care center. Long, Long, op. cit. pp. 62–66.

183 In reality, some of these boys...wield baseball bats when they hear a strange noise. Ibid.

184 Parents may actually compound a child's fears...unsupervised. Stroman, Duff, op. cit. p. 161.

184 One out of every five children...Twenty years later... leaving them alone too often when they were children. Long, Long, op. cit. p. 161–74.

184 Thomas and Lynette Long...unresponsive to children's needs. Ibid., p. 134.

184 Even though there are three million children...Lynne F. McGee, "Children: Learning to Survive on Their Own," *Washington Post*, May 25, 1982, p. B5.

184 ...only 1.6 million...latchkey children. Peggy Lewis Neiting, "School-Age Child Care: In Support of Development and Learning," *Childhood Education*, September 1983, pp. 6–7.

184 There is evidence that such child-care programs reduce abuse and neglect...Warlene Gary, National Education Association, testimony before U.S. House Select Committee on Children, Youth, and Families, September 6, 1984.

184 ...boost academic progress...vandalism. Neiting, op. cit. pp. 8–9.

185 Some experts suggest...if they were available. Gary, op. cit.

185 Children who are unsupervised...outside unsupervised. Thomas Long, personal communication, November 5, 1984.

185 In middle childhood...urge them on. Thomas J. Berndt, "Developmental Changes in Conformity to Peers and Parents," *Developmental Psychology*, vol. 15, no. 6, 1979, pp. 608–16.

185 Oregon researcher Gerald Patterson...supervision to discourage. Gerald Patterson, *Families: Applications of Social Learning to Family Life*, revised edition (Champaign, Ill: Research Press, c. 1975), pp. 118–22.

185 Authorities today report...unsupervised youth. Stroman, Duff, op. cit. p. 78.

186 Parents of latchkey children...doing his best." Long, Long, op. cit. p. 133.

186 One study...whose mothers worked...Gold, Anders, op. cit. pp. 75–84.

186 Boys have more accidents than girls...Barbara Starfield, I.B. Pless, "Physical Health," *Constancy and Change in Human Development*, op. cit. pp. 305–306.

186 In their interviews...supposedly taking care of them. Long, Long, op. cit. pp. 50–52.

186 Some experts believe that 70 to 80 percent...related to their victims. Stephen L. Luther, James H. Price, "Child Sexual Abuse: A Review," *The Journal of School Health*, March 1980, p. 162.

186 The National Center...eighteenth birthdays. Janet Rosenzweig, "You Can Help a Sexually Abused Child," *Instructor*, April 1984, p. 62.

187 Parents are likely to be more protective . . . as girls are. Terryann Nielson, "Sexual Abuse of Boys: Current Perspective," *The Personnel and Guidance Journal*, November 1983, p. 139.

187 Boys are traditionally allowed more freedom . . . frequently abused than girls are. Ibid., pp. 139–40.

187 Most sexually abused children . . . disturbance as a result. Michael Koch, "Sexual Abuse in Children," *Adolescence*, vol. 15, no. 59, Fall 1980, p. 645.

187 Often children who have been molested . . . happened to them. Nielson, op. cit. p. 141.

187 If your child should try . . . normal sex play for children. Rosenzweig, op. cit. pp. 62–63.

188 Displays guilt . . . no apparent reason. Nielson, op. cit. p. 141.

188 Seems preoccupied . . . locker room. Rosenzweig, op. cit.

188 As one mother says . . . be my fault." Bebe Moore Campbell, "Perspectives: Facing the Realities of Growing Up," *Washington Post*, November 13, 1983, p. B5.

189 . . . but boys, especially, need to know . . . vulnerable sometimes. Nielson, op. cit. p. 142.

191 Approximately 15 percent . . . tough older kids). Hechinger, op. cit. p. 15.

192 Most parents consider an eight-year-old . . . latchkey arrangement. Long, Long, op. cit., p. 23.

192 Interestingly, this is also the average age when juvenile delinquency begins. Nieting, op. cit. p. 7.

192 Michelle Seligson . . . eleven or twelve. Vance Packard, *Our Endangered Children: Growing Up in a Changing World* (Boston: Little, Brown & Company, 1983), p. 174.

192 One former latchkey youth . . . three hours . . . Ibid., p. 203.

192 Siblings who do not get along . . . alone together. Ibid., pp. 43–48.

193 It seems crucial . . . stressed. Ibid., pp. 171–72.

193 Does your son have some time . . . supervision for latchkey children. Osborne, op. cit.

194 "Checking In" is one such program . . . community is available. Judy McKnight, Betsy Shelby, "Checking In: An Alternative for Latchkey Kids," *Children Today*, May 1984, pp. 23–25; *A Guide to Operating the Family Day Care Check-In Program, After-School*

Care for Children Aged 10–14 (Fairfax, Va.: Fairfax County Office for Children, 1985).

194 Increasingly, school districts . . . rest of the bill. Packard, op. cit. p. 179.

194 A study of one program . . . after-school care. Nieting, op. cit. pp. 8–9.

194 The Wellesley School Age Child Care . . . extended care. Michelle Seligson, personal communication, January 1985.

195 It is important to give any child . . . being home alone. Long, Long, op. cit. p. 127.

195 More Americans own television sets . . . indoor plumbing. *Television and Behavior: Ten Years of Scientific Progress and Implications for the Eighties*, U.S. Department of Health and Human Services, U.S. Public Health service, 1982, p. 1.

196 Many of our children watch . . . one full day. Peggy Charran, president, Action for Children's television, personal communication, April 5, 1984.

196 Responsible studies . . . lasting over twenty years . . . Leonard D. Eron, "Parent-Child Interaction," op. cit. pp. 197–211.

196 The technical forms . . . mental processes. *Television and Behavior*, op. cit. p. 24.

196 Young children, who begin paying more attention . . . of the vocabulary used in the story.. Ibid., pp. 23–27.

197 In 1984, researchers . . . from the United States. International Coalition Against Violent Entertainment, press release, Champaign, Illinois, March 15, 1984.

197 The American Academy of Pediatrics . . . "Whoever tells most . . . tells most of the stories." Susan Okie, "Pediatricians Criticize Television in U.S.," *Washington Post*, October 16, 1985, Health, p. 16–17.

198 Sources for Leonard Eron's and Rowell Huesmann's work on television and aggression include the following:

Leonard D. Eron, "Parent-Child Interaction," op. cit.

Leonard D. Eron, L. Rowell Huesmann, "The Control of Aggressive Behavior," pp. 138–170.

Leonard D. Eron, L. Rowell Huesmann, Monroe M. Lefkowitz, Leopold O. Walder, "How Learning Conditions in Early Childhood —Including Mass Media—Relate to Aggression in Late Adolescence," *American Journal of Orthopsychiatry*, vol. 44, no. 3, April 1974, pp. 412–23.

Authors' interview with Leonard Eron, professor of psychology, University of Illinois, August 29, 1984.

200 Fantasy, make-believe . . . reading fairy tales. *Television and Behavior*, op. cit. pp. 45–46.

200 Yale psychologists . . . reading fairy tales. Jerome and Dorothy Singer, *Television, Imagination, and Aggression: A Study of Preschooler's Play* (Hillsdale, N.J.: Erlbaum, 1981), p. 151; Eron, "Parent-Child Interaction," op. cit.

200 Child psychologist Bruno Bettelheim . . . "empty-minded entertainment." Bruno Bettelheim, *The Uses of Enchantment* (New York: Vintage Books, 1977), p. 24.

200 According to the Surgeon General's 1982 report . . . aggressive in nursery schools. Ibid., pp. 45—47.

201 It can also affect his school performance . . . less TV a teenager watches. Patricia A. Williams, Edward H. Haertel, Geneva D. Haertel, Herbert J. Walberg, "The Impact of Leisure-Time Television on School Learning: A Research Synthesis," *American Educational Research Journal*, vol. 19, no. 1, Spring 1982, p. 35; *Television and Behavior*, op. cit. p. 9.

201 One physician compared . . . bright lights. Marie Winn, *The Plug-In Drug* (New York: Viking Press, 1977), p. 15.

201 Arousal refers to the level . . . tolerant of violence in general. *Television and Behavior*, op. cit. pp. 28–30.

201 Very young children may be frightened . . . as is the evening news. Joanne Cantor, Glenn G. Sparks, "Children's Fear Responses to Mass Media: Testing Some Piagetian Predictions," *Journal of Communication*, vol. 34, no. 2, Spring 1984, pp. 90–103.

202 Heavy viewers are more likely . . . "mean and scarey." *Television and Behavior*, op. cit. p. 7

202 In terms of TV viewing . . . violence in general. Ibid.

202 Boys who race . . . most of them are males. Ibid., pp. 10–11.

203 In his helpful book . . . trying to help." Fred Rogers, Barry Head, *Mister Rogers Talks with Parents* (New York: Berkley Books, 1983), p. 183.

203 One reviewer characterizes this programming . . . for resolving conflicts. Tom Shales, "The New War on Kids' TV," *Washington Post*, October 22, 1983, section 3, p. 1.

203 On the other hand . . . will not permanently harm our children. Penelope Lemov, "Why Do I Have to Turn Off the TV?" *The Washingtonian*, September 1983, pp. 4–5.

203 Manufacturers now invent . . . watch before the mouse." Shales, op. cit.

203 One psychiatrist suggests letting children help select the programs. Lemov, op. cit.

204 One commentator characterizes . . . single video. Fred Bruning, "The Perils of Rock on the Box," *Macleans*, November 14, 1983, p. 81.

204 A significant percentage . . . of a sexual nature. National Coalition on Television Violence, press release, January 10, 1983, Champaign, Illinois.

204 One rock video director . . . incredible sadism" of the presentations. Emily Yoffe, "A Day-Glo Trip Through 8 Hours of MTV," *Washington Post Magazine*, June 10, 1984, pp. 15, 19.

204 A second MTV director . . . drugs, and rock and roll." Ibid.

204 Early in 1984, the Boston-based Action for Children's Television . . . long periods of time. Peggy Charran, personal communication.

205 In the summer of 1985 . . . clean up their act." Ann Landers, *Washington Post*, August 14, 1985, p. C11.

205 Popular music is a multi-billion-dollar-a-year . . . 10 to 16 age group. Jack V. Toohey, "Popular Music and Social Values," *The Journal of School Health*, December 1982, pp. 582–85.

205 "Drugs and rock music . . . support each other." Robert Coram, Charlene P. Smith-Williams, "Hard Rock Concert: A Zoo Ruled by Youngsters," *Atlanta Constitution*, December 16, 1980, pp. 5–6.

206 Eighty-two percent of the university students . . . subconscious level. Toohey, op. cit.

206 The National PTA . . . into their homes. The National PTA, news release, August 9, 1985, Chicago, Illinois.

206 In the spring of 1985 . . . what they're getting. Parents' Music Resource Center news release, August 8, 1985, Washington, D.C.

208 As one medical expert says . . . one positive aspect." Lemov, op. cit.

208 Personal sets also make it less . . . ever present accompaniment. Okie, op. cit.

209 Over half of today's adolescents have tried illegal drugs... Georgia Sideris, "What About Other Schools?" *Woman's Day*, March 5, 1985, p. 67.

209 ...in a major metropolitan area...smoked pot. James R. Campbell, John Swanchak. "The Primary Grades: New Focus for Drug and Alcohol Education," *Early Years*, vol. 13, no. 3, November 1982, p. 35.

209 A recent study reported...older child's habit. Peggy Mann, *Marijuana Alert* (New York: McGraw-Hill Book Company, 1985), p. 72–73.

210 Males show a greater genetic tendency to become alcoholic than females. Goodwin, op cit. pp. 93–99.

210 Adopted children...problem drinkers. Holden, op. cit. pp. 33–38.

210 Boys of European...African heritage. J. Valley Rachel, Stephen A. Maisto, L. Lyn Guess, Robert L. Hubbard, "Alcohol Use Among Youth," *Alcohol and Health Monograph I: Alcohol Consumption annd Related Problems* (Washington, D.C.: U.S. Department of Health and Human Services, 1982), pp. 69–73; "Born to Drink?", *Science Digest*, vol. 92, no. 5, May 1984, p. 16.

210 Researchers have recently identified...one-quarter of all alcoholics. Holden, op. cit.

210 One expert believes...emotions and his behavior. Ibid.

210 Pennsylvania State University researchers...adulthood. Jacqueline V. Lerner, Judith R. Vicary, "Difficult Temperament and Drug Use: Analyses from the New York Longitudinal Study," *Journal of Drug Education*, vol. 14, no. 1, 1984, pp. 1–7.

211 The Chicago study...pot smokers in adolescence. Margaret E. Ensminger, C. Hendricks Brown, Sheppard G. Kellam, "Sex Differences in Antecedents of Substance Use Among Adolescents," *Journal of Social Issues*, vol. 38, no. 2, 1982, pp. 26–32.

211 A study of over eight thousand youngsters...other substances. Dean V. Babst, Sherry Deren, James Schmidler, Douglas S. Lipton, Richard Dembo, "A Study of Family Affinity and Substance Use," *Journal of Drug Education*, vol. 8, no. 1, 1978, pp. 29–40.

211 Conformity to one's peers...which society disapproves. Berndt, op. cit.

211 Boys are also more willing than girls to take risks. Huston, op. cit. p. 404.

212 When famous personalities...beer or bourbon. Laurence Shames, "When Will Teens Sober Up? They Drink, They Drive—and They Die," *Seventeen*, November 1983, pp. 75–76.

212 Recent research suggests...drank with their families. Marie D. Bloom, Michael A. Greenwald, "Alcohol and Cigarette Use Among Early Adolescents," *Journal of Drug Education*, vol. 14, no. 3, pp. 195–205.

212 Morris Chafetz...most abused drug in the United States. Stanley L. Englebardt, "Are We Teaching Our Kids to Become Alcoholics?", *Families*, vol. 2, no. 3, March 1982, p. 30.

212 Four million youngsters...accompanying other drugs." Brenda J. Wagner, "Intervening with the Adolescent Involved in Substance Abuse," *Journal of School Health*, vol. 54, no. 7, p. 244.

213 "Uppers,"...diet pills. Lloyd D. Johnston, Ph.D., Patrick M. O'Malley, Ph.D., Jerald G. Bachman, Ph.D., *Highlights from Drugs and American High School Students, 1975–1983* (Rockville, Md.: National Institute on Drug Abuse, 1984), pp. 125–29.

213 Drinking...all socioeconomic groups. Rachal et al., op. cit. pp. 69–73.

213 In fact...than in public schools. Sideris, op. cit.; Patrick M. O'Malley, Ph.D., social psychologist, University of Michigan, personal communication, June 25, 1985.

213 Children...urban and suburban communities...Rachal et al., op. cit.

214 ...but coming from a "good home"...drugs. DuPont, op. cit.

214 In many middle-...marijuana use. Jason Baron, Peggy Mann, "Kids and Drugs: New Facts, New Fears, New Hope," *Family Circle*, April 7, 1981, p. 48.

214 Recently, health officials...joints laced with it. Michael Marriott, "Local Officials Find Children Victims of PCP," *Washington Post*, August 28, 1984, p. A1.

214 Since the time...unborn child. Gold, Sherry, op. cit.

214 Perinatal mortality...*not harm a developing child*. Eileen M. Furey, "The Effects of Alcohol on the Fetus," *Exceptional Children*, vol. 49, no. 1, September 1982, pp. 30–34.

214 Nursing mothers...still forming. "A Quick Few Drinks Late in Pregnancy Can Damage a Fetus' Brain," *USA Today*, April 3, 1984, p. D1.

215 As little as one or two . . . off-spring. Christine Russell, "Alcohol in Pregnancy Found to Cut Off Oxygen to Fetus," *Washington Post*, November 5, 1982, p. A1.

215 Fetal marijuana syndrome . . . fetal alcohol syndrome. "Pride: Drug Scene Update," pamphlet published by Pride, Atlanta, Georgia.

215 Because the total number . . . response to visual stimuli. Mann, ibid. p. 142.

215 But in animal studies . . . physiological responses. Mann, op. cit. p. 154.

216 A 1985 study . . . be. Judy Foreman, *Boston Globe*, September 12, 1985, p. 7.

216 Differences in body chemistry . . . adolescents who drink. Marsha Manatt, *Parents, Peers, and Pot* (Washington, D.C.: National Institute on Drug Abuse, 1980), pp. 51–52.

216 A child's physical addiction . . . twenty to thirty days of daily drinking . . . Holden, op. cit. p. 44.

216 . . . or six months of frequent drinking. "Hey Guys, Look What Alcohol Can Do For You" (Silver Spring, Md.: National Federation of Drug-Free Youth), pamphlet, undated.

216 Alcoholism is a disease . . . recovers. Holden, op. cit.

216 Alcohol addiction . . . possibly obstructing normal growth. "What Parents Must Learn About Teens and Alcohol" (Silver Spring, Md.: National Federation of Parents for Drug-Free Youth, 1982).

216 For growing boys . . . secondary sex characteristics during adolescence. "Hey Guys," op. cit.

217 Children . . . alcohol-related. Shames, op. cit.

217 Lowering the drinking age . . . fifteen or younger. Donald P. Baker, "Lower Drinking Age Affects Schools," *Washington Post*, March 30, 1975, p. A1.

217 During the 1970s . . . responsible for the difference. Shames, op. cit.

217 Boys are more likely . . . driving. Henry Weschler, Mary Rohman, Jamie B. Kotch, Roberta K. Idelson, "Alcohol and Other Drug Use and Automobile Safety: A Survey of Boston Area Teenagers," *Journal of School Health*, vol. 54, no. 5, May 1984, pp. 201–03.

217 Any Marylander knowingly serving alcohol . . . thousand-dollar fine. "What Parents Must Learn," op. cit.

217 "Dram shop laws," . . . in 1985. Margot Hornblower, "Drunken Driving Suits Aiming at Third Parties," *Washington Post*, March 24, 1985, p. A4.

217 The federal requirement . . . even more persuasive. "Busting the Beer Bust," *Newsweek*, October 29, 1984, p. 96.

218 The pattern of substance abuse . . . or PCP. Judith S. Brook, Martin Whiteman, Ann Scovell Gordon, "Stages of Drug Use in Adolescence: Personality, Peers, and Family Correlates," *Developmental Psychology*, vol. 19, no. 2, 1983, p. 269.

218 Over one million teenagers . . . dangers. Earl Ubell, "How You Can Turn Off Drug Abuse," *Parade Magazine*, March 4, 1984.

218 From his experience . . . the top." Manatt, op. cit. p. 52.

218 But chemicals in marijuana . . . in the brain. Baron, Mann, op. cit.

218 Complete intoxication . . . can result. Manatt, op. cit.

218 Marijuana alone . . . smoke it as girls. Hardin B. Jones, M.D., "What the Practicing Physician Should Know About Marijuana," *Private Practice*, January 1976, p. 35.

218 Unlike alcohol . . . fat soluble. Manatt, op. cit.

218 THC and other cannabinoids . . . chemicals. Gabriel G. Nahas, "Some Specific Reasons to Keep Off the 'Grass'" *PTA Today*, May 1981, pp. 5–6.

218 The Boston study . . . tried marijuana. Wechsler et al., op. cit. p. 202.

219 Reduction of male hormones . . . sperm count and motility . . . Manatt, op. cit. p. 41.

219 . . . however, these effects . . . pot. Carol Grace Smith, Ricardo H. Asch, *Marijuana and Reproduction* (Rockville, Md.: American Council for Drug Education, 1982), p. 17.

219 Increased incidence . . . quoted as saying. Peggy Mann, "Marijuana Alert," reprint, *Reader's Digest*, December 1979, p. 5.

219 Reduced immune response . . . users. Nahas, op. cit.

219 Altered brain tissue . . . functioning. Mann, *Marijuana Alert*, op. cit. pp. 171–91.

219 When marijuana use . . . using marijuana. Manatt, op. cit. pp. 36–39.

219 According to a 1979 survey... unable to break them. Wagner, op. cit.

220 Chronic high dose... sleep disturbances. Meltzer, op. cit. pp. 154–60.

220 One drug expert... other drugs." Eileen Ogintz, "Cocaine's Appeal Sifts Into the Mainstream," *Miami Herald*, May 5, 1981, pp. C1, C3.

220 Cocaine may rupture... large doses. Paul Berg, "Study Establishes Link Between Cocaine, Brain Damage," *Washington Post Health*, May 15, 1985, p. 5.

220 "Large amounts... die from it." Marc Leepson, "Cocaine: Drug of the Eighties," *Editorial Research Reports*, vol. 11, no. 8, August 27, 1982, pp. 636–38.

220 Hallucinogens, like LSD... damage to users. Mary Thornton, "DEA Says It Will Outlaw Hallucinogenic Drug MDMA," *Washington Post*, June 1, 1985, A1, A7; Jane Leavy, "Ecstasy: The Lure and the Peril," *Washington Post*, June 1, 1985, pp. D1, D4.

221 Their effects... similar to alcohol's. Ubell, op. cit.

221 *Make it clear... drugs*... DuPont, op. cit.

223 One effective program... campaigns. Minuchin, Shapiro, op. cit. p. 247.

223 An unexpected drop... a boy's behavior. Manatt, op. cit. pp. 61–62.

224 In the General Mills... their own. *Raising Children in a Changing Society, The General Mills American Family Report, 1976–77* (Minneapolis, Minn.: General Mills, 1977), pp. 27–32.

8. Weathering the Storms

226 "Sometimes I think... squarely back at him..."... Harper Lee, *To Kill a Mockingbird* (New York: Popular Library, 1962 [J. B. Lippincott Company edition published in July 1960]), p. 276.

229 In some rural locations... hold their own in the field. Douglas M. Blount, Columbus, Mississippi, personal communication, June, 1985.

232 Posing questions... all about. Phyllis T. Elardo, Bettye M. Caldwell, "The Effects of an Experimental Social Development Program on Children in the Middle Childhood Period," *Psychology in the Schools*, vol. 16, no. 1, January 1979, pp. 93–100.

232 Reasoning or questions... simple prohibitions. Leon Kuczynski, "Reasoning, Prohibitions, and Motivations for Compliance," *Developmental Psychology*, vol. 19, no. 1, 1983, pp. 126–34.

232 Intensity . . . internal self-controls. Leon Kuczynski, "Intensity and Orientation of Reasoning: Motivational Determinants of Children's Compliance with Verbal Rationales," *Journal of Experimental Child Psychology*, 1980, vol. 34, 1982, pp. 357–70.

232 Accentuating the positive . . . willingness to help. Joan E. Grusec, Erica Redler, "Attribution, Reinforcement, and Altruism: A Developmental Analysis," *Developmental Psychology*, vol. 16, no. 5, pp. 525–34.

233 Being told that he is kind . . . helpful behavior. Marian Radke-Yarrow, Carolyn Zahn-Waxler, Michael Chapman, "Children's Prosocial Dispositions and Behavior," *Handbook of Child Psychology*, op. cit. vol. 4, p. 511.

233 "Rather than insisting . . . encouraged for women." Leonard D. Eron, "Prescription for Reduction of Aggression," *American Psychologist*, vol. 35, no. 3, March 1980, p. 251.

235 One male school principal . . . one aspect of his life." Harry F. Holsinger, principal, Fairfax High School, Fairfax, Virginia, personal communication, April 1985.

239 "The family is . . . administrator says. Ibid.

Recommended Books

The Child from Five to Ten
This volume by Arnold Gesell, M.D. and Frances Ilg, M.D., in collaboration with Louise Bates Ames and Glenna Bullis, is an accurate look at the school-age child. In addition to behavioral profiles, this book includes information about a child's emotional responses, school performance, relations with family and friends typical of children in their middle years. (Harper & Row, 1946)

Classics to Read Aloud to Your Children
Reading to your son even after he has learned to read himself can help him in school. This anthology of children's literature by William F. Russell is an excellent way to continue the habit of reading aloud. Selections are geared for school-age children's listening, and include approximate reading times and pronunciation guide. (Crown, 1984)

Families—Applications of Social Learning to Family Life
This little book is a course in preventing and dealing with

behavior problems, from bed-wetting, whining, and temper tantrums to aggressiveness, lying, and stealing. Written by Gerald R. Patterson of the Oregon Social Learning Center, this volume offers help to parents whose sons' behavior is beginning to cause them real concern. (Research Press Company, 1975)

The Father's Almanac
Whether you are a weekend dad or actively involved in daily discipline and child care, this book by Adam Sullivan, father of two boys, is packed with sensible information: how to help a new mother, ways to fix and build toys, what to look for in day care and nursery school, and information on outings and gardening. (Dolphin, 1980)

The First Three Years of Life
Burton White examines the child's stages of development in the first three years. White uses a forthright approach and tells parents ways to foster abilities in a young child that help him become more competent. (Avon, 1975)

The Handbook for Latchkey Children and Their Working Parents
Based on interviews with children who take care of themselves and their parents, this book by Lynette and Thomas Long not only draws a clear picture of what staying alone means to different youngsters, but helps parents deal with their own feelings of conflict. Specific guidelines and suggestions for alternative care are useful. (Arbor House, 1983)

How to Discipline With Love
The importance of love in helping rear a responsible child is emphasized in every chapter of Fitzhugh Dodson's important book. Dr. Dodson's sensible, practical advice can be used by parents of children from toddlers to teenagers. (New American Library, 1978)

How to Father
Fitzhugh Dodson explains the importance of a positive
father figure in a young boy's life. This book helps fathers understand the stages of development their sons
are going through and offers down-to-earth, practical
suggestions for creating a warm father/son relationship.
(New American Library, 1975)

Infant and Child in the Culture of Today
Written by Arnold Gesell, M.D., Frances Ilg, M.D., and
Louise Bates Ames, Ph.D., in collaboration with Janet
Rodell, Ph.D., this is the first in a trilogy of books from
the Gesell Institute that chart growth from infancy
through the preschool years. If you are rearing your first
child, this is an invaluable and indispensable book.
(Harper & Row, 1974)

Is Your Child in the Wrong Grade?
This book by Louise Bates Ames, Ph.D., can help parents faced with a decision about school placement for
their sons. Thumbnail case histories of real children am-
plify the work and illustrate specific points. If you are
not certain about your little boy's readiness for school or
his present grade placement, this book could be invaluable. (Modern Learning Press, 1978)

Learning Disabilities, A Family Affair
Written by Betty B. Osman, a learning disabilities specialist and mother of three, this book is a realistic yet
hopeful appraisal of living with an LD child and helping
him learn both socially and academically. The various
appendices offer resources and explanations of federal
guidelines for educating handicapped youngsters. (Random House, 1979)

Mother Care/Other Care
Sandra Scarr offers a fascinating historical look at the
issue of child care, as well as an up-to-date survey of
research on children of working parents. She provides

guidelines for selecting suitable child care and gives realistic examples from her own experience. To top it off, the reader receives valuable information on normal development. This helpful book for working parents is written by a thorough professional who enjoys her family *and* her work and makes no apologies. (Basic Books, 1984)

The Mother's Almanac
Written by Marguerite Kelly and Elia Parsons, this is a rich resource book packed with ideas for arts and crafts, household chores, cooking, and exploring the world outside the home. This book can help any mother—working or busy at home—enjoy raising a young child. (Doubleday, 1975)

On Being Father: A Divorced Man Talks About Sharing the Responsibilities of Parenthood
Sensitive and honest, this book by Frank Ferrara helps divorced men continue to be fathers despite the red tape of legal battles and visitation rights, or the emotional upheavals of separation. (Doubleday, 1985)

Parents, Peers, and Pot
If you aren't concerned about substance use among today's youth, you should be. This book, written by Marsha Manatt, professional educator and mother, details the realities of drug use by even "nice youngsters from good homes." Information is given on how to tell if your child might be using drugs, and what to do if he is. (U.S. Department of Health and Human Services, 1980)

P.E.T., Parent Effectiveness Training
Dr. Thomas Gordon presents a variety of active listening and other techniques for parents who want to improve communication with their children and make discipline more positive. Courses in P.E.T. are offered in a number of communities. (Peter H. Wyden, 1970)

Problem-Solving Techniques in Childrearing
Based on tested techniques, this book deals with parents' major concerns in child rearing and socialization through interpersonal cognitive problem-solving. Mothers trained to use problem-solving dialogues developed by Myrna Shure and George Spivack found that this information helped them think better, while they taught both boys and girls to find their own solutions to problems. (Jossey-Bass Publishers, 1978)

Raising Good Children
Using a developmental approach to moral growth, Dr. Thomas Lickona, father of two boys, presents a delightful commonsense guide for parents of children from infancy to adolescence. If you hope your little boy will learn the difference between right and wrong and listen to his own conscience rather than the "groupthink" of his peers, this is the book for you. Specific guidelines for television viewing, sex education, and protecting your child against drugs and drinking are included. (Bantam, 1983)

The Read-Aloud Handbook
Jim Trelease's book points out the advantages of libraries and silent reading and the disadvantages of television. Especially helpful to parents is the substantial section of the book (almost one hundred pages) devoted to descriptions of good books for reading to toddlers through teenagers. (Penguin Books, 1982)

To Listen to a Child
This is a sensitive and sensible approach to a variety of problems young children may experience, such as sadness, sleep disturbances, asthma, seizures, and bedwetting. Subtitled *Understanding the Normal Problems of Growing Up*, it is written by T. Berry Brazelton, M.D., Chief of the Child Development Unit at Boston Children's Hospital Medical Center. (Addison-Wesley Publishing Company, 1984)

Understanding Psychology
If it's been a long time since Psych. 101, or if you never had a chance to take a basic psychology course, this well-written book provides an introduction to the study of human behavior. Written by Sandra Scarr and James Vander Zanden, this is the most readable college text-book we know of. (4th edition, Random House, 1984)

Your One-Year-Old, Your Two-Year Old, etc.—up through seven years
These books by Ilg and Ames focus more closely on specific periods in the young child's life. They are especially comforting to first-time parents because they let you know what "normal" is. (Delacorte Press, 1976, 1979, 1985)

In the notes that follow, references to the following three books are listed in the following manner:

After the *first notation,*
Race, Social Class, and Individual Differences in I.Q. by Sandra Scarr is referred to as *Race, Social Class;*

Social Development, Psychological Growth and the Parent-Child Relationship by Eleanor Maccoby is referred to as *Social Development;*

and *Scientific Foundations of Development Psychiatry* by Michael Rutter is referred to as *Scientific Foundations.*

Index

abduction, 188, 189–191

accident-prone children, 172, 186

active listening, 57–58, 168

after-school programs, 185, 194

aggressiveness, 46–49, 53, 54, 57–61, 73, 76, 87, 102–103, 109, 152, 170, 176, 211

television and, 198–200

alcohol, *see* substance abuse

allergies, milk, 20, 35

alternative care, 80–82

Ames, Louise Bates, 88, 112, 234

amphetamines, 150–151, 213, 220

androgens, 6, 46, 52, 145

androgyny, 166

anger, 30, 34, 49, 57, 58, 61

attachment to caretaker, 27–28, 173

attention deficit disorder (hyperactivity), 75, 147, 150–151, 152, 154, 157, 159, 215

attention span, 91, 148, 151

automobile accidents, 202, 217

Baker, Susan, 206

bedtime routines, 68–69

bedwetting, 35

Bettelheim, Bruno, 200

blended families, 180–181

Bloom, Benjamin, 117, 166, 167

"Bluebirds," 85–86, 109

books, making of, 125–126

boys

developmental sequence in, 9–11

fretfulness in, 16

growth as variable among, 7

as larger and stronger than girls, 15–16

as more fragile than girls, 3–4, 7, 9, 20, 81

brain:

development of, 19–20, 152, 216

sex differences in, 8–9, 27, 52, 131, 145

Brazelton, T. Berry, 35

bullies, 102–103

cable television, 204–205, 208

Campbell, Sammie, 88

Canfield, Jack, 137–138

cartoons, violence in, 200, 203, 207

causal thinking, 60

central nervous system, 90, 91, 93, 147, 215

Chafetz, Morris, 212

Chess, Stella, 21

child abuse, 186–191

Childs, Barton, 149

choices, 56, 65, 157

chromosomes, sex, 5–6, 52

Churchill, Winston, 11

Clark, Ronald, 11

classroom behavior, 116–117, 118–122

clothing, 64, 65, 67–68

cocaine, 216, 220

communicable diseases, 79, 81

competence, 11, 13, 43, 77,

About the Authors

Sheila Moore is an education writer whose articles have appeared in *Parents* and the *Washington Post*. Roon Frost, also a writer, has been a columnist and contributor for the past ten years to a variety of publications, such as the *Washington Post, Gourmet, Early American Life* and the *Philadelphia Inquirer.* Moore and Frost met seven years ago when Moore was a kindergarten teacher at a Northern Virginian Montessori school. Frost's son was in her class, and THE LITTLE BOY BOOK grew out of a mutual interest in learning disabilities, early childhood years, and little boys shared by the two mothers of sons.